NET FUTURE

ALSO BY CHUCK MARTIN

The Digital Estate: Strategies for Competing and Thriving in a Networked World

NET FUTURE

THE 7 CYBERTRENDS THAT WILL DRIVE YOUR BUSINESS, CREATE NEW WEALTH, AND DEFINE YOUR FUTURE

Chuck Martin

McGraw-Hill

New York San Francisco Washington, D.C. Auckland Bogotá
Caracas Lisbon London Madrid Mexico City Milan
Montreal New Delhi San Juan Singapore
Sydney Tokyo Toronto

McGraw-Hill

A Division of The **McGraw·Hill** Companies

8 9 0   AGM/AGM   9 0 3 2 1 0 9

ISBN 0-07-041131-X

The editing supervisor for this book was Scott Amerman, and the production supervisor was Tina Cameron. It was set in Fairfield by Renee Lipton of McGraw-Hill's Professional Book Group composition unit.

Printed and bound by Quebecor/Martinsburg.

McGraw-Hill books are available at special quality discounts to use as premiums and sales promotions, or for use in corporate training programs. For more information, please write to the Director of Special Sales, McGraw-Hill, Professional Publishing, Two Penn Plaza, New York, NY 10121-2298. Or contact your local bookstore.

This book is printed on recycled, acid-free paper containing a minimum of 50% recycled, de-inked fiber.

To my little boys,
Ryan and Chase,
For the Net Future is theirs

CONTENTS

CHAPTER EIGHT. LEARNING GOES REAL TIME, ALL THE TIME   221

CHAPTER NINE. THE BEST AND WORST OF THE NET FUTURE   247

ACKNOWLEDGMENTS

During the many months we worked on this book, there were countless people who helped all along the way, to whom I will be forever grateful. First and foremost are the people of the Net Future, those executives, managers, and workers who contributed their valuable time and insights into helping formulate a view of where this networked world of ours might be going.

A very special thank you to Mary Frakes, an established journalist, who is a longtime colleague and friend. As researcher on the book, Mary got to wear many of her past hats along the way, having been an accomplished editor, writer, copyeditor, consultant, deadline manager, and now, E-business maven. To her I am greatly indebted.

For reading the manuscript and contributing to the Best and Worst chapter (Chapter 9) I want to thank long-time associates and entrepreneurs Don Tydeman, Jordan Graham, and Ellen Caravello, as well as Harry Somerdyk at McGraw-Hill for help in looking at future business models and management concepts.

A special thanks to New York–based Handshake Dynamics CEO Laurence Bunin, who is of the belief that businesses that want to be successful in the new Internet economy will have to build their technology organizations and systems infrastructure correctly, and most will have to start over. I appreciate being allowed a close-up view of some of these dramatic re-builds of companies' insides. I also want to thank Roland Desilva of Media Investment Banking firm Desilva & Phillips, Inc., for insight into new valuation metrics for E-businesses.

Others must be included on my thank you list: all my friends at McGraw-Hill, including Publisher Phil Ruppel, Editor Betsy Brown, and Publicity Director Claudia Riemer Boutote, the team that helped shape and define the book, not to mention getting it to market in a timely manner. Also, the many great agents of the Leigh Speakers Bureau for putting me in touch with such great companies and organizations throughout the world on a journey to share insights in a continual learning process.

For helping with ideas for the Best and Worst chapter, thanks to Steve Mott, Carol Page, and Steve Larsen, whom I'd also like to thank for allowing me to bounce various ideas off of.

I offer a very special thank you to Agnes Martin, my mother, for continued inspiration and in memory of Leo Martin, my father, who lived for the future of his children.

We learned a lot during the course of researching the Net Future. We found that much will change and much will remain the same. The Internet will not replace family.

I wish to offer an incredible thank you to my family, for perspective, values, and, daily doses of reality, provided by my two sons, 9-year-old Ryan and 7-year-old Chase, the joys of my life. Thank you Ryan and Chase for your patience and understanding of the balance between the Net Future and the real present. My biggest debt of all is to Teri Granger Martin, my wife of more than a decade, without whom this book truly could not have been done. For unequivocal support and keeping our family and me centered, my most heartfelt thank you, Teri.

Chuck Martin

INTRODUCTION: THE E-BUSINESS REVOLUTION

The deepening and maturing roots of the Internet are about to grab, shake, and take hold of businesses and individuals like never before. While executives of major corporations no longer question whether the Net will impact their businesses, they may not realize how much this electronic El Niño will transform customers, careers, and relationships. Many even have someone, somewhere within the organization they think is "handling" it. But they may underestimate the extent of the coming onslaught on every aspect of business life, from product concept and creation through distribution and consumption.

At issue here is the E-business revolution. For some, it will even be an issue of survival. For others, it will be an era of unprecedented opportunity and victory. Welcome to the Net Future.

The Net Future is not about selling things on the Net or about a line extension of an existing business. It is a revolution in the making. Not only will every company have to deal with those transformations, but the wins and losses will be huge; there won't be any gray areas. Companies are beginning to realize that a Web site does not an E-business make. And the Net Future truly is about E-business, which goes far beyond electronic commerce. Electronic commerce involves the buying and selling of products, information, or services over the Net. E-business involves what I call the "Netting" of the entire value chain: from product conception and creation, all the way through manufacturing and production, distribution, and ultimately consumption. Companies that understand this and are willing to undergo the close self-scrutiny involved in becoming "Netted" will be the winners in the Net Future.

WHAT'S AT STAKE

Coming is a world linked by fast, cheap communication, where speed is key, access to "the network" is ubiquitous, and virtually every business and individual is affected. This linkage, enabled by technology, will redefine the way we function at work, at home, and in the marketplace. It will determine winners and losers, both corporately and personally. The opportunity for those who capitalize on this environment will be enormous—as will the risk for those who don't. Surviving in the Net Future involves these key adjustments:

Capturing the hearts and minds of consumers. With instant access to every company and every company's products, consumers will move firmly into the driver's seat in the new Net economy. Companies that miss this will be penalized by the market itself, since another company's products and services will be but a mouse click away. And click consumers will, if not treated properly.

Reorganizing distribution mechanisms. Wired organizations will electronically reach out to suppliers and distributors and expect that the companies they buy from and use to deliver their goods will be as Netted as they are. Those that refuse, or that cannot do business in this fashion, will fall by the wayside.

Rethinking pricing. Technology will allow more and more companies to segment markets into much finer slices, skimming a competitor's best customers in the process. It also will redefine the role of price in the purchase decision.

Changing corporate culture and authority. An increasingly mobile and Net-savvy workforce will gain unprecedented access to information, including the means by which workers can determine if their particular work environment suits them and, if not, which one would. And the work environment itself will have new forms.

Integrating personal and work lives. Technology that allows anyone to communicate anywhere at any time will erase the lines between work and home. It also will change the way information is processed; real-time access to both professional and personal peers will allow people to compare notes on virtually any subject.

THE NET EVOLUTION

There are five waves of evolution of the commercial Net:

1. At the Brochureware stage, companies simply transferred what they were doing in their traditional business onto the Net. A typical example involved putting annual reports and corporate brochures on a corporate Web site exactly as they appeared in print.

2. The New Content arena took off in 1995, when companies started to create new products and services for the Net environment. This is when the true interactivity of the Internet began; for example, companies began to solicit E-mail responses to various offers. This was also when Net-only companies such as search engine Yahoo! and bookseller Amazon.com started to show how business would be conducted in the Net environment. By 1997, countless Net-only companies sprang up. Some grew, some died, others merged. Established companies started to look for payback as well as successful Net business models.

3. During the third wave, that same Internet technology infiltrated the enterprise company-wide, and the intranet was borne. By 1998, many companies started to see the power of the Internet's open technology in connecting all the workers

of a company. One of the inherent problems of this wave was that executives of some companies initially viewed the intranet simply as "plumbing" and deployed the technology for the purpose of saving money, rather than devising new ways to tap into a wired workforce.

4. In the current Business Transformation wave, this same Internet technology is used within the enterprise to connect suppliers, distributors, customers, and business partners. These closer connections between buyer and seller will enable more streamlined operations inside and outside the enterprise.

5. The true E-business wave involves tapping the end-to-end Netted enterprise so that an organization, armed with real-time knowledge from customers, can create and modify products on the fly to suit those customers' needs. It will be in this phase that the interactive environment will start to drive a company's core business. That is not to say that companies' traditional businesses will go away (though some will). But the components of the interactive environment—the wired consumer and the wired organization—will start to function in harmony.

THE SEVEN CYBERTRENDS

Over the course of this five-wave evolutionary process, seven major trends have emerged. These seven cybertrends—all driven by technology—will come into increasingly sharp focus as businesses move to the fifth wave. Each is significant by itself. Together, they define the ultimate in end-to-end electronic business, or E-business. Together, they comprise the Net Future.

The Cybereconomy Goes Main Street.   New ways of buying and selling will create a new breed of online consumer who will expect faster delivery, easier transactions, and more factual information. Traditional businesses will operate in the online arena, and online businesses will adopt traditional methods.

The Wired Workforce Takes Over.   The intranet will put more information in employees' hands and create virtual work communities, irrevocably altering the dynamics of the workplace for both individuals and companies.

The Open-Book Corporation Emerges.   Boundaries between the corporation and the outside world, including suppliers and customers, will be erased. Power shifts away from the providers of products, information, and services into the hands of the recipients of those products, information, and services.

Products Become Commodities.   New interactive dynamics will dramatically change how value is established for products. More importantly, it will mean a shift to real-time, flexible pricing as value is established moment-by-moment.

The Customer Becomes Data.   New technologies for analyzing and predicting customer behavior in real time will require companies to organize differently in order to move to a new Net-version of customer-centric.

Experience Communities Arise.   People will harness instant global communications, aggregating knowledge in real time. Collective experience will play a larger role in information-gathering and decision-making.

Learning Moves to Real Time, All-the-Time.   The new means of networking will create a new generation of empowered and independent learners—and require both self-motivation and information sharing to succeed.

A company's grasp of these seven cybertrends and its consequent willingness to transform its business will determine how well it survives in the Net Future.

THE RELATIONSHIP NETS

The seven cybertrends grow out of an interlocking series of relationships among customers, employees, distributors, suppliers, and business partners. These relationships will be facilitated by the move to an internetworked world, and the companies that are first and most adept at maximizing them will be the winners in the Net Future.

INTERNET: THE CUSTOMER RELATIONSHIP

For most customers, what they see at a company's Web site will determine their view of the company. A company already is expected to have a Web presence. This is just the cost of entry. While some companies allocate limited marketing dollars to maintain a minimal Web presence, others are forging new relationships with their customers and redefining themselves for the online world. In the Net Future, simply electronically distributing company brochures and annual reports won't cut it. The Web will provide unprecedented opportunity for companies to interact with traditional customers and to create ongoing dialogues with new customers. Companies will have the opportunity to turn these interactions into true company-customer relationships.

INTRANET: THE EMPLOYEE RELATIONSHIP

As the network of all networks, the Internet has become a place where anyone can find just about anything using a Web browser and a search engine. However, what can't be found is information contained in intranets, since they are essentially internets deployed by a company or organization for internal use only. Employees receive a password, and their access and communication within the company are handled behind a "firewall," a technology aimed at keeping outsiders on the outside. Typically, a company uses its intranet to cut the cost of distributing information, such as health plans and messages from top management. In the Net Future, smart companies will use their intranets to strengthen employee relations; to empower employees to manage, learn, and grow; to facilitate the work process; and to institute electronic programs that keep morale high and turnover low. Perhaps more important, constant online communication will keep company goals in tune with customer needs, since employees often are closer to the customers than are many top executives.

EXTRANET: THE SUPPLIER-DISTRIBUTOR-PARTNER RELATIONSHIP

The extranet is the same as an intranet, except that it is used privately *outside* the enterprise. If the Internet is the public track, an extranet is a private train that is allowed to run on that track. A company might conduct a private auction of excess inventory for its best retailers. Suppliers might be allowed to be "members" so that needed supplies are only a mouse click away. Shippers and brokers will be given access to a company's database so that it can better serve the company's needs in real time. Companies will enlist business partners, suppliers, and distributors to create and track their own records, fill out their own forms, and in effect become an integral part of the enterprise.

WHEN WORLDS COLLIDE: THE CONVERGENCE OF OLD AND NEW

Converting a company's three nets into relationship nets and then leveraging them will require totally new thinking and approaches. In my book *The Digital Estate*,[1] people in the business world are divided into two camps: those who get it and those who don't. By now, most people have to some extent "gotten it." The new fault line is between businesses that operate only in the bricks-and-mortar realm—such as many manufacturing entities and retailers—and businesses that operate in an online, interactive environment, such as online travel agents and CD retailers.

In the Net Future, these two worlds will converge, as companies in each one begin to embrace the other. This convergence will allow companies to leverage existing brands as well as create new ones, and become E-businesses. Netted companies also will be able to take enormous time and costs out of the manufacturing and distribution channels, sharing those savings with customers, suppliers, and business partners.

True convergence in the Net Future will encompass more than just hardware that delivers information, or marriages of content and technology. The new convergence will be between the digital and physical environments. And the ultimate Net Future company is one that understands that this hybrid business environment will be driven by the interactive digital, not the traditional, component.

It is this final stage that represents the Net Future. It is a phase in which the interconnectedness of everyone and everything allows the external world to transform the very notion of the corporation. It is a time when because of total, end-to-end connectivity, consumers can truly indicate to a company their product and service desires, future needs and wants, and likes and dislikes, all in real time. In the Net Future, consumption can drive concept.

As these seven cybertrends allow the enterprise to become truly customer-centric, consumers will receive more personalized and valuable services, ranging from new public services from state and local governments to deals on·virtually anything they want.

RECONCILIATION TIME

Succeeding in the Net Future means reconciling many disparate elements.

THE BUSINESS

Some companies have developed their three Net strategies in silos, each with its own approach and objectives. In other cases, the three Nets within a company really just *exist*, without any coherent strategy at all. And some companies haven't yet identified the difference, or don't see the need for the three Nets, content to use the Web as nothing more than an extension of their core business. For example, the Internet, or company Web site, might be positioned under a marketing department. The organization is based on the fact that much of the site's information involves corporate profile data as well as the company's marketing messages, which would normally flow through that channel.

The corporate intranet, on the other hand, generally falls under the eye of the Chief Information Officer or the Information Systems department. Higher security is required, since the intranet often includes corporate records and even electronic warehouses of information. While CIOs command huge operational budgets and IS staffs can number in the thousands at a big company, the focus often is on creating operational efficiencies and using information technology to create sustainable, competitive advantage. The intranet has played only a small part in those objectives. Human relations departments and purchasing agents often also will play a role in intranet content, since the automation of benefits and cost savings in procurement are two of the most obvious uses of an internal Net.

Extranet implementation might be executed by the information technology department, though it may be driven by a business unit that sees immediate benefit in linking its sales force with its customer bases or distributors. An extranet also might be driven by a manufacturing division that wants to reduce cycle time by linking suppliers into its production process.

For a company to become a Netted enterprise, the three Net strategies will, at the very least, have to be coordinated. At best, they will function orchestra-like, as a set of unified components all playing the same tune—and the tune will be composed by the customer.

THE CUSTOMER

Just as company Nets grew separately, so did customer sets. Established companies had to move so fast just to stay even with Net-only companies that very little time and effort went into analyzing who the new online customers were (or should be). The market was too new and growing exponentially.

Companies typically find that a large percentage of their online customers are new customers. While some executives view this as good news, allaying fears of cannibalization of traditional business, they often miss the new challenges and opportunities presented. These include how to reconcile new customers with a company's traditional customers, how to coordinate customer care, and how to integrate various technology issues such as linking customer billing systems with customer databases. One of the largest challenges will be creating an infrastructure and deploying robust technology to deal with a highly interactive and highly demanding customer in real time, all the time.

On the other hand, the opportunity in the Net Future will be immense. Because companies will be able to tap into connected consumers for real-time feedback, they can use this customer base to help conceive, create, test, and enhance new products. Because it is so easily obtained and because more customers will become connected, this feedback will increasingly begin to drive the direction of the company. Meantime, companies can begin to reconcile the new online customer base with their traditional customer base by introducing each to products and services in the other's world, thereby leveraging long-standing as well as new relationships with customers.

TECHNOLOGY AND THE PEOPLE

Ultimately, just about everything and everyone will be networked. Internet access will be everywhere, whether from a personal computer, a handheld organizer, a pager, or some other remote communications device. However, being wired does not change human behavior overnight. There will be both technical and cultural challenges while the technology awaits and promotes changes in the way people act and think.

- At the Millennium Gloucester Hotel in London, the removal of a bottle of Coca-Cola from the refrigerator automatically sends a message to the hotel's billing system and the debit is included on the customer's bill. However, travelers not accustomed to the invisible tracking might search through the refrigerator for a particular drink or use a container to store milk for their baby's bottle, only to be faced with hundreds of dollars in erroneous expenses at checkout.

- Ninety percent of pagers in the United States were left stranded for anywhere from a few seconds to several days when a $250 million communications satellite wobbled out of position. Doctors were left without a way to receive emergency messages. Radio and TV stations were temporarily off the air. Retailers couldn't run credit card verifications. Field personnel didn't know where their next job was. In some cases, however, people adapted by using E-mail and cell phones.

- A drugstore chain that released the names of its pharmacy customers to a direct marketing firm quickly found out that customers were outraged and was forced not only to recall the list but also to institute a policy against issuing one in the future.

The road to the Net Future will be fraught with issues related to privacy, bandwidth capacity, and taxation of E-commerce. However, companies that focus solely on the obstacles miss seeing not only the larger picture but also what their competitors are doing to take advantage of it.

THE 180-DEGREE EFFECT

Doing business successfully in the Netted environment will be challenging, especially if business is conducted using old rules and metrics. As many companies have found, the dynamics of the Net are very different from those in the physical environment. Often, an element of business is exactly the opposite from what is expected. One might say it started with Netscape, which challenged common wisdom and gave away its Internet browser software for free in order to gain quick market share. America Online used to pay content providers for appearing on AOL. Now content providers pay AOL.

In the physical world, companies created products and sold them; in the Net Future, consumers will determine what they will buy and a company then will produce it. In the past, the more information you controlled, the more power you had. In the Net Future, the more information and power you give away, the more you have. I call this phenomenon of contrary expectations "the 180-degree effect." It's best exemplified when things are not as they appear.

- When a public relations company establishes a date for an online chat, the event is over by the time the event is held. The prechat publicity generated *is* the event, not the event itself.
- Signed up to handle groceries for online retailer NetGrocer, FedEx charges dramatically less to deliver 10 pounds of groceries than it does to deliver a 1-ounce letter.
- Students attending college away from home take online classes from their college.

The ultimate 180-degree effect representation in the Net Future is that the business will be initiated by the customer, not by the business itself. The 180-degree effect means that companies cannot take for granted that the assumptions of the past hold true in the Net environment. The Net Future will belong to those who can turn assumptions inside out, upside down, and backward.

IMPEDIMENTS TO CHANGE

Any number of factors can inhibit established companies from moving aggressively and successfully in the Netted environment.

- *Lack of speed*. Does anyone feel that their company moves too fast?
- *Inflexibility*. Does anyone think their company is too flexible?

- *Corporate will.* Companies need to align executive management, the internal Net champions, and the troops so that everyone marches in the same direction.
- *Old business models.* Traditional business models do not work in the Net environment.
- *Internal focus.* The larger the company, the more internally focused it usually is. If more than 50 percent of your E-mail is from inside your organization rather than from your customers, you probably are too internally focused.
- *Skills and habits.* Since the commercial Net is only several years old, human behavior has not yet caught up with the dynamics of the Net environment. Old habits are hard to break. The next generation will change all that.
- *The desire for perfection.* Established companies with strong brands hesitate to do anything in the online world that does not match the researched, tested, tried-and-true methods of the physical world.

CRITICAL SUCCESS FACTORS FOR THE NET FUTURE

So how does a company get from here to there? Taking arms against the factors listed above is a start. In addition, businesses have three core tasks:

1. *Understanding the end-to-end nature of E-business.* The seven cybertrends are not independent of one another. Looking at each in terms of how it interacts with all the others reinforces the understanding that an E-business is dramatically more than the sum of its parts.
2. *Aligning the organization to tie it together end-to-end.* Understanding the nature of E-business does no good unless the enterprise reflects that understanding. Because E-business is so interconnected, implementing many of the changes required can seem an overwhelming process. How-

ever, learning from mistakes based on rapid feedback is the right model in this environment. E-business is a destination and a journey.

3. *Make sure that alignment is centered on the customer.* Connectivity allows customers to drive companies.

In the Net environment, so much seems to happen so quickly that it's often difficult for companies to step back and see how the various pieces fit together. There are so many disparate parts, and yet all the pieces interconnect, much like the Net itself. Changes in consumer buying patterns will affect which products get developed. The products that are developed will affect the operations side of a company. A change in operations will affect the way a company relates to its business partners and what is needed from its workforce. Workforce requirements affect corporate training needs and employment patterns. Employment patterns affect consumer buying.

The E-business revolution is just around the corner. This is the Net Future!

THE CYBERECONOMY GOES MAIN STREET

The Internet economy can be viewed as a massive underground complex. There are buyers, who scour the Net labyrinth for the best deals, and sellers, who reach out in new and innovative ways to attract those buyers. Sometimes deals leave the buyer the winner; sometimes it's the seller. Even those who get the short end of the stick may find another deal that's as good or better. The millions of consumers and producers in the above-ground world who don't even participate in these transactions—yet—are those who truly lose. This is about to change.

Internet commerce has begun to take off, but the potential has scarcely been touched. Consider:

- About 40 percent of new Web site traffic growth is from new users connecting from home.[1]

- By the year 2002, 60 percent of U.S. households will have a personal computer.[2]

- One study of 100,000 Web users reported that those users were spending as much time online as watching TV.[3]

- Spending on the Web is expected to reach more than $200 billion annually by the year 2001—almost one percent of the global economy. E-commerce in Western Europe alone will hit $30 billion by the year 2001.[4]

- Vanderbilt University, the University of Texas at Austin, and others are allowing MBA candidates to specialize in electronic commerce.

- The Internet is growing faster than any other medium in history. It took radio 38 years to acquire 50 million listeners. Television took 13 years to get to 50 million viewers. The Internet achieved 50 million users in just four years.

Whether this mainstream role for the Internet is good or problematic depends on one's viewpoint. For buyers, commerce on the Net has meant an additional way to find things they want and discover things they didn't know they wanted or needed. Sellers and producers face a greater challenge; in many cases, they must live in both the underground world of the cybereconomy as well as in the physical world. And in many ways, aspects of these worlds will compete with one another for some time until they are reconciled in the Net Future.

A company may choose to operate solely on the Net, to ignore it completely, or to become a hybrid of the two. Each choice has its own set of challenges. Since the commercialization of the Internet began, there has been a chronic chorus of "no one is making money on the Net." Not only does this complaint totally miss the point, but it threatens to stifle some of the very companies that otherwise could face the best opportunities.

WHY THE NET ECONOMY IS GOING MAINSTREAM

In the early days of the Internet economy, E-commerce meant creating a Web site and trying to attract consumers by spraying banner ads and reciprocal links around the Net, so that when a person searched for a particular word or subject, he or she would be driven to the appropriate site. In the Net Future, marketing will be taken to the next level, targeting sophisticated buyers by providing access to all information at any time.

There are four elements that, in combination, will drive the underground cybereconomy aboveground and into the mainstream:

1. *The market.* The audience of millions of Internet users has widened beyond the "under-30 males interested in comput-

ers, CDs, and porn" stereotype and has begun to align itself more closely with the profile of the mainstream population. The fastest growing segment of Web users encompasses teenage girls and women over 50.[5]

2. *Timing*. The problems posed to older computer systems because of the year 2000 present companies with an obvious opportunity to migrate internal technologies to the technology of the Internet. Rather than trying to jury-rig old systems, some companies are choosing simply to convert mainframe applications to Web-based systems.

3. *Behavior*. As companies adopt intranets and convert to E-businesses, corporate consuming will be dramatically altered. Companies will be training employees to order online. These same people will then be prepped to electronically shop for personal wares on their own.

4. *Value*. By far the most important factor is the economics of buying and selling on the Net. Inventory and distribution costs can be dramatically lower. Global reach can be achieved at far less cost than with usual marketing methods. With the growth of new ways of buying and selling, online auctions, automated recommendations, and automatic supply replenishment will emerge. These will forever alter the relationship between buyer and seller.

SUCH A DEAL!

The main reason that the cybereconomy is going mainstream is that everybody loves a bargain. The value proposition and the case of buying are just too strong for cost-conscious buyers to ignore. The channel from product creation to consumption is compressed, and doing things digitally simply is cheaper. In many cases, online prices will be lower than what consumers can find elsewhere.

- Some of the best bargains on air travel are available at the last minute over the Net. Airlines post their deals on their public

Web sites; others notify registered users by e-mail at a designated time each week. The savings? US Air offers round-trip fares from Boston to Philadelphia for $89, half the price of a regular coach fare purchased from a travel agent.

- Because it maintains no warehouse and routes book orders directly to distributors, Amazon.com can deliver a book at a price that, even including shipping costs, is below what traditional bookstores can afford to charge. And Bargain Book Warehouse goes even further, charging a flat shipping fee, so someone with a lot of books to buy can batch the orders and ship them all for just $4.25.

- Online auctions such as Onsale.com and Auction Universe allow consumers to bid on items in a variety of categories. Egghead offers SurplusAuction.com, where remnant software is auctioned at discount prices.

- Dealaday.com sells discounted brand-name clothing over the Net, operating in much the same way as Loehmann's and Marshalls in the physical world. An Ann Taylor silk body suit might sell for $10, a Ralph Lauren sweatshirt for $29. And after 10 purchases, shipping and handling are free.

- Countrywide Home Loans Inc., the largest independent mortgage lender in the United States, cuts 1.25 points off the closing costs for a home loan for people who take out their mortgage using the company's online service.

- Investors who want to find out about the quality of an annuity can use A.M. Best's BestLine to check out its rating. Using the Web avoids the $2.95 initial charge for the same service over the phone.

PRODUCTS BY THE SLICE

The Net allows companies to create entirely new product sets that are not economically feasible in the brick-and-mortar world. In many cases, these products are subsets of existing products, disaggregated from the whole.

In the Net Future, as mechanisms for micropayments

become more widespread, consumers will increasingly be able to buy products and services in small slices. This is particularly true for information products, which can be combined and recombined endlessly.

This slicing and dicing of product will bring some higher-priced products within the reach of a broader audience.

- Law firms that normally would have to pay thousands of dollars for reference books and CD-ROMs from legal publisher Matthew Bender use the Net to get access only to the material they need. Called Authority On-Demand, the program allows purchase of specific sections of Bender publications for anywhere from $5.95 to $35, depending on the size of the individual section. Transactions are handled by credit card. The same is true for West Publishing.

- NewsLibrary allows readers to search newspaper archives around the United States to find past stories. A story that looks appealing based on the first few lines can be purchased for a dollar or two.

- Music companies explore how they can let consumers buy individual songs online. Capitol Records pushed the envelope of music delivery when it released a song by Duran Duran on the Internet site. The trial effort infuriated the retailers that have traditionally been record labels' distribution outlet. The uproar caused the company to back off, but the experiment demonstrated that channel conflict, not technology, was the primary obstacle to distributing music more directly than ever before. It also underscored the Net's ability to revive the concept of selling music by the slice (the Duran Duran song went for under $1). SuperSonic Boom, owned by CDnow, offers thousands of music tracks; users can download files and create their own CDs.

- Companies that can't afford to install network conferencing equipment can rent virtual conference space from online community organizer GeoCities, which allows small businesses to hold online conferences with clients or business partners at minimal cost.

ENTER THE E-CONSUMER

New ways of buying and selling will create informed consumers with high expectations born of the Net. I call this new set of savvy, online buyers and shoppers "E-consumers." This new E-consumer, plugged into his or her peers, will demand faster delivery, easier transactions, and more factual information even in non-electronic arenas.

The new E-consumer defies the early wisdom about the Internet audience. With 64 percent of online shoppers between the ages of 40 and 64, one-third of the households with online access have made a purchase on the Web.[6]

E-consumers are not one-dimensional in their behavior. The overlap between Web sites that people access at home and at work is only 13 percent, largely representing gateway or portal sites such as the search engines and Netscape. Business users access the same Web sites more frequently at work than they do at home, where they tend to roam over a more varied selection. What will the E-consumer of the Net Future look like?

E-Consumers Will Be Well-Informed.   The Net Future is an age of all information available to all. The overwhelming majority of consumers with online access already say that online research is valuable in making buying decisions. And if businesses don't supply the needed information themselves, consumers will find it somewhere else—and possibly buy there as well. The opportunities to compare prices and products are everywhere. Partnerships between a company such as search engine Yahoo! or Netscape and subject-specific sites give the new E-consumer the ability to search for precisely what he or she wants. Other services do the comparison automatically for consumers. WebPricer allows consumers to enter information from their own phone bills to get an automated comparison of the rates offered by seven long-distance companies and see which carrier would be most cost-effective for them.

E-Consumers Will Have Higher Demands.   Roughly half of E-consumers report that lower prices and convenience are the two most important reasons they shop online, followed closely by the greater variety available. And those demands are not likely to stop at the computer keyboard; customers who get used to finding the book they want and having it delivered overnight are not about to wait patiently for a week offline.

E-Consumers Will Compare Notes with Others.   Personal recommendations have traditionally been a powerful influence on consumers, especially for bigger-ticket items. Chat rooms, bulletin boards, newsgroups, and personal Web pages all offer the opportunity to factor word of mouth into a buying decision. New technologies, called recommendation systems, allow consumers to get automatic recommendations based on the opinions of other consumers like themselves (see Chapter Six).

BEHAVIOR MODIFICATION AND CHANGING EXPECTATIONS

When the ATM was introduced, people said they wouldn't use it, preferring instead to deal with "real people." Consumers now *pay* to use those same machines. But it took time and a change in habit. Once people realized the benefit, the habit of using an ATM was integrated into the routines of their lives. The Net will be no different. Consumers who try Net buying are increasingly likely to do so again. For example, 50 percent of the customers of Music Boulevard, owned by Net-only music retailer N2K, are repeat buyers.[7]

Consumer behavior does not change overnight just because someone has access to the Net; it evolves with the individual's familiarity with the Net. New users tend to move through four stages of E-commerce involvement:[8]

1. The Information Giver agrees to enter information about himself or herself in exchange for free services.

2. The Information Sorter signs up for services that automate the process of getting the most appropriate information. Such services include personalized pages such as My Yahoo! and recommendation services.

3. The One-Time Buyer makes individual small purchases, such as books or gifts.
4. The E-consumer is comfortable with more complex transactions, such as online brokerage services and regular participation in auctions.

The behavior of E-consumers depends on where they use the Net. Other than to search sites, there seems to be relatively little overlap between where users go on the Net when they're at work and when they're at home.[9] At least some of the difference may have to do with the fact that many people can access the Internet more quickly at work, where pages often transmit over high-speed T1 lines rather than dramatically slower residential lines.

There also is a hidden dimension to Internet commerce, which stems from the fact that millions of consumers—nearly two-thirds of consumers with Net access—already research purchases online before going to the store to execute the transaction.[10]

WHAT A MAINSTREAM CYBERECONOMY CHANGES

COMMERCE EVERYWHERE

It used to be that people did banking in a bank, shopped for groceries in a grocery store, contacted a broker to trade stocks, and bought videos at a video store. In the Net Future, all that can change.

- Southland Corp., which owns the convenience store chain 7-Eleven, teamed with NCR to install kiosks called financial service centers in 37 Austin, Texas stores to provide round-the-clock banking, including bill paying, money transfers, and check cashing.
- At least one bank is putting Web kiosks in supermarkets, malls, and other retail locations. The kiosks give customers the ability not only to access their checking and savings

accounts, but also to check on loans and investment information and have a live videoconference with a bank service representative. Moreover, the system allows the bank to deliver site-specific marketing messages.

- Shell Oil is looking at converting credit card transaction machines at gas pumps into full-blown ATM machines, so that busy motorists can get cash while they fuel. The company already has developed automated, robotic gas-filling machines.

- Streamline of Boston will, for free, install a Streamline Box in a person's garage or basement. When people electronically order package pickup, grocery staples, and even frozen foods, the company will deliver them to keep customers from having to go out to shop. How does the company know which brands you prefer? When a customer signs up for the service, a Streamline representative bar-code scans all the groceries in the customer's kitchen cabinets to capture brand preferences into a database.

COMPETITION AROUND THE CORNER

The new players in an industry may not be the competitors you expect. Companies that are leaders in developing E-commerce for themselves are in some cases finding new businesses in selling those products to other companies.

- Electronic component wholesaler AMP sells to other companies the Web-based system it developed for updating large quantities of information in its online catalog (see Chapter Four).

- Cherokee National Life Insurance Co. partners with software company nFront to market a Web banking system to the 800 bank clients for whom it already offers credit life insurance. "We were looking for additional products to sell and decided that they didn't have to be insurance-related," says a Cherokee officer.

- First Chicago NBD supplies its customers with an Internet access kit that includes a primer on Internet use and a news service. When the software is started, First Chicago's home page comes up. What Internet access provider would view a bank as a competitor?

• Artists such as the one formerly known as Prince are beginning to sell their music directly to the public, bypassing the music industry entirely. Rock musician Todd Rundgren plans to allow fans to subscribe to Rundgren's music and download audio files. In addition to charging a subscription fee, the PatroNet service might also eventually include other bands.

NOT IN MY INDUSTRY!

Every company and every industry will feel the impact of the Net Future, but some will feel it sooner. Take, for example, the car business. All car-buying habits will be changed as consumers have at their fingertips dealer cost and retail comparisons as well as the ability to buy directly, to shop dealers globally, and to play dealers against one another.

Industry officials estimate that by the end of the century, 50 percent of all new car buyers could use the Internet for some part of their purchase or research. Chrysler Chairman Robert Eaton jolted the National Automobile Dealers Association by telling them the "customer is going to grab control of the process, and we're all going to salute smartly and do exactly what the customer tells us if we want to stay in business."

To help serve that newly empowered customer, Chrysler is putting its entire nationwide inventory on the Internet. People will be able to select the car they want and be directed to the nearest dealer that has one available. Individual dealers also have found ways to make the Net work for them. A dealer in Kellogg, Idaho, reportedly sold 4000 Jeeps over the Net. Manheim Online, which sells cars to wholesale dealers, lets dealers search its CyberLots for a specific make, model, and year. The wholesalers can purchase what they find immediately; they can also research cars to be sold at an offline Manheim auction.

Focusing on consumer-direct sales, Auto-By-Tel has sold more than a million cars through its Web site. Toyota wants customers to be able to order cars from the factory exactly as they want them, to be delivered two weeks later through a dealership.

THE NEW WALL STREET

As we have seen, the Net is transforming every area of life. However, banking and investing will be particularly affected. Because finance is based on interactivity that involves large volumes of rapidly changing statistical information, these institutions will be dramatically altered in the Net Future—and indeed, will be instrumental in driving that future.

One company that is leading the charge of change is Silicon Alley–based Wit Capital. The company was founded after the first-ever IPO for Spring Street Brewery raised $1.6 million on the Net from 3500 online investors. As the Net economy matured, Wit Capital brought in a new team, headed by Chairman and CEO Bob Lessin, former vice chairman of Salomon Smith Barney. Lessin quickly brought in a group of seasoned executives, including Ronald Readmond, former vice chairman of Charles Schwab & Co., and Beth Polish from KPMG, the former CFO of iVillage.[11]

"Wit Capital is focused on the empowerment of the individual," says Lessin. "I want to build a franchise, where there is the implication that if we underwrite a deal it is solid." Lessin sees an opportunity to bring previously unattainable IPO stock to online investors on a first-come, first-served basis.

Unlike online brokerages, Wit raises capital for companies. Its customers are individual investors with average orders around 800 shares.

"In 20 years, parts will be different and parts will be the same. There won't be road shows for IPOs and you'll have the ability to micro-market to those who matter most," says Lessin. "The individual becomes more important. When you have a Cleveland Indians IPO, we'll market to Ohio people. I want to know preferences and how people spend their time online. [When we can do that,] we'll be able to market more efficiently than any institutional house. We're lowering the cost of capital.

"Some percentage of the world's capital will be raised online. This is true pioneering stuff. This is the new versus the old. Wall Street has a lot of legacy to break down before it can get close to this. Traditional Wall Street will feel threatened when it's too late. This is so utterly right for a certain number of people."

Lessin expects to involve the online brokerages as Wit attempts to create a digital stock market. "This is a game largely about capital, and whoever has access to the capital is key. In the future people will be able to buy and sell to each other when the market is closed. Everyone will have at least one online account. IPO and capital raising stocks will have to come to us."

In the all-the-time world of the Net Future, it will be only natural to expect that buying, selling, and trading of everything will occur well beyond the hours of traditional markets. The millions of newly wired E-consumers in the game will become a new economic force. The dramatic impact that online brokerages have had on traditional firms is only the beginning, as mainstream consumers get both greater access to financial information and the ability to act directly on that information in real time.

Three additional trends play into the transformation of financial services in the coming decades:

1. *The desktop tickertape.* The Net provides inexpensive access to information and services formerly available only through financial services companies like brokerage houses. Consumers are being empowered to make more of their financial decisions unassisted. At the same time, consumers who still want advice or someone to make the decisions for them have more information to validate or undercut that advice. The Net not only allows content owners and distributors to send a constant and unlimited flow of data to consumers but also lets those customers take immediate action on that information.

2. *The boomer bulge.* The emergence of Net-based financial services comes precisely when baby boomers are increasingly focused on the financial world. With children in or heading for college and a hoped-for retirement following shortly thereafter, the pig-in-the-python generation will be increasingly obsessed with how to get the money to pay for those big-ticket life choices. And in the Net Future it will be those same boomers who manage or inherit the estates of their savings-conscious, Depression-era parents, a responsibility that requires a greater need for financial savvy.

3. *The invested workforce.* Corporate America's adoption of 401(k) retirement plans that include stock mutual funds and company stock as options for that money will only gain momentum in the Net Future. This has meant and will continue to mean participation in the stock market by a greater segment of the population than ever before.

Online investing and banking are not new. Many brokerages and banks have offered their customers software and information dial-up services for several years. Strategies for capturing the Net Future customer are now on the front burner for them all.

The growth has already been dramatic. By spring 1998, 60 percent of commissionable trades at Fidelity Investments were made using PCs; a year earlier, it was 7 percent. By June of the same year, 52 percent of the total customer trading volume at Charles Schwab & Co. was done online. With 14.4 million online trading accounts worth $688 billion forecast by the year 2002,[12] those affluent, frequent traders are precisely the investors who are most profitable for brokers.

When it comes to trading, the discounters that led the way in dial-up and phone transactions—Schwab, Fidelity, Quick & Reilly—have been joined in their no-frills strategy. Net-born, online-only operations such as E*Trade carried the revolution begun by the discounters one step further by cutting the cost of trading dramatically. Others followed, and ultimately trades that used to cost $25 to $30 minimum—the definition of "discount" only a few years ago—were made available for $8 or less. Breakpoints that cut fees for bigger trades are giving way to flat prices that apply whether a person buys 100 or 1000 shares. WebStreet Securities offers free trading on NASDAQ orders of 1000 shares or more.

The actual transaction in the Net Future will be a commodity and the new battleground will be service. Accurate, fast trading is critical, but sophisticated investing information that empowers customers and encourages them to trade actively will be an increasingly important competitive weapon in the Net Future.

Those active traders who generate the vast majority of brokerage profits demand extensive, timely statistics. Full-service brokers such as Paine Webber are anxious to make this kind of information available. Microsoft Investor, Quicken.com, DBC, and Quote.com all have aggregated individual information services from Standard & Poor's, First Call, Zacks, Morningstar, and others into content-rich packages. Online investors also can find help with interactive financial planning calculators (smartcalc.com), fundamental information (Quicken.com, Quote.com, DBC), analysis and commentary (TheStreet.com), company profiles (Hoover's), SEC filings (Disclosure), analyst recommendations (Zacks), price history (charts), and earnings estimates (First Call).

Those services in turn are being private-labeled for Internet search engines such as Yahoo! and Lycos, media companies, financial services companies, and others. These companies have discovered that the constantly changing nature of financial information has the power to draw repeat visits from the kind of affluent user that is most likely to be followed by advertising dollars.

This emphasis on supplying information sets up an interesting dynamic. On one end of the spectrum are the full-service houses that offer the handholding of a broker who uses access to all this information to provide investment recommendations, earning a commission in the process. On the other end are the superdiscounters; they offer low trading prices, but if there's a problem with a trade, the investor gets little in the way of unpaid service.

In the Net Future there will emerge a new kind of brokerage whose services and pricing are the meat in the middle of the other two market slices. The E-investor, accustomed to researching purchases online, will become increasingly comfortable with doing investment research and financial planning, and trading there as well. Yet many people will still want to be able to talk to someone in person if there's a problem with a trade. To address that large market, a brokerage might offer:

- Superior customer support, both online and phone
- A wealth of information to support customer decisions, including online data and serious financial planning tools or services
- Prices that are lower than the full-service firms but that are not based on "you're-on-your-own-kid" service

It's not only the giants that are moving into the Net Future. U.S. Clearing, a subsidiary of Quick and Reilly that handles the trades of smaller brokerage firms, offers its affiliated brokerages a mass-customized turnkey Internet investing site that can supply customers with quotes, charts, company news, and a portfolio tracking tool.

As traditional sources of information become more available to the average investor, new sources of investing information will emerge. Added to the online editions of traditional investing publications have been such online-only publications as TheStreet.com, which features the commentary of well-known Wall Street observer James Cramer. The Motley Fool began on America Online with David and Tom Gardner, two brothers who figured they were just as likely to outsmart the market as any of the more established pundits. In addition to offering their own commentary, the brothers started investing forums where investors could ask questions, post comments, and generally engage in the kind of I-made-a-killing braggadocio that avid investors live for.

The Motley Fool is now one of the most popular online investing areas. However, investors looking for information do well to remember that, to paraphrase the famous *New Yorker* cartoon, on the Internet, nobody knows your stock's a dog. Stock touts paid to promote the value of a stock have been known to generate tidal waves of investor enthusiasm by spreading the word of a hot stock on the Net, whose price skyrockets and then collapses.

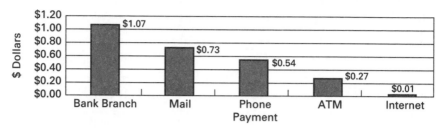

What's a Transaction Cost?

FIGURE 2.1

THE NEW BROKERS OR THE NEW BANKS?

The case for online banking is compelling, both for customers and for the banks themselves. The cost of a transaction on the Internet is roughly a penny, dramatically less than that of any other distribution channel.[13] By the end of the century, 90 percent of North American banks will be able to handle Web transactions. So it is no wonder that banks as a whole are ahead of brokerages and insurance companies in offering Web-based transactions. There are even Internet-only banks, such as Atlanta Internet Bank and Houston-based CompuBank.

Even banks reluctant to go that far are weaving the Web into their other services.

- Canada Trust allows customers with the proper equipment to reach the call center directly and chat with a representative. The rep can walk the customer through such online tasks as applying for a mortgage while the customer is still online. The rep also knows which page of its Web site the customer is on, and can send information to the customer's computer screen as he or she is using the site.

- Huntington Bancshares gives customers the ability to check, via personalized pages, information about all their relationships with the bank. Users can monitor money market, checking, and savings accounts; credit card accounts; mortgages and other loans; mutual funds; and CDs. Adding the transactional capabilities has doubled the bank's customer acquisition rate.

- NationsBank Direct, a service of Charlotte, North Carolina–based NationsBank, handles treasury services for its corporate customers over the Net. Foreign exchange wires, treasury management, digital check image viewing, notification of bad checks, and receivables data are all available online.

- In a pilot project, Pittsburgh Power & Light automatically debits the accounts of corporate customers for the amount of their utility bill.

- Citibank will work with car dealerships to approve or deny car loans within 90 seconds of a loan application being submitted. Both customers and dealers will be able to check on the status of a loan.

- Chase Manhattan customers are able not only to view their account information and transfer funds on the Web but also to view and pay bills from retailers and other institutions that participate in the program.

- Austrian bank Sicherheit und Privat (Security and Privacy) offers a virtual Swiss bank account online, complete with digital cash transactions and a privacy-protected MasterCard.

In addition to putting bank services on the Net, banks will increasingly blur the lines between themselves and brokerage houses. However, rather than panting after the day traders that brokers hunger for, banks will try to position themselves as "one-stop shopping" centers for financial services. By offering brokerage services, financial planning tools, and news, companies such as Wells Fargo, Chase Manhattan, Wachovia, Citibank, and Compass Bank of Birmingham, Alabama are positioning themselves as the new bank-broker to beat, in hopes of luring new customers and increasing retention rates.

CROSSING THE CHANNEL

Beyond contending with legacy business and legacy infrastructure, established companies moving into the Net Future have to be concerned with their traditional partners, most notably their sales channels. Traditional full-service brokerage companies face the dilemma of whether to jump on the Net bandwagon and alienate the brokers that own the direct customer relationships and generate most of their business, or to ignore the Net while Net-based retail stock transactions approach one-fourth of all trades.

The airline industry, a significant part of the travel industry, gets about 80 percent of its U.S. travel booked through travel agencies. Traditionally, airlines paid travel agencies 10 percent of the revenue for each ticket booked, with the obvious benefit of requiring fewer ticketing agents at the airlines. They had effectively deployed their business directly to the travel agents, which functioned as if they were parts of the airlines themselves, including being armed with terminals that linked the agents directly into the airlines' reservations systems. Some interactive travel systems, such as the Sabre Group's Net-based Sabre Interactive Travel Service, fulfill Internet orders from consumers through a contract travel agent, to keep the agent channel involved.

However, travel agents were powerless as they watched consumers flock to Web sites such as those from Delta Airlines to book their travel directly. Delta in turn reduced commissions to travel agents to 6 percent, further eroding one of the travel agents' core revenue streams. Rather than joining the Net revolution by looking for ways to transform their businesses into cybercorporations, many travel agencies decided to charge travelers a fee to issue airline tickets.

Instead of siding with the travelers and offering new and innovative services, these agencies aided in driving value-conscious travelers directly to the airlines' Web sites, where they could not only get tickets booked for free but also see the latest deals across all airlines. In the short term, the effect could be to drive the most profitable traveler, the business traveler, away from travel agents, leaving those same agents with time-consuming, low-profit holiday travelers. Travel agents might have rethought how to better service their customers, and aggregate the online airline efforts into their service offerings.

BRIDGING THE CHANNEL

1. *Force the issue.* Avon decided that the potential to sell on the Net was too great to ignore. At the same time, it didn't want to alienate the army of Avon ladies who held the link to the customer. Company research showed little overlap between existing customers and potential Net customers. The company also then looked at ways to help reps set up their own Web sites. Liberty Mutual asks online customers up front whether they buy directly or buy through a financial adviser. If the answer is "through an adviser," customers are routed to the appropriate area and told that information about their needs, based on what they do on the Web site, will be relayed to their adviser.

2. *Sell around them.* Gibson Guitars found that though dealers were outraged when the company tried to sell guitars directly to consumers, they didn't object to direct sales of accessories such as guitar strings and parts. Other companies have found that items not profitable in the physical world of distributors are perfectly suited to online distribution. Though J. C. Penney sells on the Net as well as in stores, one of its Net strategies might be adopted by retailers facing channel conflict. Penney offers coupons on its Web site that can be printed and redeemed at its stores; a similar strategy might work with franchises or distributors. Store 24, a convenience store chain, also offers online coupons for its stores.

3. *Back off.* VFCorp., the makers of Lee and Wrangler Jeans, decided it would rather not compete with major retail stores. Instead, it uses the Net to help customers with size and fit—and to help them find nearby retailers.

4. *Play on a level field.* When Sega of America decided to sell its products online as well as by phone, it was determined not to undercut the traditional retail distribution channels. Online customers do not get discounts; they pay the same price on the Net as they do in a store. In addition, online customers must pay for shipping, making online purchases a bit more expensive than buying from stores. Sega's occasional online promotions offer products unavailable from retailers, not discounted prices.

In other words, Sega decided not to take advantage of the economics of the Net at the expense of its distributors; there is no great cost incentive to shopping online that would threaten the traditional distribution channel and possibly cause them to stop carrying Sega products.

E-COMMERCE MEETS THE REAL WORLD

The Net Future will create not only a buyer's but also a seller's market. Part of the appeal in moving to an E-business world is the close connection between buyer and seller in all categories. Nowhere will this be felt more strongly than in business-to-business transactions (see Chapter Four). As consumers continue to migrate online because of great deals, so too will businesses discover that the economics of E-commerce are compelling: 85 percent of 1997 E-commerce revenues were derived from business-to-business transactions.

That close connection between buyer and seller, whether the customer is a business or a consumer, will change the role of the sales force, placing salespeople in the role of consultants rather than order takers. For example, bank tellers will increasingly handle exception cases rather than routine transactions.

"We'll be able to use our salespeople in a higher-value capacity," says Jim Smith, executive director of electronic commerce for John Hancock. "They may specialize in a particular type of product rather than a geographic area. But that means we have to give them the tools to fulfill that role."[14]

One of the biggest hurdles in some areas of electronic commerce is the existence of state regulations. For example, the sale of life insurance often still requires a physical exam, and only a handful of states allow the purchase of car insurance online. However, as the value proposition of the Net becomes increasingly compelling, both businesses and consumers will begin to press for dramatic changes in that environment.

RETAIL MEETS THE E-WORLD

Having an established business can make it all the more difficult to move headfirst into the Net Future. Take, for example,

E-Commerce Lingo

THEY SAID . . .	THEY'LL SAY . . .
Check number	Check routing number
Name	Customer ID
PIN	Password
Paperless office	Paperless cash
Ticket	E-Ticket
Cash	Cybercash
Direct response	Clickthrough
Checking account	Digital wallet
Small change	Micropayment
"The check is in the mail"	"Payment is being routed through my ISP"

Egghead, Inc. When the software store chain faced a horde of computer superstores, rather than devote huge resources to trying to compete in the physical world, it closed all its 80 stores to focus on Internet-only selling. The $100 million retailer decided to chase part of the online software sales, which promised to move well past $1 billion by 2002, accounting for more than 30 percent of all consumer software sales. The firm laid off four out of five workers, and saved more than $20 million in annual overhead by the move. It even changed its name from Egghead, Inc., to Egghead.com, Inc.

THE DON'TS OF THE E-COMMERCE WORLD

There are some potential pitfalls for companies moving into the Net Future. Being too overt with sales pitches or too narrow-minded about how to use the Internet can either stall potential useful efforts or bring down those that are well intentioned.

Don't Be a Hero. Team up wherever possible to enhance product or speed delivery. Take advantage of real communities, rather than trying to force-fit groups of people. Some companies developed elaborate Web sites in an attempt to build communities around a product, forgetting that just because people use the same brand of deodorant doesn't mean they are likely to congregate. A stronger approach is to find a way to sell products through true communities whose interests are similar to those in the target market. In the case of our hypothetical deodorant company, a good fit might be a community interested in sports and health information.

Don't Be Two-Faced.   Make sure your online and real-world brand identities match. If one of your key value propositions as a retailer is convenience, make especially sure that your public Web site design is easy to navigate. If you're an upscale retailer, you'd better find some way to add serious value online—without destroying your corporate image—to compete with discounters that are only a click away.

Don't Stand in Cement.   Just because something hasn't been profitable in the past doesn't mean it's not a business opportunity now. Camelot Music began to sell overlooked music selections on the Net. The cost of distribution was low enough that it was worthwhile to offer titles that sell only a few copies a year—not enough to justify stocking them in Camelot's stores. N2K's Music Boulevard has had the same experience; roughly 80 percent of its sales are "deep catalog."[15]

Don't Use the Old Metrics.   It will be increasingly important in the Net Future to compare marketing costs against the potential lifetime value of a customer. The ability to tailor a user's experience to his or her needs creates a powerful dynamic that can ensure an ongoing revenue stream. Give the customer a reason to supply you with the information you need to deliver a personalized service, and you create a customer who probably won't want to go to the trouble of reentering the same data somewhere else. Who do you want to put you out of business, you or a new competitor?

Don't Be Fooled by the Lag Time!   Because Internet connectivity has been more widely adopted in the United States than elsewhere in the world, some observers thought commerce on the Net would be limited to the U.S market. However, companies are finding that U.S. experience can be an important preview of what will happen elsewhere. And the lag time between the two will be dramatically shortened in the Net Future. Consider the case of Encyclopaedia Britannica, which shuttered its American sales force in favor of its pay service on the Net way back in 1996. It was not until 1998 that the era of door-to-door Britannica sales ended in the United Kingdom. By mid-1998, more than half of all U.K. college students had access to Britannica's Web site, a paid service. The U.K. transition lagged but the market dynamics of the Net value proposition were too compelling to keep companies doing business the old way, in any market.

Don't Take Without Giving   When Lucent Technologies created its MapsOnUs product on the Net, it wanted to capture as much information as possible about its users. However, it knew that too much interrogation would turn people away from the service, which allows consumers to pick any location in the United States and receive free mapping and detailed printed directions. The solution? As individual travelers continue to request more detailed information about route to destination, they are gently prompted to provide additional personal information to the company. This quid-pro-quo approach can help companies fill their databases with detailed consumer and business information, so they may provide even more relevant information or service to users who return. Lucent, which ultimately sold MapsOnUs, was able to promote traffic and goodwill by gently prodding travelers to provide small pieces of information that bring large returns in service.

GETTING TO THE OTHER SIDE

Companies of all types and sizes are discovering that the dynamics of retail in the Net Future are quite different. Smart Kids Toys, a toy chain based in Greenwich, Connecticut that specializes in educational toys, changed its entire business model to prepare for the Net Future. Here's the view from Mary DeSilva, owner of Smart Kids Toys:

Back in '96 we had three stores and found it was difficult to run them all centrally from our location in Greenwich. The others were in Fairfield, CT, and Scarsdale, NY. We were seeing this at the same time that the Internet was beginning to take off. Our oldest son happened to have a software business, so we had him create a Web site for our store.

After he set up the original site, we found it was inventory tracking that we really needed, because someone would want to buy an item on the site and we found we didn't have it in stock. So he wrote a program to administer the inventory, manage the orders, and make additions to the site itself. Then we had to upgrade our retail point-of-sale system to communicate with this Web system. We run the retail business upstairs and the Web business downstairs.

Our choice of retail computer systems was driven by our Web site business. With the two integrated, our strategy is set for the future. We are conservatively planning on the Web business to be 30 percent of our total sales in '98, twice that in '99, and who knows beyond that. In the meantime, we figured out the business model. We just take the 500 top-selling products from our stores and put them on the Web site; it's an easy feed off a running business. We do fulfillment here and just keep feeding the Web business. It's really the fulfillment part that's expensive—the warehousing and shipping of the toys. So combining the retail and Web in one location really makes sense. We finally closed two of our three physical stores and now use the Greenwich facility as the central point for our global Net business, which is what it instantly became. The Net let us expand our business without new locations.

At first, we got most of our orders from all over the world. Our first order was from a grandmother in Rome who said to us, "You'll probably never be able to get the toys to me in time for Christmas," but we did. She sent us a nice E-mail, she was so happy. We actually got so many orders from outside the United States, we had to increase the international shipping charges to try to drive the business domestically, at least until we can ship more cost-effectively. Out of the international orders, about 50 percent were from Asia. This was interesting, since a fair amount of the goods being bought were manufactured in Asia. So we were receiving goods from Asia and people from Asia were buying them back!

We also get a tremendous amount of requests from around the world from people who want to be dealers. They want to buy direct from us and then sell to others. We really target the educated and concerned parent, not children. The grandparent market is going to be a tremendous market for us, I can see it already. Counties around the country are educating the elderly, especially how to shop online. Most of our marketing is electronic because it's so efficient.

I'm amazed at how personal buying on the Net is. We get parents and grandparents who send notes to their nieces and grandsons with the gifts and we often get messages back from the buyers. We have running correspondence with people we've never met.

You also can tell when people have time. Sunday night is a big order night and Monday morning is the busiest day of the week for us. Our Net business will become its own entity, and now we're looking for a larger facility to fulfill the orders we expect from the Net. Net commerce is tremendous and now we're looking at going beyond retail.

The best way for existing companies to succeed in the cybereconomy will be to understand that the Net is a new medium, that the rules of business are different, and that transitioning into the environment will take an integrated effort. Customers will not be served in one arena alone, so it is important for companies to incorporate Net efforts with traditional business.

MERGING WORLDS

- Office Depot didn't launch its public Web site until 1998, having waited until it felt its customers—those in home offices, small businesses, and individuals—were ready to shop online. But two years earlier, the company created one of the first pilot projects for procurement of office supplies on the Net. Office Depot set up a private Web site for buyers at

Massachusetts Institute of Technology. It later opened the site to many of the customers of its business services division. It ended up with hundreds of customers, ranging from universities to corporations such as Motorola. The world's largest office products retailer tackled business-to-business commerce first, integrating it with the core business rather than simply trying to market its wares to consumers at a Web site.

- Consumers can buy online from CompUSA, but when they have a problem with a computer purchased online, they can either pack it and ship it back to the company or simply take it to the nearest store.

- In a pilot project at Sam's Club stores, independent insurance agencies set up sales kiosks in 88 of the discount retail giant's outlets. Unlike the Allstate agents, which used to be located in Sears stores and sold only Allstate insurance, agents will be able to offer coverage from several different insurance companies. Using a system from Insurance Holdings of America, agents will access the Internet for data and execute sales transactions electronically from the store. If successful, the program, dubbed Group Advantage, will be expanded to the 400-plus Sam's Club outlets.

- When Playboy Enterprises decided to go online in August 1994, it also decided not to replicate the experience it had when it launched the Playboy Channel.[16] The television effort, now the most profitable aspect of the business, took years to prove itself, and the company spent millions getting it on its feet. With Playboy Online, the company took the opposite tack and started small. It ran the business on a breakeven basis for two years to prove that a business was indeed there. While starting early made this strategy easier, it proves that profitability on the Web does not necessarily require investing and losing lots of money first. The media company also went online without cannibalizing its traditional business. In fact, online subscribers can browse Playboy's archives—not easy to do in the physical world even if readers still have that collection of old issues in the attic.

Some companies are finding that their core businesses adapt especially well to the new environment:

- Ticketmaster's profitable online ticket sales operation represents a growing share of its revenue, with 22 percent of those online sales coming from new business. USA Networks, which owns Ticketmaster, hopes to integrates the company's transaction-processing capabilities with its other properties, including the Home Shopping Network.
- ValPak coupons, which distributes packages of local business coupons through the mail, created an online operation to distribute electronic coupons via its Web site in 24 U.S. cities.
- Discount broker Charles Schwab & Co. offered Internet access for customers in its 270 branches. It also started offering online trading to all its nearly 5 million account holders rather than making the service available only to its top-tier clients.

Other companies are crossing the boundary between new and old channels only in selective areas. Many Net-only companies, such as Amazon.com and CDNow, are utilizing traditional advertising mass media—TV, radio, and print—to lure online users. Auto-by-Tel advertised on the biggest mass-market ad buy imaginable: the SuperBowl. Amazon.com also is increasing its physical warehousing capabilities after storing almost no books on premises.

EXPAND THE BUSINESS

Companies may be able to find unexpected markets related to existing brands.

- Party Creations of Georgia started selling packages of customized party decorations for children on the Web. However, the owner found that she was getting requests for highly specialized theme parties for grownups. The people who asked her to supply them regularly with themed weddings and corporate event planning became an important part of her business.

- UPS reinforced its image as a shipping company by developing an online delivery program to guarantee the security and authenticity of digital messages. UPS OnLine Dossier is designed to allow financial services companies, health care institutions, law firms, and companies with global distribution to send sensitive documents over the Net. It verifies the identities of both sender and recipient, confirms delivery, and insures the transmission for up to $100,000. A less expensive service is designed for less sensitive documents.

- Like many other financial services companies, Telekurs processes financial transactions for its customers. Those relationships are enabling it to develop additional services processing E-commerce credit card transactions for the same customers. It also supplies customers with digital certificates that guarantee the authenticity of electronic documents. Telekurs morphed into a company that goes beyond financial services.

- M&M's sells mugs, T-shirts, and hats with the M&M logo online. J. C. Penney also sells items online that are not available in stores. For example, computers would be a slow seller for Penney's usual customer base, which is 80 percent mature women; on the Net, the retailers can appeal to a new and different customer set.

NOTHING BUT NET

It will be possible to make significant revenue in the Net-only environment, but not as easily as in the traditional world. You can't see the competitors coming, while the competitors can easily track your efforts and leapfrog them at any desired turn. A dramatic illustration of the Net's power as a platform for leapfrogging is the Web site of the National Center for Supercomputing Applications at the University of Illinois, where Netscape was born. The site's archives show that of the commercial sites listed as new in 1993, only a smattering still exist.

The most successful Internet-only companies will be those whose business models are driven by Net-enabled customization, speed, and community.

- Shopping.com sells a wide variety of consumer goods, offering extraordinary discounts on selected items. By reintermediating distributors suffering from the tiny margins allowed them by superstore retailers in the physical world, it could offer discounts such as 60 percent on books. Chief Operating Officer Douglas Hay's background in traditional retailing enabled the company to put together a network of 250 distributors of everything from consumer packaged goods to household furnishings. Because of the economics of selling on the Net, distributors can make more selling through Shopping.com than through traditional outlets, Hay says.

- Banks used to build ornate Greek Revival structures, whose sturdy columns spoke of permanence and were often a dominant physical presence in small-town America. Not so with CompuBank. Customers of the Internet-only institution do everything online; the bank has no physical presence. Checking and savings accounts and bill payment were the first services, to be followed by brokerage accounts and credit cards. As with any bank, deposits, which are made by mail or by direct deposit from an employer, are insured by the FDIC.

- NetGrocer is rethinking the food chain —literally. The online grocer takes advantage of the Net's unlimited geographic reach by delivering supermarket staples across the United States via Federal Express. By selling only nonperishable items, NetGrocer avoids having to deal with local groceries as other online grocery services do. Buying directly from wholesalers and manufacturers keeps the company's cost of goods low, so it doesn't have to charge membership fees.

- When Michael Kinsley, former editor of the New Republic and CNN's *Crossfire* host, left to join Microsoft, it was to launch *Slate*, an electronic-only political commentary publication. By 1998, the free publication had about 150,000 online readers a month. With 30 employees and annual advertising revenue of about $1 million, less than the cost to produce, the publication decided to charge a subscription fee.

- Rather than maintaining an inventory of its own, eBay became profitable by putting buyers and sellers in touch with each other in an auction environment. The company takes a percentage of every transaction.

E-EVERYTHING

Online commerce has only begun to demonstrate the power of the Net to connect sellers to Main Street, USA. Following are a few examples of the new retail environment indicating that the cybereconomy is, in fact, on its way to Main Street. This is just the tip of what lies ahead.

E-MUSIC

- Streamland.com, sponsored by Levi's, provides a pick-your-own music video jukebox.
- Sony Music is taking a hybrid approach, selling traditional albums via the Net.
- EMI Music lets visitors search an online database of song lyrics.
- N2K, owner of Music Boulevard, plans to seek out artists not currently under contract whose music they can distribute directly on the Web.[17]
- BMG Music Service has expanded its direct-mail music club to the Net. Three months after the company launched a revised online service, 400,000 of the company's 8 million catalog customers were online members as well, and BMG found that online club members tend to buy more CDs than direct-mail customers.

E-TRAVEL

- Already one of the most successful E-commerce categories, travel will continue its rapid growth, with the dollar value of airfares, hotel rooms, rental cars, and vacation packages booked online reaching $8.9 billion by 2002.[18]

- Airlines now automatically issue paperless tickets unless customers request a paper ticket. One reason: handling costs are $1 for E-tickets compared with $8 for a paper ticket. Superdiscounted last-minute airfares available only online and sold directly by the airlines will require use of E-tickets.

- United Airlines is going beyond simply selling its own flights online. United Connection allows users to enter a date, desired flight time, and destination; the service not only retrieves a list of matching flights from multiple airlines but also allows consumers to buy the ticket and choose a seat.

- Microsoft's Expedia sold more than $100 million in online bookings in the first year after it started.[19] It is expanding into the business travel market by offering a version of the service that can be used by corporate travel departments.

E-MONEY

- QuickenMortgage, E-Loan, and HomeShark partner with banks and mortgage companies to allow consumers to compare home mortgage rates and apply for loans over the Net. The dollar value of home loans issued by Internet Mortgage, a subsidiary of Ameri-National Mortgage Co., was between $2 million and $3 million a day six months after the service launched.

- Bank Rate Monitor provides automated comparisons of credit cards, money market account rates, and more.

E-CARS

- Using information entered about a specific used car, the Kelley Blue Book's online service will tell users or potential buyers what the old clunker is worth.

- Edmund's, which has supplied car buyers with information about car invoice prices for years, posts information about manufacturers' holdback allowances—a 2 to 3 percent profit for the dealership, which is built into the invoice price—as well as an up-to-date list of rebates and sales incentives on individual models.

- Ford started selling used cars online.

E-Food

- Local Girl Scout councils have begun selling Thin Mints, Tagalongs, and Samoas over the Net. Instead of learning business by selling cookies directly, the scouts in many cases put up the Web sites and handle online sales.

- Antonelli's Meat, Fish, and Poultry Shop in San Francisco, a local butcher shop, ships its products to vacationing customers around the globe.

- KosherGrocer.com thought its business would come mostly from rural customers who didn't have access to kosher products.[20] In fact, urban customers and institutions that want convenience proved to be a strong market for the Internet start-up.

- Papa John's offers takeout pizza ordering online and partners with Cybermeals for delivery. Cybermeals in turn has signed agreements with Yahoo!, Excite, Lycos, and America Online; customers can order online from more than 20,000 local restaurants in selected cities around the United States, and Cybermeals will deliver the meal.

E-Postage

- The U.S. Postal Service is testing a Web-based system to allow consumers to buy postage online using a credit card or transferring money from a bank account. The system, developed by Internet start-up E-Stamp, downloads the postage and prints it directly on the envelope, eliminating the need for stamps. A bar code is included to prevent fraud. The current system requires a security device that is attached to the user's computer, but E-Stamp, Pitney Bowes, and others are developing systems to enable purchase from any computer.

E-Pix

- The Wedding Photographers Network allows users to browse an online database of the photographers' portfolios.

E-Grills

- The Iron Works, a $2 million family-owned business, made its largest sale ever online: a $35,000 custom-built gas grill.

E-Mom, E Apple Pie

- If you have an old photo of Mom that needs sprucing up, Artshots Graphic Studio will make the photo look like new. And Pie Gourmet will ship a frozen apple pie anywhere in the continental United States overnight for $44.95.

NET RESULTS

E-commerce is the lead and often most visible part of E-business, but it is just the tip of the iceberg. The challenge for established companies will be to look at their electronic commerce efforts and see how they tie in to the rest of the traditional business. How can knowledge gathered in real time from consumers be used to streamline manufacturing and distribution processes? How can this knowledge be used to enhance product creation? Who are these new customers and what are their new needs?

In the Net Future, it will be difficult for companies and individuals to live in one world alone. Successful companies will look at the networked environment not just as a new distribution channel, but as a totally new way to do business that affects all four of the traditional marketing "four P's"— product, price, place, and promotion.

The companies that win will be those that have looked at the Net in terms of what it means to make their entire organization an integral part of the E-business community.

THE WIRED WORKFORCE TAKES OVER

Employees and managers are about to be interconnected throughout the enterprise as never before. However, the connections themselves are not what will dramatically change business; it's what companies can and will do when they tap into a totally wired workforce. And it's what that workforce, empowered with more instantly retrievable knowledge than ever before, may do with that newfound power.

The move to a wired workforce is being driven by companies realizing the potential of corporate intranets, allowing everyone in the organization to use the same user-friendly interface of the World Wide Web. These company-private intranets will reach out as tiny tentacles to virtually every employee and manager anywhere in the world. Providing instant information dissemination and new ways of internal collaboration, this new capability will change corporate communication and employee interaction like nothing since the introduction of the IBM personal computer in 1982.

This interconnectedness will give companies true competitive advantage, while empowering workers to drive their own career destinies. With a wired workforce, company executives will have the ability to instantly broadcast messages to all, and employees will have unprecedented power to reach out and electronically communicate among themselves.

Corporate intranets continue to grow rapidly; with intranet servers expected to outsell Internet servers 4.6 million to 440,000 by the turn of the century.[1] One reason for the rapid adoption has been the payback in cost savings and increased productivity. The typical return on investment can be more than 1000 percent.[2]

The more obvious uses of technology that links workers are to provide employee benefit information, such as 401K tracking and health benefit changes and updates. By 1998, roughly half of all U.S. companies enabled employees to do some sort of human resources–related business over the Web, and 38 percent were using it to link their global operations.[3] However, companies that link their workers only for HR applications will be missing the boat.

The newly wired workforce will affect:

Managers.   The wired workforce, with its dramatically altered way of working, will create new challenges for digital managers, who will need an updated set of skills to function as team leaders, publishers, censors, and proponents of rapid adoption of new ideas.

Human resources personnel.   HR departments will face new challenges: tougher competition for mobile knowledge workers, reliance on more non-employees, and tougher decisions about what labor skills are needed in a networked world and how to train an employee base in them. They also will face an increasingly vocal staff of workers who will make new demands of their employer based on the basis of mountains of electronic information available to them. Those demands will include ongoing training for lifetime employability rather than lifetime employment.

Home-based workers.   In the Net Future, work goes home and home goes to the office. Intranets will allow employees to work anywhere, anytime, all the time, and will require new management processes to monitor employee performance, create bonding mechanisms, and deal with offsite workers interactively and electronically.

The organization itself. Creating, managing, and using the info-flow will be a major challenge for the intranetworked organization. There also will be internal struggles over control of this powerful new medium. The wired organization will be positioned to turn on a dime, and the paperless office may come one step closer to reality to keep up with the office-less worker. And as companies expect their workers to do more work outside the office, such as weekend E-mails, employees will come to expect more of their corporations, such as being allowed to do more "home" work at the office.

REVOLUTION IN THE RANKS

At the heart of the coming workforce revolution is a fundamental shift in the distribution of the information that is the lifeblood of a corporation.

As with the larger Internet, intranets make possible widespread distribution of information at low cost, accessible whenever and wherever an employee needs it. Instead of distributing reams of paper that may or may not one day be read, companies are finding it far simpler to post information on Web pages that can be updated quickly and easily. In addition, departments and even individuals can have their own pages; their colleagues have access to the information if they need it and ignore it if they don't. AT&T's 500 linked intranet sites, which include more than half a million pages, may seem overwhelming until one considers the tons of paper they have replaced.

Almost any kind of company that has a reasonable number of employees can benefit from connecting those employees to one another, and to management, though specific benefits will vary.

• Companies whose business involves extensive documentation and lengthy product development cycles will find that intranets help cut the red tape. Because representatives from each of Dallas-based Baylor Health Care System's four hospitals had to approve a contract and could meet only once a month, the process of negotiating pharmacology purchasing contracts took anywhere from three to six months. Using the intranet to coordinate contract reviews should cut that time to three weeks, and the organization hopes eventually to transmit the contract to the vendor electronically.

- Many companies rely on large numbers of entry-level workers with a high level of turnover to handle call centers and customer inquiries. When rapid expansion required the Amdahl Corporation to absorb a large number of new employees, it needed to get them up to speed quickly. By putting training materials on the company intranet, where employees could access them whenever they needed, the company dramatically cut training time. And Cadence Design Systems found that new intranet-trained sales reps were able to meet their quotas within two months of being hired instead of four.

- As companies that operate around the world face the constraints of multiple languages, highly variable technology capabilities, and geographic disbursement of their workforce, they will increasingly look to the Net as a means of disseminating information. This dynamic will become a self-fulfilling prophecy. As the Internet becomes more widely used around the globe, it will in turn be easier for businesses to function globally. And as more companies go global, the move will drive an even greater need for corporate intranets, which will in turn make it easier for businesses to function globally . . . you get the picture.

- Financial services companies, oil companies, investment bankers—all depend on highly detailed, constantly changing information. Again, as the Internet makes up-to-date information more available in the world at large, it will drive the necessity of having the latest internal information available on demand. Southern California Gas Company representatives must deal with frequently changing prices when making sales calls on customers. The company's intranet, linked to a legacy database, provides real-time information.

However, the next generation of workforce will have more than employee manuals, phone directories, newsletters, and benefits information online. Consider:

- Nearly two-thirds of employees expect to videoconference at least once a month by the year 2000.[4]

- Applied Materials Inc. of Santa Clara intends to use its intranet to remind managers automatically when salary reviews for employees are due and help them create what-if scenarios to assess the impact of various raises on departmental budgets. Early tests of the system have helped managers get reviews in more accurately and on time.

- Some intranetworked companies facilitate purchasing of supplies and equipment by simply featuring Web-based catalogs that include vendors' names and contact information. However, the future will look more like Advanced Micro Devices' system, which allows employees to order certain supplies online and which will be expanded to include more suppliers as well as more employees. Such systems let the company track purchases precisely and prevent maverick buying from companies that are not part of corporate purchasing agreements. The next step for many is to link directly to the ultimate supplier, who becomes part of a corporate extranet (see Chapter Four).

- Ford Motor Company lets its workers buy cars online at a discount. Using the company's intranet, employees can see whether they're eligible to buy. They can select a model, check which options are available and see how the car would look in various colors. Employees use an online calculator to see what their monthly payments would be on a car loan. They can then place an online order and check electronically on delivery status.

Intranets not only offer an effective way for companies to communicate with employees; they also empower employees to communicate with one another. Companies that adopted groupware during the 1990s developed some skills and habits that will be enhanced and expanded in the Net Future as organizations move to corporate intranets. Teams that learned to operate virtually will migrate that work to the corporate intranet, using bulletin boards and chat rooms to conduct business across geographic and temporal boundaries.

The concept of teamwork has received a lot of lip service. In the Net Future, as work becomes more complex and technology provides a way for team members to collaborate regardless of time and distance constraints, it will become the norm. For example, Dow Chemical Co. made Microsoft NetMeeting document sharing software available to 30,000 employees at 120 locations worldwide, giving work groups of up to 25 the ability to view documents at the same time while talking with one another on the phone.

The goal was to cut down on the number of trips and to shorten the cycle time of information sharing on a project. The virtual teams share presentations, work on the same document together, and even conduct global meetings. "We estimate that we've saved between $15,000 and $20,000 in travel and related costs on one business team project alone since the corporate rollout," says Harold Bennett, manager of Dow's desktop conferencing project. Maybe more important, 85 percent of employees surveyed said their productivity had increased with the virtual approach.

Even small companies can use services on the Net that will set up virtual interactive offices for them. These areas let visitors hold virtual conferences, send and receive messages, and exchange data files. Put this increased availability of information into the hands of employees who are part of an information-based economy, and you have a newly empowered workforce: ready, willing, and most important, able to second-guess management decisions.

As organizations decentralize to give themselves increased flexibility, more workers have more information that directly affects how their jobs function. A flattened hierarchy takes those at the bottom of the pyramid and effectively moves them up in the organization. And those newly promoted workers are likely to want a greater voice in how the business is run—particularly when their jobs are so much more directly affected by what goes on around and above them. They may very well use the Net to flex that muscle.

In many cases, the true wiring of the workforce began as a lot of individual grassroots installations of Web browsers and unofficial Web pages put up by individual employees who wanted to streamline knowledge management. Some even had other motives, such as the Borders employees who attempted to organize a union by hosting a Web site for other employees to visit where they could track the history of the organizing campaign.

This monumental shift in who has the information will forever change the dynamics of the contract between employer and employee. The intranet of the Net Future will continue to eviscerate the manager who leads only by virtue of greater access to information. In the short term, of course, the supply of experienced technical workers at all levels has tipped the balance in favor of the employee. But even when this supply-demand disparity is righted, employers will find that the newly empowered workforce, connected by the intranet that the company set up for sound business reasons, will be reluctant to return to the days of "mushroom management," which, for various reasons, left many employees in the dark.

Distributed information also takes on a new meaning when the company's ability to control the distribution of information within its walls is reduced. A wired workforce will have access to any public information available about the company, from whatever source. Want to know what the company president makes? Go to one of the company's SEC filings. Curious about whether you're underpaid relative to your peers in other companies? Check out JobSmart, which lists salaries by title, region, and experience level. This totally informed workforce will be newly empowered to, if not make, then at least understand decisions as they're being made.

Or browse the online job posting services to see what other jobs in your field might be open. If an employee posts a negative newspaper article on the company bulletin board, it can be quickly taken down; not so for something that is a few keystrokes away on the public Net—a public that includes colleagues and employees. And even if employees don't have access to the information at the office, they are likely to have it at home.

However, the new contract also means that employees will bear the responsibility for their own advancement. At Dow Chemical, employees traditionally learned about advancement opportunities through an old-boy network of friends and relatives working in the same plant. The company now electronically posts openings and job descriptions at factories around the globe, expanding the base of applicants. It also includes career development reference materials. However, it's up to the employee to monitor the openings.

DISINTERMEDIATION OF MANAGEMENT?

New tools that permit collaborative computing will empower companies to create employee virtual communities for specific tasks or events. They also will empower employees to organize their own communities. The new technologies will create new "virtual" mentors and peer groups, which may be inside the company or outside.

At Eli Lilly, a course on combinatorial chemistry was adapted as a prototype online course.[5] Rather than sitting through traditional instruction, chemists study materials online, examine and solve case studies, and submit proposals for experimentation based on their current real-world research efforts. The most promising projects become part of an integrated reference desktop from which others can benefit. Experts serve as online and in-person mentors and facilitators, reviewing and making suggestions about the materials, case studies and proposals. The system includes an extensive online reference library and discussion groups.

One challenge in implementing such a system is to create the kind of cultural environment that encourages such collaboration. "Researchers as well as others in the business world focus primarily on individual production; collaboration outside their immediate area tends to take a back seat," says Lilly's Josh Plaskoff, who is in charge of developing the system. "We need to take a lesson from basketball and track assists (when a player's pass helps another player score). In business we downplay assists." Plaskoff is working with other areas of the company to develop systems for rewarding and encouraging cross-functional collaboration and shared learning.

TRW's 9000-person Space and Electronics Group has a "mentorship databank" that helps pair up mentors and those seeking a mentor.[6] When the system launched on the division's intranet, 130 mentors had agreed to serve. Since then, an additional 70 mentors and 230 potential protégés have entered their names and other profile information in the databank. Pairings are done blind.

Protégés do a keyword search of the databank on a topic about which they'd like to have a mentor. The search returns a list of mentor profiles, which give previous titles, divisions where candidates have worked, and areas of expertise, but not mentor names. When a mentor is selected, the system notifies that individual of the protégé's interest, again without divulging the protégé's name. Once a mentor accepts, the protégé is given the mentor's name to contact independently. The rest is up to the individuals involved.

"We felt very strongly that we didn't want this to be a program where people had to account for their participation," says Bob Esposito, who is in charge of the databank. "We do everything we can to preserve the natural process of getting people together."

The response to the original program, which encouraged ongoing relationships between mentor and protégé, has led the company to develop the Minute Mentor system, aimed at facilitating short-term networking. Minute Mentors agree to have their names made public in the database for shorter, one-time information sessions. That way, people who don't need an ongoing mentor relationship can still benefit from a mentor's experience.

Mentors outside the company also are only a click away, through both experience communities (see Chapter Eight) and online career advisers. Roughly 2000 Hewlett-Packard employees participate in an E-mail mentoring program with high school students, helping them with projects in science and math as well as research skills. One mentor worked to develop a student's interest in math by linking it with baseball, his passion. The pair worked to construct a statistical model of a baseball player's performance that could be tested against actual game statistics.

Or consider this exchange from a bulletin board at *hard@work*.

> *Question:* I am the executive assistant at a small start-up company. We are moving offices, and I have been given only seven days to find a new office and hire movers. Although this time frame isn't very realistic, it's the moving itself that concerns me. My boss told me that I must unpack our computers (by myself) and set them up again. Our 10 computers are heavy, and I feel physically incapable of unpacking them. I'm also concerned about lifting heavy boxes. I am a small woman and I don't feel this sort of assignment is reasonable. But I am afraid to tell my boss because she might fire me. What can I do?
>
> *Answer:* How can she possibly fire you when "lifting 75 pounds" wasn't in your job description or in the ad you answered? If your boss is stubborn, ask about the workers' comp plan before you do any lifting. She'll get the hint. I recently told my company that I wouldn't travel with the laptop because it was extremely heavy, and the last time I had to carry it on my shoulder it was sore for a week. They quickly made other arrangements.

The wired workforce not only uses the intranet as a way to operate in teams; it also sometimes uses it to actually form the teams themselves.

Consultants at Booz, Allen & Hamilton often need to include specific areas of expertise on cross-functional teams. The company had traditionally relied on word of mouth to locate expertise within the far-flung organization. In the highly competitive culture of consulting, where admitting to a lack of knowledge is problematic, finding the right person was not always an easy task (certainly not for associates new to the company). The company's intranet, called Knowledge On-Line, allows employees to search the company's résumé database by keywords that may help them turn up someone who has expertise outside their current job function, such as a consultant who currently focuses on bioengineering but who has a background in pharmaceutical development.

THE NEW LAWS OF DIGITAL MANAGEMENT

What type of manager will be required to deal with the wired workforce? One who understands that dealing with a newly empowered, geographically mobile wired worker truly is very different. Organizations will have to grapple with issues that go far beyond developing and deploying the appropriate technologies throughout the enterprise.

NEW RESPONSIBILITIES

When IBM Chairman Lou Gerstner decided that the company should aggressively pursue wiring the company's 270,000 employees scattered throughout 165 countries, he created an internal group called Enterprise Web Management focused on Web-enabling the company's major business processes, including E-commerce, online service and support, and Net-based procurement. In addition to targeting savings in the company's $40 billion-a-year procurement budget and setting up new methods of serving customers through the Net, the group started a Net-based "e-care" initiative for employees.

"There's no doubt there is a workplace revolution going on," says 22-year IBM veteran Jonathan Judge[7], who was tapped as general manager of Enterprise Web Management, to start the internal group. "We now have about 100,000 mobile workers. When you become highly mobile, you need very good tools, combined with all the capabilities of the Net to provide increased productivity and information for employees."

The company found that while the technology enables a workforce to work from anywhere at any time, it brings with it other responsibilities and management issues. "It used to be that you could walk around the office and find things out, sometimes by accident," says Judge. "Now, you need to think about who else needs to know and how do you keep them informed.

Walking around doesn't work when part of your department is mobile or remotely located. You need to keep them informed electronically. "In a wired world, a whole new set of work standards need to emerge. In the old days, I could go back and just tell the five or six people in the office about my last meeting. Now, if I forget to send an E-mail, people who might need to know won't find out directly. There is a whole new set of management responsibilities. If there's a problem and I send an E-mail at 7 p.m., do I transfer the problem to the employee without alerting them via phone? Do I expect 24-hour availability? What's my responsibility as a manager, and as an employee now?

"We need to deal with work-life balance, elderly care, and even issues like what is the proper etiquette in the remote environment."

IBM found that employees who started working remotely actually worked more hours, not less, but the workers were grateful for the opportunity to spread the work over a long period of time.

"There's always more work to do than there is time within a 24-hour period," says Judge. "It has to be OK to say 'I don't take calls at 7 in the morning.' The real issue is that all companies have a culture and value system, and how do you embed that in a remote employee? We've had to rethink the employee-manager responsibility. Going remote and going mobile requires a certain amount of human interaction.

"Some of our people got lonely out there. People actually start to drift and they long for human interaction. They like to go out for a drink after work or go to a promotion party."

The company views its internal Net initiative with a unique measuring stick. "The metrics of this world are totally different," says Judge. "This is an interactive world we're in, but we're absolutely committed to benchmarking with the outside world. I view the Net to be, not a soup-to-nuts solution, but a very valuable component of a hybrid approach. The Net will be used extensively for distance learning.

"To achieve sustainable competitive advantage, you have to be careful about selecting the things that the Web will enable. We have customer self-service with 400 support sites. Software people pride themselves on knowledge of their area. They may be more interested in going through a database to find the answer to a problem without talking to a person. You bring customer service costs down and the customer is satisfied."

IBM also sees a change in speed to market as a bonus benefit to the wiring of its workforce. "The ability to get to all our employees in a matter of hours and to reach the world at large is incredibly powerful," says Judge. Once the group was established, it became part of the office of the CIO.

PERFORMANCE MANAGEMENT

In many industries, the employee of the future will not be required to sit in a cubicle or an office, and will not be constricted to regimented time shifts. Companies and managers will become more focused on getting the job done, leading to more team or group accountability. And employees will be provided with electronic tools and time to use them.

One organization that has started down this road is The Boeing Company, the aerospace giant in Seattle.[8] Like most large companies, Boeing has a public Internet site that describes the company's divisions, products, and financials in great detail. Also like most large companies, Boeing has an extensive intranet infrastructure that sits behind a "firewall," an electronic moat that keeps the information available only to internal staff. The company supplies employees with news items related to their technical specialty, and individuals can select categories of news to which they want to subscribe.

An internal electronic commerce group of about a dozen people helps the company's many divisions steer along the same internal, online course. The group is headed by Linda Fischer, manager of electronic commerce, whose charter was to create a process for intelligence transfer into reusable components and link Net systems to legacy databases. The electronic commerce group hosts monthly electronic forums with about 200 Web developers to share code and foster education. The group intends to stay relatively small so that it can move quickly enough to ensure that the knowledge transfer keeps up with the pace of change.

"Our company encourages employees to have their own Web page," says Fischer. "The employees do it themselves. Some do it from their homes and have family Web sites, some do it at the office. You can now just take a Microsoft Word document and place it on the Web. Then, when a manager is going to a large internal meeting, he can simply look up the people attending in advance."

Not all employees accept the idea that they should have their own page. "A lot of analytic engineers feel that 'broadcasting' is offensive," says Fischer, and the company doesn't force employees to create an electronic presence.

Boeing also sponsors telecommuting throughout the company, and Fischer's entire group telecommutes three days a week in self-managed teams. "When we get a request for service through our intranet, and a customer asks for support, within seconds it goes to the entire team. I can log on to the system and sign up for any in-house course. If there is a seat available, I can sign up using E-mail. We also have online courses," says Fischer.

"The president used to send out VCR tapes each month, but now that information is just broadcast on the Net. It costs so much less to use streaming video networks rather than sending videotapes to all departments. We have full online audio-video, online courses and online certification. The president of Boeing said he now communicates more with his team and sees them less."

Although most of Boeing's divisions are in the high-tech arena, not all employees and managers will leverage the capabilities of the wired workforce. "The people who know how to take advantage of the technology are the informed. Those who don't, well, there's a gap," says Fischer. "Some people still expect a blue sheet to come in the mail, but it doesn't come in the mail anymore. Now, you have to go out to the Net and get it."

The transformation to a wired workforce technologically is relatively straightforward. It is the rest—the changing of habits, behaviors, and procedures that employees and managers do day after day and week after week—that sometimes causes the gut-wrenching. Says Fischer:

> This has challenged management. A lot of people have difficulty with telecommuting because it's away from line of sight management to management by performance. As a digital manager, my goal is to have a fully functional, self-managed team using the Web. With NetMeeting, [a conferencing product], employees can work on a project together from their homes. Those that are not technologically astute will be at a distinct disadvantage. They will move slower than anyone else. The non-digital manager tends to manage in a more controlled environment. All of my people have the same performance objective. Most, if not all, individual performance and MBOs have to be group based. The manager of the future can't be the same as today.
>
> The telecommuting employees have to understand what hours they will be working. For a manager, it requires that you can look out the hallway at 3 o'clock in the afternoon and not see anyone and still know that I have to sign off on time and sign off on overtime. I have to manage by objectives, not seat time. If you don't see the employee at 8:05 a.m. you don't assume they're not working.
>
> Managers are going to be extinct. Middle management does not help a process move forward. All middle management does is inspect, check and review. It stops the process.

While not all companies have so many employees in the high-tech environment of a Boeing, the challenges and opportunities of dealing with a wired workforce have many common elements.

THE GREAT UNWIRED

Creating a wired workforce, with all its implications, does not come naturally to all companies and industries. Some companies even face the challenge of getting their workforce to accept that the enterprise *should* be wired.

The real estate industry has traditionally been slow to adopt new technology. A leading exception to this rule is Re/Max of southeastern Pennsylvania and Maryland.[9] The company, with annual sales of about $5 billion, sells nearly 40,000 properties a year. Like the other offices of the nationwide franchise owner, the company is independently owned and operated, and deploys 1500 other independent contractors scattered throughout its 80 real estate offices. The challenge for the company was to convince these fiercely independent and competitive contractors that being part of a wired workforce was beneficial.

With a consolidating and competing real estate industry, Re/Max of Southeastern PA, Inc. views the Net as a competitive advantage for its brokers. Says CEO Michael Stefonick:

> There will probably be only around seven primary realty companies in America. It will be a brand business. The question I had was, how do I make it easy for my agents to do business and make a living? Our rationale was to provide the tools for them to do this. We needed to make all information accessible to them when they want it, and to utilize push technology to send things to them electronically. We installed an intranet and let the agents dial in from anywhere. They get property data and various other things, like marketing information and templates to market a property. There's no end to the innovation; it's almost like a fairy tale. But the proof is in the pudding. I'm 55 years old and the Net is the most amazing thing I've ever seen. In our company the agent is the customer so I'm in the sales associate business. I need to give my customer what he or she wants. There needs to be more than just hiring the best people and paying them what they're worth, with just a commission on a property sale. The Net is all about getting back to taking care of your customer. It's a challenge to stay ahead when someone else can just leapfrog you. Innovation is every-

where. I try to lead. The Net provides us with operational efficiency. It involves better time management, cost savings. In the past, real estate companies built large offices. The office of the future involves remote computing. We won't need all the office buildings. Half of our regional staff already telecommutes. Our headquarters went from 4400 square feet to 1600 square feet. Intranet acceptance was pretty easy. We already have 25 percent of the agents using it. People don't like to read any more. They just want to know, how does it enhance their lives or help them make a living? It's all been word-of-mouth marketing. Agents will listen to another agent they see succeeding. You can't tell an independent contractor what to do.

For companies such as Hewlett-Packard, which implemented an intranet early on, the challenge is not getting employees started on an intranet but rather managing the volume of information already accumulated. Implementing a search engine for the intranet has helped, but in some ways, says one HP manager, "it has made more visible how unorganized and overwhelming the intranet is for people." The company now is looking at better ways to catalog and evaluate the quality of information, including both automated filtering techniques and human intervention.

Whether the Net Future manager is dealing with geographically removed independent contractors of real estate companies or employees at corporate headquarters, many of the needed skills will not be dramatically different from the skills that have always made a good manager. Good communication skills have always increased a manager's value. However, in the Net Future, when working relationships rely less on daily face-to-face interaction, communication skills become essential.

No longer will a manager be able to rely on a likable personality to mask poor managerial skills. E-mails and telephone conversations can all too easily be misunderstood on both a tactical level and an emotional level.

THE ONLINE REVIEW

Managers of the future will look to the Net for tools to help them do their jobs. One company created a tool that automates the employee review-writing process.[10] KnowledgePoint, a developer of knowledge-based, human resource software in Petaluma, CA, estimated that with more than 10 million managers writing anywhere from 1 to 10 employee reviews a year, there would be a huge market for a Net-based review system.

Written employee reviews often are last-minute or rushed, and at many smaller companies, they are barely more than a standardized one-form-suits-all. By targeting smaller companies, KnowledgePoint created a Net-based program that walks a manager through a roughly 15-minute process. The manager selects from 36 performance elements, such as job knowledge and initiative, and the program then asks the manager a series of questions.

At the end, the site generates an official evaluation, which the manager can have E-mailed back or printed immediately. The electronic version then can be routed to the HR department, to a supervisor or even directly to the employee. Within months of the product's launch in 1998, about 10,000 reviews had been completed at the site. "Performance reviews for many companies are off the radar until you really need them," says Michael George, the company's Internet product marketing manager.

Strategic Resource Solutions, Inc., a North Carolina company that provides multi-site facilities and energy management products and services, sees online reviews as the only way to handle such functions. The company has more than 500 employees and 100 managers, with offices throughout the United States. "We just give the Web address to all the managers with some brief instructions and they begin using the system," says HR specialist Gary Bossert. "The learning curve is very short; the managers just go to the site and point and click. We don't worry about security because it resides on their server, not ours."

No one really knows yet how much things should cost in the Net Future, although companies are already realizing the effects of cost benefits. Leading companies will experiment and let the market decide. Initially KnowledgePoint charged various fees, ranging from a by-the-review fee of $9.95 to a full annual subscription of $89.95 for unlimited use. The company ended up with more individual users than corporate customers.

"We might have 10 managers in 10 different departments at the same company using the program," says George. "This is a line manager's tool. The guys in the trenches know exactly what the technology can do for them. Managers can end-run their internal process; there's no software installation, and they come to our site, do the review, and just get the result they want. Disintermediation is a possibility for the former HR expert."

KnowledgePoint initially expected to create a large outsourcing business, storing the employee performance reviews. "What happened is that many companies came back and said they wanted the tool for their managers, so we had to release a corporate version of the program," says George. "This has compressed development time, because we got so much feedback from customers we ended up developing this from the outside in. It has taken the guesswork out."

E-Management Style

THE GOOD MANAGER	THE GOOD DIGITAL MANAGER
Communicates well with employees	Helps employees communicate with one another
Acknowledges memos	Acknowledges E-mail on the same day
Knows the number for the help desk	Knows the one person on the help desk who can actually fix your computer
Sets clear direction	Gets the group to achieve consensus on direction
Tries to accommodate employee's personal needs	Represents the department on company telecommuting policy committee
Doesn't stand over employees' shoulders	Doesn't stand anywhere near employees
Conveys important policy information from higher-ups	Makes sure members of the department are on important E-mail distribution lists
Trains employees to do their jobs well	Trains employees to do their jobs well and builds their career skills
Has a sense of humor	Has a sense of humor

As companies get more comfortable outsourcing more and more of their internal applications and processes, KnowledgePoint, growing its Net business at 50 percent a month, hopes at least to get part of the performance review portion.

E-mail Personalities

The Egocaster.   E-mails a constant barrage of news articles across the corporate network to demonstrate how connected he thinks he is.

The Avon Lady.   Insists on speaking by phone instead of using E-mail.

The Commentator.   No matter what the group E-mail is about, she always has another two cents' worth.

The County Dump.   Every push channel is automatically downloading on his desktop.

The Copy Machine.   Has to cc: EVERYONE on EVERY E-mail sent.

The Archivist.   Hasn't cleaned out her electronic in-box since the first day on the job. After all, she just might need to respond one day to that message from HR welcoming her to the company.

The CYA.   A master of the art of ambiguous E-mail.

The Limelight Hog.   Why is credit grabbing so much more obvious in a short message?

The Deer.   Can't figure out how to respond to an E-mail and just stares and stares at the message.

HOME GOES TO WORK; WORK GOES HOME

As the workforce gets wired, both corporations and workers will find that home and work become increasingly seamless. As intranets begin to incorporate wireless technology, workers will be able to get information—E-mail, alerts when a stock hits a target price, voicemail—anytime anywhere. The combination of technology and the potential savings in operating costs from reduced need for office space will produce savvy employees who will find new ways to integrate their personal and work lives. An overwhelming number of people say they would like to work from home at least two days a week[11], and companies in the Net Future increasingly will accommodate that desire.

E-mail, already a staple of most offices, will grow even more, with the number of electronic mailboxes reaching 112 million in 1999.[12] E-mail has become so pervasive that in Singapore, you can even hail a taxi by E-mail. The request is sent to an automated dispatch system, which sends back an E-mailed confirmation. But the taxi drivers are also a wired workforce of sorts. When a crime is spotted, the police have direct, electronic access to the taxi drivers' network, so that the drivers all are on the lookout for a police-described felon immediately after a crime.[13]

There are many factors that point to the integration of home and work life.

- In North America, 74 percent of companies expect their use of telecommuting to increase by the year 2000.[14]

- By 1998, 55 percent of AT&T's white-collar workers were considered telecommuters by AT&T's definition: people who work out of their home regularly at least twice a week.

- The company that employs Alrie Daniels and 14 other people has about 200 square feet of office space. Daniels and her colleagues collaborate on keeping corporate databases and Web sites constantly refreshed, operating in teams that depend on a given client's needs. They are paid on an hourly basis and have full benefits, but they meet in person only about once a month. That's because their employer, Outsource Solutions of Waltham, MA, is a virtual company. Except for Livia Givoni, vice president of strategic development and marketing, all employees work out of their homes. The parent company is in the process of expanding its services nationally and into Europe; eventually it plans to go global. And why not? In the Net Future, the digital commute is a lot shorter.

- The New York Stock Exchange (NYSE) is deliberating about how to implement a rule that requires member firms to monitor their employees' home E-mail to prevent securities fraud. The NYSE could allow employees to send employers a copy of all electronic correspondence, or demand that employees route all their home E-mail through their employers' networks for review. Securities firms protested the rule, saying it affects the privacy of employees' families.

- Using call forwarding and a system tested for Paul Bunyan Telephone Co. of Bemidji, MN, parents can be notified at work when their children are about to get off the school bus. The BusCall messaging system notifies families over the phone, by E-mail, or by personal pager. In the Bemidji program, the telephone company calls the home phone with a distinctive ring. Whoever picks up the phone hears a message like, "School bus number 44 will be arriving at your bus stop in 10 minutes and 35 seconds." If a parent has call forwarding, the call can be put through to the forwarded number.

- A prototype system notifies employees of Burlington Northern and Santa Fe Railway Company when railroad crossings have power outages, broken or stuck gates, or other maintenance problems. Before installation of the system, information had been sent manually over telephone lines to maintenance crew dispatchers. The new network, which uses wireless communications, can deliver status alerts to multiple locations by Internet, E-mail, pagers, fax, and direct intranet connection. Dispatchers can make decisions and assign crews from virtually any remote location.

- Eugene Tsiang, an astrophysicist at the Harvard-Smithsonian Center for Astrophysics, is part of a team building a radio telescope on Mauna Kea in Hawaii. The telescope has been designed so that Tsiang and his colleagues do not have to be at the site to make observations. Using a software program he can operate from his laptop, Tsiang can tap into the center's network, adjust the telescope's settings, make the astronomical observations, and retrieve the information without leaving his home in Cambridge, MA.

- When travelers call America West to make an airline reservation, the responding agent who is so knowledgeable about flight times and availability may be sitting not in a large bullpen surrounded by coworkers, but in bunny slippers in a cozy home office. Using software that taps their home computers directly into America West's system, employees in the airline's Home Agents program receive calls that are automatically routed from the company's 800 number to a remote site—in this case, an agent's home office. The Home Agents program enables the company to tap a more diverse workforce, including disabled people who can now work from home. It has been so successful that the company plans to expand to 120 the number of agents participating.

- Electronic organizers that can automatically synchronize information with a user's computer now access E-mail and Web-based information in mobile workforces.

- Bob Gordon, CEO and President of New England's The Store 24 Companies Inc. and chairman of the National Association of Convenience Stores, says that convenience stores may need to change what they stock and carry more office supplies to reflect the fact that more people are working at home. And if more ordering is done over the Internet, convenience stores could serve as a pickup point to allow more efficient distribution by online merchants.

- Systems developed by Cisco are now being used by Global One—an international joint venture of Deutsche Telekom, France Telecom, and Sprint—to provide worldwide intranet access for corporations without their own dedicated network. Traveling and telecommuting employees as well as remote branch offices can dial a local number and use a virtual private network to check the Internet, their E-mail, and their corporate intranets. Global One offered the system in 50 countries in Europe, Asia Pacific, and the Americas in 1998, the launch year.

THE VIRTUAL EXECUTIVE

Omar Leeman, who is responsible for business operations within the business markets division of MCI, is on the road roughly

260 days a year.[15] His office is in Atlanta; his home is in Houston; his direct reports are located everywhere from Atlanta to Seattle. How does he coordinate all the scattered parts of his life?

> I use E-mail, voicemail, cellular service, a pager. I've set up a profile with my phone service so that when people call me, the service knows to try Houston first. If I'm not there, it will send a message to my cell phone number, and if there's no answer, to my assistant in Atlanta. I do video-conferencing at my home, and audioconferencing a lot.
>
> Today my first call started at 9 a.m. Eastern, 8 Houston time. Someone had sent an electronic presentation. I went through it on a conference call with a dozen other people. Later in the day I did a Net meeting; people called in from all over the country. A moderator ran the presentation and was responsible for advancing all the slides. Through lunch, calls were forwarded to my cell phone. If nobody's around, I have an interactive two-way pager that lets me reply to a page, or send a message to other pagers or to E-mail addresses.
>
> My assistant in Atlanta keeps my appointments, schedules conference calls. I use a handheld computer for all that information. She updates my schedule; then we hot-synch the handheld to get updates into my calendar. Sometime she'll call on a Saturday or Sunday and tell me to be sure to hot-synch over the weekend because there have been changes for the next week. I've got to be virtual. In some ways it's almost a nuisance, because other people aren't necessarily as electronically virtual as I am.
>
> We've really empowered our field people with the same kinds of tools to allow them to do their business anywhere any time. Basically it's not the hardware or software that's the issue; it's to get people to use them. That was the biggest challenge when we rolled out laptops to all the sales and service folks. You have to get people to change the way they go about their business. It is not easy; you have to make sure your assumptions are correct. For instance, we assumed everybody would be able to operate in a Windows environment. In some cases, people thought opening up a window meant literally going to the window in the room

and opening it up. We had to make it a prerequisite to get basic PC skills. The other thing is that you have to sometimes go cold turkey in the way you distribute information. People have to learn that if you don't open your laptop, you don't get the information you need to do your job.

The next step would be to get a lot of information that is in multiple devices into one. I had to get interactive paging and my calendar into one device, integrating paging and cellular in a way that is easier to use.

How do I balance my personal life with my work life, being on the road so much? To me it's not even a question of balance. To others, I think it's almost viewed as an invasion of privacy. I guess you could say I work seven days a week, 365 days a year. I've been able to utilize the tools to be able to stay in touch with friends and family. With the pager or E-mail, we can send messages any time; it's pretty instantaneous. It allows me to get to my family and communicate on a daily basis. My two twins are 14 years old. I've found that with my kids, when they first started sending me E-mail messages, they weren't thinking as they were writing the message; it was almost like sitting at the dinner table saying something. Sometimes I had to get them to put in the context for what they were saying; now they're pretty clear and direct. For the two kids that are away at college, it's really easy to E-mail back and forth.

My spouse has a pager, and I page her just like she pages me. I remember when I got my first digital pager; I would see my home phone number, and I would have to stop whatever I was doing till I could get to a phone to see if there was an emergency. Then it evolved to an alpha pager; now it's just another form of two-way communication.

I can't even imagine going back to paper, not having the ability to do what I do today. It's the only way I could do the job. I either have to move everybody who works for me to the same place, or use the tools that are available to let me do what I need to do.

Though Leeman's perpetual-motion schedule may be extreme, the ways he has learned to balance the demands of his work and home lives offer lessons for the workforce of the future.

The newly wired workforce offers new economic possibilities for more than workers and their employers. Small communities with sagging economies are investing in sophisticated infrastructure development, hoping to lure telecommuters to relocate in rural areas that may be far from their parent companies.

In the United States, what is believed to be the nation's first telecommunity is planned for the 8600-person town of Nevada, MO. A British developer is building on 729 acres of land that used to be a state hospital for the mentally ill and disabled until budget cutbacks closed it in 1991. The hospital had been the town's single largest employer. Each of the 38 residences in the initial phase will have fiber-optic wiring connected to its wall sockets that will link occupants' computers to one another, to corporate networks, and to the Internet.

A former hospital building, once used for drug and alcohol abuse rehabilitation, has been converted into a high-tech "telecenter" of communications lines, videoconferencing facilities, conference rooms, computers with high-speed data links, scanners, and satellite transmissions. Interestingly, the British developer responsible for Acorn Televillages found out about Nevada from a query posted on the Internet asking for feedback about the idea of wooing homesteaders to the community.

A similar project is happening in the medieval village of Colletta di Castelbianco, near Genoa, Italy. When developers began restoring the village, which had been uninhabited for 30 years, they decided that to lure residents, they would make the redevelopment project a "televillage."

A state-of-the-art telecommunications infrastructure being installed in the renovated fourteenth-century buildings will enable telecommuters to work from their homes. The village has its own intranet that uses fiber-optic cable and is protected by a firewall. A cybercafe in the town square provides Internet access and is connected to the village's own private digital telephone exchange. In addition, each of the 60 renovated apartments inside the old stone walls has an ISDN phone connection through the village's LAN, a digital voicemail system, a mobile cordless phone system, and a satellite TV hookup. The first residents moved into the village in March 1998.

Jobs To Go

It's no secret that as company loyalty to employee is being dissolved by competitive pressures, so is employee loyalty to company. The company network may make internal job postings more visible throughout the company, but they're only a mouse click away from listings by a company's competitors on services such as Monster Board and Career Mosaic, two of the largest online career sites. These Web sites use search technology that sorts through hundreds of thousands of job listings, providing deep, categorized listings by industry, geography and salary. More than a million electronic résumés are available online,[16] and companies are expected to spend $218 million on Internet recruiting by the year 2000.[17]

Geography is no longer an impediment in a job search. Newspapers across the U.S. have banded together to protect their position in the future of employment advertising by creating CareerPath. The site aggregates want ads from newspapers ranging from the *New York Times* to the *Los Angeles Times*. And the *Wall Street Journal* partnered with executive recruiter Korn/Ferry International to create Futurestep, an online service where individuals register their credentials while potential employers tap into the rich database to fill management positions.

As more résumés and job postings hit the Net, the process of matching the two will become more automated. Human resources departments use software that automatically finds résumés as soon as they hit the Web and delivers to the job seeker an E-mail from a recruiter. It also works the other way; a service called CareerCast automatically copies job postings from a participating company's site and sends them to multiple job listing services such as Monster Board and Career Mosaic.

Not all applicants will have to do the work of looking for jobs. An E-mail service from SkillsSearch Corp. lets employees enter details on the kinds of jobs that interest them, and a list of matching positions is sent back. These wired workers will have at their fingertips a smorgasbord of job and career opportunities from which to choose. New challenges arise for companies trying to keep these employees from jumping ship. Part of the solution for many companies will be to make sure they get the right employee to start with.

"Now, depending on the number of people applying and the number of candidates you want to spend time with, you can mathematically reach just the people you want to spend time with," says Randy Madden, CEO of SHL Aspen Tree Software.[18] The company makes a Web-based interviewing system to prescreen job applicants. The online interviewing system—currently being used by companies such as US West and Coopers & Lybrand—can screen 10,000 applicants, eliminate 40 percent up front, and route the remaining 60 percent to face-to-face interviews.

"You get more applications now than in the pencil-and-paper days. The Web sort of turned the résumé system into a monster," says Madden. "People were looking to get more people into the system, so now when companies advertise for a job they get thousands of résumés when they were expecting tens. Depending on your recruiting needs, you could even make a cutoff at the top 50 percent. Getting the right fit is hugely important; then keeping that talent with you a long period of time will be more and more important."

It's no surprise that the typical online applicant is a college student or technical staff, because such a large percentage of students have Net access. "Nearly every company has a problem getting and retaining technical people." And in the Net Future, the same technological capability that allows candidates to find jobs easily will allow them to change jobs easily. More pressure is placed on the organization to get the right people—and then to keep them happy. "It doesn't seem to be any one thing in particular that makes people change jobs, but job satisfaction is still the big reason to stay," says Madden.

In the Net Future, companies will have to come to grips with a wired workforce with continually more job and career choices because of the ability for others to aggregate them on the Net.

THE COMPANY STORE

As one might imagine with a corporation the size of General Mills, the company has a lot of people who need a lot of stuff. There are more than 2000 separate approval processes for everything from office furniture to computers to supplies. To streamline the process, the company is implementing an online purchasing system that not only makes ordering easier for the 1500 employees who use it but also integrates the entire procurement process.

Under the system, employees use a Web browser to search the corporate catalog for items that meet their specifications. Once located, the items are put in an electronic shopping cart, much as they would be gathered at consumer shopping sites. Depending on the user's profile, which can include a limit on the amount that person can order without approval, the electronic requisition is automatically routed to anyone who must sign off on the request. Designated approvers are notified by E-mail or alerted automatically about any requisitions waiting for their OK. Employees can also check the system to find out the status of their order, eliminating repeated calls to the purchasing department to find out where those requisitioned laptops have gone.

- Chevron Corp., which spends nearly $3 billion annually with about 200 regular suppliers, plans to move its procurement system onto the Net, giving company buyers access to manufacturers of oil and refinery components, as well as to service providers for various plant operations. The company ultimately hopes to expand the online procurement to its entire global purchase budget of almost $10 billion.

- MasterCard wants to have all its domestic employees doing online procurement by the year 2000; in 1998, its first year of operation, it added about 200 workers to the system every three months and expected that $2 to $3 million worth of purchases would be made online.[19] James Cullinan, the company's vice president for global purchasing, envisions going

beyond the initial ordering of office supplies and PC equipment. He'd like workers to be able to buy marketing collateral
materials, hire temp workers, and arrange for transportation
services online. "In some areas, we anticipate being able to
save up to 15 percent," says Cullinan.

However, wiring the workforce to the company store can
involve a cultural change. "We had to change people's attitudes
about using the system," says Cullinan. "When I came here,
people were going out on their own buying whatever they wanted. That's how they felt they had to work to get the stuff they
needed. We started to say, `OK, let's assume people will follow
rules as long as it makes sense to them.'"

Cullinan's group started using their suppliers' proprietary
tools and introduced online ordering in bits and pieces: first
electronic forms, later electronic catalogs from individual suppliers. "We knew it wasn't where we wanted to end up, but we
needed the workforce to begin to trust the technology. They
needed to trust that we would really develop things that would
be much easier for them. At the end, they have to really see and
feel that what they're doing is delivering a result to them."

MasterCard's system is relatively advanced—something you
might expect from a company that depends on people buying
things, and that is located in a New York town named Purchase.

Many companies are just beginning to streamline the procurement process. In some cases, empowering the workforce
can be as simple as making sure people have access to the right
information. The corporate purchasing department at Time
Warner did a great job at negotiating deals on commodities that
the company used in large quantities—paper for its magazines,
for example. However, it sometimes actually wound up paying
higher prices than were available under a negotiated contract
simply because individual buyers within the company weren't
even aware that the contract existed. With the establishment of
a Web database that includes more than 200 contracts, users
can view the terms of each and make a more informed purchase.

Automated procurement will require a new way of thinking
for purchasing managers. Tim McEneny, CEO of American

Tech, worked with Time Warner on its system and has been involved in automating purchasing processes for more than 15 years:[20] In his words:

> The first phase is streamlining the internal process; the current process is very cumbersome and paper-based. The typical company process from the time an individual says "I need something" till the time the requisition gets approved and to the purchasing department is four weeks. Automating that process allows companies to collapse that time to 24 hours. We try to take people out of this approval process.
>
> Studies have shown that the cost of generating a purchase order and getting approval for it are an average of $150 per purchase order; we're trying to get that cost down to $10 to $20. But there's going to have to be a change in the mindset of management to say that it's really not that important that we capture every single transaction and that every transaction flow through the purchasing department. One of our clients used to work at a financial services company where everybody in the company was allowed to order their own stuff; as a result, everybody had lots of extra inventory lying around. Some of our clients have worked for years to get control over these things to prevent waste like that. But the absurdity of a purchase order costing $150 for $50 worth of office supplies is starting to sink in. Controls need to be in place so that the system knows from your user profile that you're authorized to order $50 worth of stuff at Office Depot but you're not going to be able to go out and buy a Jaguar and have it delivered to your house.
>
> It means giving up some degree of control, empowering employees.

The savings from wiring the workforce into the company store will not come solely from saving workers time. In many cases, it may come from enabling purchasing employees to focus less on processing paper or resolving discrepancies between invoices and purchase orders, and more on fulfilling higher-level responsibilities—for example, negotiating better deals with suppliers.

"The purchasing department of the future will hire people who are not administrative, who are college-educated and have good analytical skills, who are able to sell, to craft legal agreements, who are good at influencing, and leadership," says Patrick Guerra, vice president of corporate supply management for Advanced Micro Devices.[21]

"They will be able to study a marketplace and figure out what the competitive advantage of each supplier is. They will strike a deal, negotiate a contract, and have that contract be represented in a catalog you can procure from. Then they will back out of the process and go work the next deal, leaving the people who need the items to requisition them themselves."

One company, SQL Financials International, studied its customers to determine the savings per employee from Web-based procurement systems and found that in business services companies with revenue between $50 million and $1 billion, the savings was $250 to $500 per employee per year. In a $2 billion financial services company, with dramatically more paperwork to streamline, annual savings was $5000 per employee per year.

In the Net Future, there is a window of opportunity for companies prepared to develop online catalogs that can be integrated with their customers' intranets. Companies anxious to implement online procurement are still having difficulty finding suppliers who can help them achieve that vision. A company that is prepared to supply the wired workforce has a near-term opportunity to capture market share, and such a strategy could provide a foot in the door with companies that might otherwise be happy to stick with their existing suppliers. Procurement is another example of how a Netted company will have a competitive advantage when it comes to managing inventory for a real-time world.

THE CORPORATION AS PUBLISHER

In the Net Future, companies will be forced to act somewhat like publishing companies as they grapple with new ways to disseminate information and adequately serve an audience of employees. With the market for intranet content growing to more than $1 billion by the year 2000,[22] companies will be looking for new sources of information to keep their employees informed and even entertained. Most companies do not have the inherent skill sets of traditional publishing companies, though many of these skills will be required to properly serve a wired workforce.

Traditional magazine and newspaper publishing companies basically are in the business of organizing an audience and delivering content or service to that audience. Newspapers organize audiences geographically, since they serve local constituents by providing readers with news and information about that specific community. Magazines generally organize audiences by interest, such as hobby or sports magazines, providing information about a specific area.

As a result, newspapers are predominantly local, or confined to a specific geographical location, while magazines serve people with specific interests no matter where they live. Success is measured by how well the publication serves the reader, and revenue is generally derived from advertisers—those companies that want to reach the specific community with their commercial message. Revenue is usually based on advertising or subscriptions.

Finally, success is measured by repeat business: satisfied readers continue to derive useful or interesting information, while advertisers are pleased as the audiences buy their products. Relatively simple, and tried and true. Great publishers make it look easy.

But when companies whose primary business is, say, manufacturing, begin doing business over the Net or trying to implement internal knowledge management online, they may find themselves grappling with processes that are completely unfamiliar. The four basic parts of publishing—content creation, manufacturing and distribution, advertising sales, and circulation (customer acquisition and retention)—often work like a well-oiled machine. Corporations will be faced with mimicking some of these models to keep their audiences of employees satisfied.

Content Creation

- *Maintain credibility.* Companies that want employees to trust the information they distribute should be honest.

Whatever is disseminated inhouse can easily be copied and E-mailed outside the company.

- *Quickly review content.*   This is the real-time Net, and HTML pages can be changed easily if there is a well-understood procedure in place. Companies shouldn't get so caught up in details that the entire process bogs down.

- *Launch and learn.*   A company that waits to get all its content onto its intranet before launching will lose the benefit of starting small and learning from mistakes. With a plan for adding new content regularly, employees will help direct what works and what doesn't through constant feedback.

- *Keep it timely.*   A "cobweb" site will lose an audience quickly. Constant updating is the norm on the Net.

- *Provide context for information and services.*   Supplying links to other relevant content and making the intranet an interactive convenience center makes company content more attractive.

- *Don't forget that you're not alone.*   Many content providers are interested in licensing their content for use within corporations. A news service that can automatically post information about a specific industry not only might be useful for employees but can help streamline knowledge distribution. And one of the most efficient ways to generate content is to have users create it themselves.

- *Stay in touch with your audience.*   The wired workforce will help shape the way a company shares information if people have a forum for expressing what they like and don't like.

- *Tease the user.*   Alerting your audience to what they can expect to see in the future on their intranet gives them a reason to check back.

- *Maintain quality.*   Just as a magazine has a visual identity, so should a company's intranet pages. Develop some easy-to-use page templates and graphics as well as a set of style guidelines that offer users flexibility while maintaining a consistent look.

- *Have something for everyone.*   Communications professionals as well as information technology staff should be involved in deciding what the intranet will include. One large financial services company found that its intranet was not used much because the information on it pertained largely to information technology.

Content Circulation

- *Use the strengths of the Net.*   Employees will have the ability to control and in some cases create the programming that is broadcast to them. I call this a "pullcasting" approach, in which the individuals pull the relevant information to themselves, in effect creating their own networks of information.[23] Timing and context as well as content will affect whether they choose to pull in a given message. Technologies such as collaborative filtering (see Chapter Six) can automate getting the right information to the right people when they need it.

- *Remember: celebrities sell.*   Employees are more likely to use an intranet if they see that key executives participate actively in its use.

- *Be everywhere.*   Companies have found any number of ways to promote intranet use to their audiences offline as well as online, from running contests to name the system to appointing departmental "correspondents."

- *Tap into niche audiences.*   Encourage individual divisions to create their portions of the intranet to suit their own work needs. Too great an insistence on corporate uniformity can come at the expense of usefulness.

- *Create communities of interest.*   If people post a comment on a bulletin board, chances are they'll check back to see if there's been any reply. Employees who have a genuine interest in specific job-related subjects—innovative use of the Internet in your industry, perhaps, or day-care problems—can be encouraged to develop communities around those topics.

Content Manufacturing and Distribution

- *Establish a process for copy flow.*   The process will flow more smoothly if all the stakeholders are involved in thinking through how information will be updated, who will do the updating, who will review content if it needs it, and who will implement changes.

- *Set a publishing schedule.*   Publishers often work on several issues at once, each issue being in a different stage of production. They may be developing the content of one issue, editing another, printing a third, and mailing a fourth, all at the same time. It helps to have a well-defined but flexible schedule, including a backup plan for when things go wrong.
- *Update.*   Make sure the process includes very frequent information updates.

Ad Sales Management.   More companies will be faced with the issue of allowing outside advertising to their employees on their intranets. Some issues to think about:

- *Document usage and audience.*   Advertisers and advertising agencies want the same kind of information about a publication that corporate sponsors need to support the intranet financially. Both will want documented information about how useful the publication is for users, how often they use it, what the most popular features are, and how much it will cost to get their message out.
- *Develop guidelines for the types of ads to be accepted.*   Some companies might decide not to carry ads of competitors that are trying to hire away employees; others might have prohibitions about liquor or cigarettes.
- *Keep expectations realistic.*   Most Internet ad dollars have traditionally gone to companies that could deliver the biggest number of page views. Even a highly targeted audience may or may not be able to command premium ad prices. Be prepared to be flexible on pricing.
- *Track page views.*   The number of page views generally determines how much ad "space" or ad inventory is available. An advertiser may buy 100,000 page views, for example.

- *Hire an outside ad sales representative.* The corporation-as-publisher usually has other things to focus on besides advertising. And just whose budget does the advertising revenue hit?

Just as the corporation will be acting as a publisher, so too will it be playing the role of the corporate circulation department for outside publishers. One Internet start-up company, Rowe.com Inc. in Cambridge, MA, saw the opportunity for creating the Net Future version of employee subscriptions.[24]

The company created a Net-based subscription service that is totally automated, including electronic payments and claims. Once Rowe.com has signed an exclusive arrangement to provide subscriptions to all employees of a given company, an executive of the corporate client, typically the CFO, sends a companywide note saying that all other subscriptions will not be company-reimbursed. Rowe.com creates a virtual company store for the enterprise, providing one-stop shopping for all publications needs. When employees visit the company's internal Web site, they can subscribe to whatever publications they choose.

Rowe.com's system includes E-mail notification telling employees when their subscriptions are about to expire as well as capabilities for linking clients' intranets link directly into Rowe.com's database. The company eliminated a middle layer, and created a new business model for corporate subscriptions.

In the pre-Net world, an agent might offer a similar assortment of publications to a corporation. The difference is in Net economics. The agent would act as an intermediary between corporation and publisher. The agent used to charge a company list price plus a fee, generally in the range of 2 to 5 percent. The agent would also receive a 5 to 10 percent discount from the publisher, and the fee and discount would comprise the profit for the agent.

In the Net economy, the new agent gets the same discount from the publisher but passes the entire discount through to the employees at a subscribing corporation. Where does the new agent make its revenue? It charges a transaction fee on every subscription, no matter what the cost. Within a short period of time, Rowe.com signed exclusive contracts to provide Net-based subscription services to Coopers & Lybrand, Massachusetts General Hospital, Deloitte & Touche LLP, Ernst & Young, Arthur Andersen, Hewlett-Packard, Coca-Cola, and the Federal Reserve Board.

"We changed the rules," says CEO and founder Richard Rowe. "The publisher gives the same discount but it's all electronic." The subscribing corporation is able to make an electronic payment direct from its own account or to place funds at Bank One. Money is transferred to the publishing company once a subscription is processed. The entire process is paperless and comprises five steps.

1. The employee finds a desired publication and subscribes. Electronic notification is sent to the buyer's trusted third party bank.
2. A "trusted third-party bank" receives notification of the purchase request.
3. Bank sends the funds to the sellers' bank and debits the buyer's account.
4. The order and the payment confirmation are sent to the seller
5. Seller confirms that the buyer received the order and payment.

The cost to Rowe.com for the bank to process the entire transaction? Twenty-five cents!

A side benefit for the client is that it can receive a full view of what its employees are receiving as printed information. The data later can be used to find similarities in patterns, relations to jobs, productivity measurements, and the like. For example, employees might use collaborative filtering technology (see Chapter Six) to check what others within the company are reading and receive a recommendation of what they might also be interested in, based on the reading behavior of others.

THE CORPORATION AS BROADCASTER

As technology advances get introduced and adopted throughout the enterprise, many companies will find themselves becoming not only internal publishers but also internal broadcasters. A leading example of how a company can become a global broadcaster to its employees is Lucent Technologies.

The company created internal Net-based radio programming. With professional disc jockeys, catchy jingles and news from around the world, Lucent Web Radio closely resembles traditional radio.

"We created a product marketing group and found we had a distribution problem with getting materials out," says Robert Yurkovic, Director of Advanced Business Management at Lucent and creator of Lucent Web Radio.[25]

Yurkovic created a Web-only radio station with several channels that use standard Internet technology, such as RealAudio. He negotiated re-broadcast deals with the BBC, National Public Radio, the Associated Press, and CNET, then packaged the news and music with internal messages. Regular interviews, including employee and divisional success stories, are heard regularly, so that company employees in different parts of the world at least get to hear about one another.

Lucent Web Radio reaches more than 50,000 employees, who listen an average of 156 minutes a day.

"We get E-mails from people in Poland, Singapore, and Brazil who say they now feel connected," Yurkovic says.

The company found that the Web radio station's greatest impact is in training and communications. "We had a $6 million recovery of training costs because now we do teletraining. We also set up a communications channel so we can bring in business executives for interviews," says Yurkovic.

What's the ROI on the company's intranet effort? More than 750 percent, with a savings of $15.5 million a year!

HOW WIRED IS YOUR WORKFORCE?

- Do you have rewards in place that encourage online collaboration?
- Do employees automatically check the intranet as their first stop in researching employee or job-related information?
- Do you provide career-planning resources online?

- Can employees check benefits information online?
- Can your employees enroll in benefits programs online?
- Can employees review an online catalog or ordering information for buying office equipment or supplies?
- Can employees actually submit purchase orders online?
- Can employees order directly from suppliers?
- Do you have a mechanism for employees to share knowledge electronically?
- Is automated information specific to your industry delivered directly to employee desktops?
- What percentage of your workforce is connected to the public Internet at work?
- Do you have chat rooms and online discussion areas for employees?
- Do your employees have bulletin boards on the intranet? Were they sponsored by the company or did they begin as grassroots efforts?
- Does your intranet include multiple languages for employees overseas?
- Do you sponsor an online mentoring program?
- Are employee evaluations distributed or reported online?
- Do employees have access to company-sponsored online training?
- Does the CEO hold online forums or participate in bulletin boards?
- What percentage of your workforce works outside the office at least two days a week?
- Do you provide increased technical support for telecommuters?

TURNING THE COMPANY ON A DIME

In an era when technology can create new competitors virtually overnight, the ability to communicate rapidly and effectively within the organization can mean the difference between winning and losing. With a wired workforce, companies will be able to better keep up with the increasing pace of change, and those that embrace the concept of a totally wired workforce can thrive. Companies that resist will find not only that they have missed the flood tide of history but also that the tide threatens to drown them.

THE OPEN-BOOK CORPORATION EMERGES

Companies have been talking about being consumer-driven for years. Of course, every company and most executives have a different vision of what that means. When a company pronounces that "the customer is in charge," it might mean that the company has, through various research methods, found or created products that the customer is willing to buy. The process has been a relatively static one, based on a snapshot of customer behavior at a given time or a series of such snapshots over time.

In the Net Future, the customer really can get into the driver's seat, if the producers of products and services are willing to sit in back. And the customers actually *will* drive the business on behalf of the producing company. It is this reversal of the balance of power—as well as the companies who leverage this 180-degree shift in power—that will drive the Net Future.

PUSHING IT OUT

In the traditional business world, knowledge is power. In the Net Future, dissemination of knowledge is power.

The more other companies understand about your business, the greater your ability to ensure that the market marches to your drumbeat. Why would Netscape decide to distribute the code underlying its Web browser—the software equivalent of printing the formula for Coca-Cola on a billboard in Times Square? To encourage other companies to develop their own products and services based on that standard. If a company can get the rest of the world to use something it produced, it can then develop other products and services that take advantage of that fact—products and services for which it can exact a premium price.

By disseminating information that enabled small accounts to do much of the work themselves, electronic parts manufacturer AMP was able to reduce its reliance on distributors that had paid more attention to larger customers. In this case, dissemination of knowledge equaled the power to grow a previously underperforming market segment.

The dissemination of knowledge can also equal the power to improve performance. By contributing to the aggregation of knowledge, you increase your own ability to set benchmarks and goals. And what do companies do after they have undergone the first and second levels of opening themselves to their customers? They start to look for additional ways to extend the push-it-out philosophy.

After opening its package tracking system to its customers, FedEx decided to continue its philosophy internally by developing a system for comparing an individual driver's performance with that of other drivers. As drivers get recipients to sign for delivery of their packages, that information goes into a constantly refreshed database. Not only can the company compare driver performance, but the drivers themselves can see where they stand on their delivery schedule and how their performance compares with that of other drivers. This is how an open-book corporation can extend methods developed externally to assist in wiring its workforce, as previously discussed.

In the traditional economy, the more information people controlled, the more power they had. Managers were protective, even secretive, about their strategies, plans, and ideas. In addition to promoting job security, privileged information gave an individual a sense of true power: "I *am* the person in the know. Without me, this project cannot succeed." The Net changes all that.

In the Net Future, the more power a person gives out, the more that is made available to all, the more power he or she will have. Power will be in knowledge dissemination, not knowledge collection. This will be true of companies as well as of individuals. There used to be a chant of "open systems." The new chant will be about what I call the "open-book corporation." The Net Future will be the age of open everything.

An increasing number of companies will find that by opening their databases to the world, as FedEx and others have done, they can get others to do much of the work. Moreover, customers and suppliers love it! Taking a company's intranet to the next logical step—by allowing customers to get the information they need more quickly by directly accessing the corporate database—benefits both customer and company.

With the open-book corporation, the wiring of the workforce evolves into the wiring of multiple workforces. This linkage means more than simply exchanging digital information. It will require companies to revise business practices to link themselves more closely with customers and suppliers. In essence, customers, suppliers, and distributors will actually begin to help *run* the corporation.

THE NEXTROVERTS

The open-book corporation means more than simply sticking up a sign on a company Web site that says, "Order here." It means connecting and extending the enterprise like never before. It means taking into account legacy technology as well as legacy ways of conducting business. And it means leveraging the internetworked customers, suppliers, and distributors in new and innovative ways to drive the core business, as well as to seek new revenue and cut costs.

The next generation of Net-savvy companies will find every way imaginable to tap into external forces to make the enterprise more successful. They will leverage their customer base. They will link suppliers together. They will act as the glue to aggregate new groups of people, creating totally new customer sets for products they will be quick to provide. They will use these outside forces to help drive their traditional business as well. I call these next-generation, outwardly focused, and Net-astute companies "Nextroverts," and they will be the new force to be reckoned with.

The Internet traditionally can be used to find new revenue streams from customers. The intranet can be used to cut costs, by streamlining the inner workings of the corporation. The extranet can be used for both: for finding new revenue streams from new customers as well as for cutting costs by leveraging the traditional, core business. Two companies that have figured this out are 1-800-Flowers, Inc., and Office Depot.

A NETWORK OF FLORISTS

The Long Island-based 1-800-Flowers has grown into the world's largest florist, with sales of $300 million, and 40 percent compounded annual growth rate for several years.

The company was started in traditional fashion by Jim McCann, who owned a chain of 14 flower shops in the New York area. In 1987, McCann acquired the 1-800-Flowers phone number—and the rest, as they say, is history. In addition to its 150 company-owned and franchised outlets, 1-800-Flowers partnered with another 2500 florists, based on ability to meet certain volumes.[1]

The company entered the Net arena in the mid-1990s, and its online business has evolved from providing $30 million in annual revenue to the company to starting to change how the company does business. The interactive portion of 1-800-Flowers includes a team of 20 technology, marketing, and Internet experts (the company employs more than 2000 people throughout its retail flower shops), and it launched on the Net in 1994.

The company is probably best known for its ability to serve flower buyers by phone, by fax, in person, and visibly on the Net. Less visible, however, is what the company has done with its delivery system to speed orders and link florists with one another. "The Net has been extremely powerful for us," says Donna Iucolano, director of interactive services. "This will be a $50 to $100 million business, but the less sexy part, the extranet, can be even bigger."

On its Internet site, 1-800-Flowers can receive up to 100,000 unique visitors during a busy time, like around Mother's Day. Of the people who visit the Web site, about 20 percent order flowers. And no order takers are needed to help. In true open-book-corporation style, the customer does all the work. An added benefit is that some people use the online site as a catalog, then still use the 800 number to call. "We're seeing more of this every day," says Iucolano.

Noticing this and other factors, the company decided to start linking its traditional business more closely with its online efforts. When callers order through the 800 number, they're asked if they would like to receive marketing offers via E-mail. The company found that 20 percent of callers per day were happy to give the company their E-mail addresses. "We're seeing more of the traditional customers moving online," says Iucolano.

But the company sees even greater opportunity in leveraging its network of florists. The first step was to allow florists to tap directly into 1-800-Flowers to receive orders and questions in real time. Communications were established so that when an order is placed from 1-800-Flowers to the florist, the florists can ask questions instantly about substituting various flowers or alternating delivery times. The network of florists then was more closely networked, or aggregated, by 1-800-Flowers, which became essentially the technology platform provider for all the florists.

To encourage florists to use the system, 1-800-Flowers let stores confirm order delivery over the Net-based system, giving the store 10 cents on each order. (Traditionally, local florists pay 50 cents for each order that 1-800-Flowers sends them for fulfillment.) And since people buying flowers use various methods, such as ordering online and checking the order by phone, the database is always up to the minute. Further, because the company integrated its phone and Net-based ordering channels from the beginning, everyone is always working from the same set of information.

To speed the process of connecting flower buyers and sellers, since many orders are for same-day delivery, 1-800-Flowers launched chat capability so that consumers and retailers could instantly communicate with each other about a specific order. The process avoids tying up a customer service operator on the phone and gives the consumer the information more quickly.

So where does 1-800-Flowers go in the Net Future? The company has launched an online product to its 2500 partners providing state-of-the-art capability for florists to communicate with one another over the Net. Included in the online product are wholesale buying opportunities and training courses offered by 1-800-Flowers.

The company also will enter the distance-learning business by offering courses led by horticulturists and flower designers. Once the florists are all interconnected, 1-800-Flowers will have a solid customer base and will offer reach into this group to third-party sellers trying to market goods to florists.

A NETWORK OF TRUCK DRIVERS

Office Depot is a $7 billion retailer that stocks 7000 office products throughout 620 stores and 20 warehouses in the United States. The company wanted to leverage its distribution capabilities into the Net Future, since it already had 2000 delivery trucks and 2500 drivers for its physical operations. So it was no surprise that when it launched its public site on the Web in 1998, it decided to take an end-to-end approach, linking its core business with its new digital environment.[2]

Elizabeth VanStory, known for creating weather.com at The Weather Channel, was named Vice President of Online at Office Depot. She set up electronic operations in San Francisco, so she could tap into the Internet talent pool. In her words:

> Retailing on the Internet takes more than strong merchandising and brand awareness, although they're both essential. At Office Depot, we took a holistic approach to entering the Web, looking at all aspects of our business and how they

might impact or be impacted by a Web site. We wanted to create one of the best E-commerce sites on the Web and to satisfy our customers.

We actually asked our customers what they would expect and what they would want, and they said they wanted to be able to buy office products and have them delivered the next business day. They also wanted access to order history and the ability to create custom shopping lists. For our small business target, the key benefit they hoped to derive was convenience, since many of these people traditionally have had to take time away from their business to go get office supplies.

We then determined how we could best leverage our existing business systems. We evaluated several Internet commerce software solutions, but decided that we didn't need a packaged end-to-end solution. We already had licensed or built some of the critical components to conducting commerce. We were already using an address validation and correction package as well as a tax package, and had built components for order entry. These existing systems not only support our stores, but also our multi-billion dollar catalog and delivery business.

In building our site infrastructure, we integrated our Internet site with our back-end systems, including inventory and customer databases. This allows customers to check for products at a local store or at the warehouse closest to them and confirm availability. We also check their address in real time to ensure that it's a real delivery address. We catch typographical errors as well as avoid sending our drivers to a non-deliverable location. We also verify credit card information in real time. This means that our customers won't get a message from us hours after ordering indicating a card problem.

Since our customers place orders in real time, our service reps have immediate access to the order information. By integrating our systems and providing real-time validation of products, charges, and delivery, we're able to provide excellent service to customers. There aren't many Web sites that are as integrated yet.

We also leverage our extensive delivery infrastructure. These distribution points support next-business-day delivery on our own trucks with our own drivers to over 95 percent of the country. Also, we can accept COD orders for those customers still concerned about security and offer painless returns by sending our drivers to pick up items from customers. In addition to increased customer responsiveness and satisfaction, we're moving more volume through an existing capital infrastructure, resulting in cost savings.

We had customers use the site to perform a series of shopping activities. This individual, hands-on research was instrumental in refining several areas of navigation. But, as with all Web sites, we continue to get feedback from our customers and enhance the site based on their input.

To promote OfficeDepot.com we're leveraging the numerous vehicles the company already distributes to customers such as catalogs and direct mail pieces. We've also added the URL to all print ads, including weekly newspaper inserts and our extensive television campaign featuring the cartoon character Dilbert.

Many of our traditional large catalog customers transitioned from ordering through phone or fax to placing orders online. We estimate that if it costs 100 percent to take an order over the phone, it costs 40 percent via fax and 10 percent online. So we're effectively driving down the cost of sales. In addition, we've steadily acquired new customers. We've noticed many online customers shopping when physical retail locations are closed. We're also witnessing many repeat sales to customers.

On the Web, we're able to track merchandising and marketing efforts in detail. In the future, we look forward to utilizing customer information, both explicit and implicit, to continuously improve how we sell to our customers through all channels. We've been very aggressive at integrating our site activities with the rest of the company and leveraging our previous experience and significant infrastructure investment.

NEW MARKETS, NEW METHODS

The case of AMP demonstrates how becoming an open-book corporation can require rethinking pricing, the value of various customer sets, and channel-to-market strategies.[3]

The Pennsylvania-based corporation is the world's leading supplier of electrical and electronic connectors, selling more than 130,000 products to 88,000 customers in 46 countries around the world. It adds as many as 200 new products daily. Product information has traditionally been distributed in 400 paper catalogs, paid out of the company's $16 million printing budget. With 400 catalogs published in eight languages, such changes are not only expensive but also a logistical nightmare. That is why each print catalog can be updated only once every two years, making it out of date the day it leaves the shipping dock.

Jim Kessler, Director of Global Electronic Commerce and AMPeMerce Internet Solutions, says AMP turned to an open-book approach in part out of concern over slowing growth:

> We had a need to track orders once they've been placed. When we realized our growth was beginning to taper off, we began to look at the way we serve our customers, which are grouped into three tiers. Tier 1 includes our 80 largest customers, who were exhibiting slow growth. Because of their size they had become relatively low profit margin accounts. The other end of the spectrum, Tier 3, which includes 80,000 customers, seemed to have much higher growth potential, as well as higher margins. But we found that our distributors had begun to look away from them—many of the dollars in this segment came from customers giving us small orders—and were focusing instead on the larger accounts. We asked ourselves, "What is our channel-to-market strategy here?" We decided to find a way to better serve this customer segment, the one that seemed to represent our best growth potential.
>
> A private network would not have been cost-effective. But we had created a search technology for our CD-ROM pilot effort, so we took that technology, which allowed customers to describe the part they were looking for in intuitive ways, to a Web conference to see what the reaction would be. It was so positive that we went back and patented the technology.
>
> At the time, the Internet was still being viewed as something for kids to play with. We decided to find out how involved our target customers were with the Internet. We

thought about 5 to 10 percent would be using the Internet. In reality, it was closer to 30 percent. We decided that was sufficient to justify developing a way to provide product information online and allow customers to order parts online.

When we began development, our management insisted we not go live until the number of parts available online was enough to generate 80 percent of the revenue from the targeted market segment. They also required us to offer a global system, available in multiple languages and able to support regional part-stocking methods. And they insisted that we develop in-house expertise to handle the system.

The pilot program involved 12 customers—companies such as AT&T, GE, IBM, Siemens, and Xerox—plus two distributors. We asked these companies to critique the system once it was developed. We wrote improvements into the site within two weeks and asked them to review the changes.

We debuted our online catalog, *AMP Connect,* with 32,000 product part numbers available in five languages. It currently features information on 90,000 products in eight languages and records 115,000 hits per day. Repeat use of the catalog is growing at a rate of 10 to 15 percent per month, with 250 new users a day signing up.

Previously our prices varied from country to country. Because customers could now see all of these prices, we had to develop a single base price that worked globally. We then specified tariffs and logistics costs as add-ons rather than incorporating them into the prices. We didn't have a choice about standardizing base prices, and we had to educate our customers about what went into calculating the base prices.

We also learned that electronic commerce challenges the value proposition of distributors. Geographic proximity and the ability to supply product information had been big parts of the value proposition provided by distributors. With the Internet, that value disappears. Some of our distributors realized that and developed new ways of adding value. One distributor developed customer-training programs; that makes the distributor a more valued partner in the supply chain. Others are exploring becoming master suppliers of multiple products and taking on the role of finding ways to reduce costs for customers overall.

As a bonus, we saved more on publishing than we spent on developing the electronic channel. It cost us $1.4 million to build the online system. But $800,000 of the total was invested in the searchable database, which we also now use to generate print catalogs. That alone has cut our print catalog costs by 60 percent.

Everybody wants to know how much revenue will be generated over the Internet. That's an important measure of success, but the costs that are avoided, such as those related to the printing and publishing of paper catalogs, are just as important. The transition to electronic commerce is well underway.

Besides offering customers convenience, better decision-making capabilities, and easier tracking of orders, becoming an open-book corporation provides significant competitive advantages. Once a customer is used to ordering through your system, you're much less likely to lose that customer to a competitor. Moving requires dislocation, retraining, and going through the initiation process all over again. Inertia can be a powerful force in favor of a company that has bonded with its customers.

However, as the AMP example illustrates, the move can involve significant rethinking of business issues. The customer is now more firmly settled in the driver's seat. AMP customers clearly would have rebelled if the company had not revamped its pricing structure.

GETTING EVERYONE ON THE SAME PAGE

Some customers are realizing that by raising barriers to exit, a supplier extranet can give the supplier a distinct advantage. And as more companies make the move to open-book operation, they can find themselves confronted with multiple suppliers, each with its own ordering mechanisms, technology, and automated systems—which may or may not integrate with other supplier systems and a customer's own internal accounting and resource management systems. As a result, in the Net Future large companies will start to try to take control and force suppliers to integrate into their own open-book procurement systems.

Boston Edison's 3400 employees generate about 70,000 purchase orders a year for spare parts, equipment, and maintenance/repair/operations supplies. The company's automated ordering system allows employees to order supplies directly online; for example, a worker can get next-day delivery of office supplies to his or her desk. Moreover, the company can incorporate many different supply partners into its own system rather than force employees to learn multiple systems for ordering online.

Companies like SNS are trying to address the problem by providing one-stop shopping for both buyer and supplier in specific industries. SNS's original business was processing credit card authorizations for customers of Canadian financial institutions. It now is morphing into a company that provides end-to-end electronic commerce services.[4] The company has a transportation tracking service. If a supplier, shipper, or freight forwarder wants to check on the status of a shipment, it can fill in a Web form to request information about when to expect delivery. SNS translates the information into a form that a carrier such as a major airline can understand, delivers it to the airline, which in turn checks on the shipping status, and delivers the information back to the shipper's Web browser. It also alerts a retailer about details of an expected delivery from the supplier.

"From the buyers' point of view, they need to be able to have a common interface between their many supplier catalogs. Suppliers also will need management, maintenance, and cataloging of their products offered for sale, along with electronic interfaces into their inventory and fulfillment systems," says Fred Douglas, executive vice president of business development for SNS.

THE SELF-SERVICE STRATEGY

Much of what people want—and can have because of the Net—is self-service. The ultimate in becoming a service organization is to create the platform for customers to serve themselves. Companies ranging from financial institutions to airlines have started to aim their businesses in this direction.

At the base level, there will be really two kinds of self-service approaches in the Net Future. In one, the customer does the work, such as customers ordering their packages to be picked up by FedEx. In the other, the customer pays, such as an individual buying a CD online at Music Boulevard. "Customer" here refers to any customer, whether business to consumer or business to business.

One of the latter is American Skandia Life Assurance Corp., the U.S. subsidiary of Skandia Insurance Company, one of the largest insurance companies in Scandinavia.[5]

Only 10 years old, the Shelton, CT–based corporation had an advantage when it jumped into the highly competitive field of packaging and selling variable annuities. The company's customers are brokers at investment firms scattered throughout the country. They include Everen Securities, LPL, Dain Rauscher, Legg Mason, Fahnestock, and R.W. Baird.

American Skandia basically assembles various financial packages and markets them to these brokers, who in turn sell them to individual investors. In the Net Future, the company sees itself as being able to streamline the process through its corporate extranet, providing its broker customers with direct access to all its financial planning tools. Says Wade Dokken, President of American Skandia:

> Yesterday, when a customer interfaced with you, such as when the customer wanted to make an investment transaction, add or withdraw funds, change allocations, or whatever, they all required the broker to go through us. We were the first to just put all this on the Web. We're motivating our customer, the financial adviser, to become more Web proficient. Now he can electronically download all his client's portfolios and holdings.
>
> The financial adviser used to have to call one of us, which took both of us time. We thought, if the adviser can look up all his clients and download their entire holdings, we're not just a packager and intermediary. The Net is ruthless to the low-value intermediary.

When you're not buying commodity products, the Web is weak. When there's a motivated buyer, the Web is great. We have a very Web-friendly company, since we're relatively new and have no legacy systems.

We're putting videos of our money managers on the Web, and a financial adviser can submit an application directly to us on the Net. What this really does is let the brokers spend as much time as they can with their customers. Seventy-five percent of our business comes from financial planners who are excessively high-tech, and because they are high-tech brokers, they embrace the technology. We once created a CD-ROM product with a series of experts in it. Financial planners don't use videotapes, because it makes them observers. Computer presentations make them an integral part.

The Net saves our customers money in their business. It's that simple. We're trying to create the value that our people want to help bring them with us into an electronic relationship.

American Skandia found that the more it became an "open book," the more its customers gave it high marks in independently conducted ratings—in virtually all aspects of customer service.

CUSTOMER AS WORKER

Following its foray into being an online banker for consumers, Citicorp took the logical step of putting credit card account data in its Web site. Meanwhile, BankAmerica fashioned its Web site for credit card holders to check current balances, several months of statements, and credit limits. Delta, United, and most other airlines allow their frequent fliers to check their account balances, while e*Trade, Charles Schwab, and other online brokerages let consumers manage their own online accounts. Hyatt Hotels offers online reservations as well as account status information.

Auto manufacturers generally are supporting the dealership infrastructure through which vehicles have traditionally been sold. However, some are experimenting with selling directly on the Net and using their dealer networks as a distribution mechanism. At the Ford Motor Company Preowned Showroom, customers can go online to buy a used car. All models are less than 3 model years old with fewer than 36,000 miles. In addition, each has a 12-month, 12,000-mile warranty and comes with 24-hour roadside assistance.

To buy online, customers search the inventory by entering their zip code and what they're looking for. Once they've found a car they want, they enter personal information, and then put down a $300 deposit by using a credit card or by calling a customer service representative.

A dealership for a test drive and delivery is then selected. If financing is needed, the customer can apply online. The order is then confirmed online and again within 24 hours by a call from a customer service representative who has checked for credit card authorization. If the purchase is not confirmed within 48 hours, the order is canceled. Once the car has arrived at the dealership, the customer is notified to come in for the test drive. Unless the buyer decides against the purchase after the test drive, the purchase is completed at the dealership.

Truckers are a much more wired population than one might imagine. More than 55 percent of truckers own a PC; 35 percent go online daily.[6] That's why Volvo decided it made sense to allow potential buyers of its 770 model truck cab—which sells for about $120,000—not only to configure their vehicle online but to apply for a loan and buy online as well. The user can pick the color, wheel base, engine, transmission, and interior trim as well as designate the dealership where the truck will be picked up. The trucker can then fill out a credit application, which Volvo's finance arm tries to evaluate within 24 hours; the application's status can be tracked online. Once the loan is approved, a credit card can be used to make the down payment. The truck cab can be picked up about two months later at a dealership.

In some cases, the open-book corporation actually is two corporations. Fidelity Institutional Retirement Services Company, a division of Fidelity Investments, is the largest administrator of retirement and other benefits plans for 2500 companies and their 5 million employees.[7] Rather than putting benefits information online themselves, those companies can include Fidelity's NetBenefits service as part of the online access they provide to employees. In some cases, companies simply provide a link from their own intranets to Fidelity's site; in other cases, Fidelity customizes NetBenefits for incorporation into the client's intranet.

Retirement plan participants must call Fidelity's 800 number to get access to NetBenefits for the first time. Once they've been given a password, they can look up their account balances, change the way their retirement savings are invested, plan their retirement savings strategy, and check on the price of their company's stock in real time. Eventually, if their company agrees, participants also will be able to enroll in their company's plan online.

- The Bank of Montreal allows customers not only to apply for mortgages online but also to track the status of their loan applications. The same is true for student loans.

- Counsel Connect, an online communications and information service for the legal profession, allows lawyers from different firms to hold virtual conferences in a secure, private online environment. The service, which also provides personalized legal information, online continuing education seminars, and extensive legal libraries, enables lawyers to meet with clients in cyberspace as well.

- Ford's Annual Meeting On-Line allows its shareholders to vote their proxies electronically.

- Before Mobil Corporation began using the Net to communicate with its network of 300 lubricant distributors, transactions were handled by a computer system that required the distributor to purchase and install software. Updates on products and programs were done by letter, fax, or phone, and distributors had to call the company before ordering to double-check that the information wasn't outdated. Purchases and product information are now available in the same place, and information is current when a distributor needs to order.

- Many people originally thought the Net revolution would be confined to the United States. Such is not the case. When Pennsylvania-based Unisys planned its twenty-fifth Unisys Airline Users Association conference in East Berlin, it provided all the information on the conference on an extranet. Executives from airlines around the world, such as British Airways, Air France, Finnair, Iberia, SAS, Delta, United Airlines, and cohost Lufthansa, simply tapped into the Unisys extranet. There, they received the three-day conference agenda, background on the organization, contacts, conference registration forms, and even Berlin travel tips and tour information.

- KinderCare, a large chain of child-care centers, plans to allow parents to check a local center's schedule, find out what's on the daily lunch menu, and review their child's progress and development.

- Howard Press, which handles annual reports, stationery, and business forms for many Fortune 500 corporations, automates the ordering process by allowing customers to order online directly from the company's warehouse. The system gives the corporations quick response time to customer needs while eliminating the need to store materials onsite.

- In addition to maintaining purchase records for nearly 100 large corporate customers, Dell Computer tested a similar system for small businesses and consumers. Going beyond the system that allows customers to configure and purchase a computer online, the new interface would enable customers to check on what they bought and when, as well as remind customers about repairs performed and warranty information.

- Members of Kaiser Permanente, the large California HMO, will be able to schedule nonemergency appointments with doctors, get a personalized health assessment on the basis of their health habits and history, and consult a nurse.

- The Boston Globe and other newspapers allow subscribers to go online to subscribe, place classified print ads online, and contact customer service if the newspaper isn't delivered.

Creating a self-service model for customers has several advantages for a company. First, it cuts down on customer-service costs, since fewer people call or contact the company directly, other than through the Web site. More important, in the ultimate extended enterprise, customers get exactly what they are looking for when they want it. Customers have more resources at their fingertips at a lower cost to the providing company. Which competitor will want to be the one without this capability?

Self-service can go awry, of course. Consider the case of Kansas City Power and Light. In its commendable eagerness to give the customer the ability to contact the company directly about service problems, it allows the customer to electronically send in a service outage notification from the company's Web site. What is wrong with this picture? Think about it. How do you use your computer when the power's out?

CUSTOMER AS PAYER

Consumers have been able to pay their bills electronically for several years, but typically that has meant either authorizing their bank to pay the bills automatically or using a software package to pay bills received in the mail. However, what will become increasingly common in the Net Future is the ability to call up your bill online and pay it using a credit card.

MCI uses electronic invoicing, a service that allows customers to pay their bills at the MCI Web site. The AT&T Universal card and BellSouth also allow their customers to view their accounts and pay bills directly on their sites.

A second option for online payments is E-checks. Fifty U.S. Defense Department contractors are helping the Federal Reserve Bank of Boston test an electronic version of the paper check. In the test, the Defense Department creates electronic checks that are signed digitally and E-mailed to the contractors. The contractor then digitally endorses the check and E-mails it with an electronic deposit slip to its bank, which verifies both check and endorsement signature. The electronic check information is processed by existing bank systems that use an

Internet-enabled front end. The pilot will serve as a test case for how companies that deal with the federal government may be paid in the future. The U.S. government has mandated that all its suppliers be paid electronically.

Similar technology ultimately would enable consumers to sign an E-check with a smart card that contains an encrypted digital signature. Using an E-check would simplify the transfer of electronic money between individuals, who usually have no real electronic payment capabilities.

Electronic deposit of paychecks has been around for some time, but the Cummins-Allison Corp. worked with Glenview State Bank of Glenview, IL, to develop a system for electronically paying stockholder dividends to its shareholders. Instead of mailing out paper checks, the company was able to transfer the money directly into shareholders' bank accounts.

GOVERNMENT ON DEMAND

In the Net Future, the concept of the open-book corporation will extend to government, directly linking constituents with services. In Massachusetts, for example, residents can skip long lines to register their vehicles and can even pay speeding tickets by going to the state's Express Lane at its Web site and paying online by credit card. While there, they can get an absentee voter ballot and even form a corporation. Nearly every state is starting to open the government and the myriad of government services available. A few examples:

- Missouri has opened its books to the public by providing detailed information on children's treatment services and parental help stress lines. It also provides an "adoption photo listing." Potential parents can peer into the open book of the government and see details by age on boys, girls, and siblings who are candidates for adoption, complete with photos.

- Need to contact a government employee? Kentucky opened the books on its telephone directory by allowing residents to search for anyone at any time. Residents and visitors also can search on state facilities, such as parks, and immediately see photos and information about the attraction.

- The state of Connecticut aggregates the executive, judicial, and legislative branches of government and instantly routes citizens to any of the 169 municipalities that matter to them at the moment.

- Want to check on a tax refund? Residents of West Virginia simply go to the state's Web site, enter their social security number and refund amount, and push a button. Like many other states, West Virginia also opened its statewide database of all jobs available, categorized, searchable, and detailed, complete with application forms online.

Most of the activity at the state government level is being headed by a state chief information officer (CIO)—a common fixture in large corporations, but a relatively new phenomenon in state government. In the early 1990s, there was barely a handful of state CIOs. Now, nearly every state in the U.S. has one.

One of the more progressive CIOs is John Thomas Flynn, Chief Information Officer of California. Flynn was one of the first state CIOs in the country when then-governor of Massachusetts William Weld appointed him to the office in 1994. In California, whose total revenues rank behind only GM, Exxon, and Ford, he oversees 8000 information technology workers and manages a $2 billion IT budget.

The state has 280,000 employees; a half-dozen technology projects, each greater than $100 million, are under way. In addition, Flynn is president of the National Association of State Information Resource Executives, the official society of state CIOs. He envisions enormous changes in the structure of government[8]:

> The organizations in the states are undergoing a big change. Everything the government does can be done quicker, more cheaply, and more easily electronically on the Net: licensing, fee structures, payments of benefits, virtually everything we do. We're going to totally change how we do business.

Virtually anything we do can be done more efficiently by computer. Every service and all of delivery of government is going to change.

In San Francisco, if you want a vanity plate, you fill out a form with your three choices. You wait in line and at the end of the line, a clerk enters the choices into a computer and it might reject all three. You then go back and create another form and start in the line all over again. Now we have an online database of every plate number; you can download a form over the Internet and send it in. Then we'll be taking credit cards with the form. This kind of change pays for itself in a week.

If you want to go to a campsite, you can visit the camp virtually on the Net. With a recommendation engine, we can suggest that you might be in need of a fishing license, which we'll prompt you for. And maybe you'll need a hat or shirt while you're there. I doubt in 10 years we'll all have the numbers of employees we have now, because we're not going to need as many folks to deal with the public.

Outsourcing hasn't even touched government yet. Government is always relatively slow to get into these areas, because of bureaucratic inefficiencies and a strong resistance to change.

In the future, there won't be as many staffs to get things done. The whole structure of government is going to change. A few years out, we'll get upset if we can't E-mail our kids' teachers. These schools have Web sites. My son is 12 and he wants to get a part-time job doing Web sites. I just don't see a downside to it.

Some companies are starting to look at ROI. They don't think this through very well. In government, about 15 percent of our residents are active government customers, those who get some kind of benefit, like unemployment benefits. People are eligible for dozens of other programs, like energy fuel projects and so forth. But no one knows the number of beneficiaries—the programs and databases are separate—so we have islands of automation. For example, a digital driver's license for everyone, whether they drive or not, could be beneficial. You could use it for food stamps.

> We have a backlog of $7 billion in unpaid child support. The Net can be used to help identify and find these offenders. This is an opportunity for the government to do better.

The state provides living and learning areas for students to participate in digital and virtual teaching and even offers a selection of other Web sites specifically for children. California has taken a lead in opening its government to citizens, so that they can get government services when they want them.

THE PERFUME SYNDROME

The open-book corporation will be open not only to customers but also to their business channel partners as well. This open distribution of information means that corporations and their suppliers will work together more closely to figure out strategies for boosting sales. It also means that in the Net Future, the term *partner* will be a more accurate reflection of the business relationship than it is now.

The open-book corporation will enable manufacturers and retailers to become more closely aligned in making decisions about such things as marketing strategy and inventory planning. With wider information distribution, more decisions can be made more rapidly in the field. In short, extranets can create a full chain of operational integration. Just as the complexity of the world will require individual workers to work in teams, so it will demand that Netted companies work in teams with suppliers.

For example, Land O' Lakes, which sells more than 400 dairy products through 30,000 retail grocery stores and wholesale clubs, is integrating food brokers with its sales force by giving them the ability to pull customized reports from the company's database.[9]

Using real-time data, brokers can generate reports to show to supermarkets that stock the company's dairy products (Land O' Lakes does not sell directly to retailers). A broker can show a store manager how Land O' Lakes brands are selling in other stores in the same supermarket chain, how they are selling against other dairy products, and how they are selling in competing stores. The information enables brokers and retailers to work together to change pricing and placement of products to encourage sales. Coupled with sophisticated datamining techniques that provide rapid-response reporting on product performance, this tight integration has the potential for profound impact not only on retail sales but on product development.

In the Net Future, marketers of any consumer product may confront the "Perfume Syndrome." Perfume companies know that a perfume's fate is determined within the first few months after it is introduced; if it doesn't make a big splash then, it never will. With retailers and suppliers able to take quick action on the basis of immediate feedback, merchandise may have an even narrower window of opportunity to prove itself.

Consider how quick feedback affects products sold in a Dayton Hudson store.[10] The department store chain provides real-time information on sales to its suppliers, enabling them to monitor how their merchandise is selling in each of the chain's stores. Armed with this information, individual store managers and suppliers collaborate on how to stock, price and promote products. The supplier's reps may suggest to store managers strategies that have worked in other Dayton Hudson outlets: a special offer, perhaps, or a targeted marketing campaign. And store managers can make the best possible use of shelf space on a day-to-day basis.

This kind of distributed decision making based on quick feedback means that merchandise in the Net Future will need to make an immediate impact on sales. If it doesn't find its market rapidly, it may well be jerked off the shelves or relegated to a more obscure display than something that generates a big splash when it is introduced. Already, books whose sales are not deemed adequate within 90 days are being returned to publishers; in the Net Future, that time frame could become even shorter.

REVOLUTION IN THE OTHER CHANNELS

The extended, electronic enterprise will impact more than marketing time cycles. The dramatic changes that occur in relationships with distributors, retailers, and manufacturers will enable

the entire supply chain to cut inventory costs and reduce manufacturing cycle time, including real-time product modifications.

An example of the process at work is InfoTEST, a consortium of companies from a variety of industries that are jointly
exploring the uses of new technology. In a real-life test of a
hypothetical scenario, corporations including Caterpillar, 3M,
Digital Equipment Corp., Hughes Electronics, Sprint, Hewlett-
Packard, and IBM worked through how to cut the time needed
to respond to a customer's demand from weeks to five days.

The test involved figuring out how manufacturers could
work simultaneously with their suppliers and customers to speed
the process of modifying a product to meet the customer's
requirements. On the basis of that test, product development in
the Net Future might be as shown on pages 116 and 117.

The group hopes that the ability to bring products to market
more quickly will cut costs more than will moving manufacturing operations overseas.

Another dramatic example of how an open-book corporation
might work is the Automotive Network eXchange (ANX).[11]
Piloted in 1998 by the Automotive Industry Action Group
(AIAG), a consortium of more than 1300 North American
automakers and suppliers, ANX ultimately will link not only
U.S. companies but their counterparts in Europe and around
the globe.

ANX is essentially a business extranet for the automotive
industry, a private network that uses Internet technology to create a single, massive communications link among all segments
of the auto manufacturing supply chain. The pilot project
included the Big Three automakers, Caterpillar, PACCAR, and
28 top-level suppliers. However, the system is expected to make
life easier for smaller suppliers as well, less than 50 percent of
whom are currently doing electronic exchange of information.

The system would allow manufacturers and suppliers to
exchange E-mail, share Computer-Assisted Design (CAD)
drawings, meet via videoconference and communicate production schedules more easily than they can now. According to Tom
Hoy, Executive Director of AIAG during the pilot program, the
ANX service is the largest of several industry supply-chain

streamlining projects that have the potential to save the industry $2 billion annually:

> Right now it takes 4 to 6 weeks for the North American auto industry to pass scheduling and production information down to the lowest tier of a supply chain—roughly a week per tier. And when it gets there, it's useless! The information is old. It's incomplete. And it doesn't help the lower tiers, such as individual parts manufacturers and materials companies, in their planning. Even with all the technology at our disposal, I could walk from Chicago to Detroit with a message in less time than it takes to move information down a typical supply chain.
>
> When researching connectivity options for design data and business information, we realized that data sharing, virtual design, videoconferencing, E-mail, and other applications were becoming more important to the automotive industry. We wanted to streamline not only manufacturer-to-supplier communications but supplier-to-supplier as well. ANX will eliminate the need for the many different phone lines and data communications technologies that exist today. Some dedicated lines can cost hundreds—even thousands—per month to support. Suppliers can also use the ANX system to build their own internal networks or eliminate redundant telecommunications systems dedicated to one automaker or application.
>
> To get an idea of the potential time savings, consider how efficient it would be to have multiple trading partners that use multiple applications access all those many programs using a single connection. Right now a supplier may have individual connections to Ford, GM, and Chrysler, and other connections to smaller suppliers. Having a single pipeline to connect to all of them is quite a departure from having a dedicated phone line for each of several trading partners.
>
> Unlike the public Internet, the ANX has a central management structure. An overseer communications company, Bellcore/SAIC, will certify and monitor Internet Service Providers who meet ANX standards for performance, reliability, and security. Suppliers and automakers would sub-

Product Development in the Net Future

DAY ONE: THE REQUEST	DAY TWO: THE SEARCH
Customer faxes request to Caterpillar dealer	Team members meet electronically after reviewing situation
Dealer faxes request to regional rep, who scans it and sends over the Net to product support group	Team members make decisions about how to help resolve the request
Product group team leader: • Uses pager, E-mail, voicemail to alert global team to need for late-afternoon electronic conference • Starts electronic folder, accessible to all team members, that will include all project info	Team leader makes duty assignments, updates workflow plan
At meeting, team members—engineering, manufacturing, accounting, product support, and suppliers—review information, assign research responsibilities, set up workflow plan	Team members work independently to explore possible alternatives.
Team leader: • Schedules electronic conference for following day • E-mails dealer with overview of action plan	At end of day, team members • Confer electronically and decide to design a new component that can be built into tractors • Assess design alternatives • Review cost and scheduling implications Team leader incorporates information into project folder

DAY THREE: THE ENGINEERING	DAY FOUR: THE ANSWER	DAY FIVE: THE SHIPMENT
Component supplier, who conferred overnight with staff about ability to modify component, gives team details about his research	Product team members work concurrently via electronic channels to finalize the change and general work flow	Supplier delivers casting to Caterpillar for final machining and shipment to dealer for installation on customer's tractor
Team refines design alternatives, using E-mail and desktop video conferences and info from component supplier	Team leader • oversees release of the work plan • checks with supplier on casting of the needed part • updates project folder and workflow plan	Information generated by project is captured on a customer and product database for future reference
Team meets electronically to • compare design analysis results • decide which options to pursue for the needed component		
Team leader updates project folder and electronic workflow plan		

scribe to one of these providers to gain access to the ANX network. If companies have problems with the ANX, they can turn to the overseer to get them resolved. This structure provides reliability, security, and performance that the public Internet doesn't have.

Pilot studies have already shown that streamlining communications can cut time end-to-end from 4 to 6 weeks to 4 to 6 days. That translates into a savings of $71 per car.

- Eastman Software, whose products help automate document management and image processing, found that being an open-book corporation was a significant competitive advantage in recruiting and retaining the distributors that would actually sell and install its products.
- Fed Ex's widely recognized extranet, which allows customers to track their own packages, also lets customers incorporate the service within an intranet. Rockwell's RWEB, the intranet that includes Rockwell information, incorporates the FedEx tracking system, giving FedEx a second layer of customer penetration.
- The Boeing Company has a parts page at its Web site where all buyers can order parts and track them at all times. With its tight electronic linkage to Federal Express, buyers think they are looking at the Boeing parts page, but they're really looking at FedEx.

THE CUSTOMER IS THE ENTERPRISE

Opening up the corporation to customers puts additional pressure on companies to make sure that their operations meet customer expectations in terms of efficiency and responsiveness.

- In developing leadership among its managers, Silicon Graphics asks their peers, employees, and supervisors to assess the managers by filling out an extensive questionnaire. The only problem is that the forms must be returned to the company administering the program for scoring. Personnel Decisions International, which administers the program, now lets respondents fill out the questionnaire online and respond electronically. E-mail is used to notify participants that they've been selected to assess a colleague, and reminds them if they're getting close to the deadline for submission. The process has increased response by 30 percent.

- When Russell Inc., a Toronto marketing communications firm, created an extranet for Mutual of Omaha's Canadian division, it set up a password-protected Web site that allowed the client to view the work in progress as it was being created. The insurance company was able to track the status of the project and make comments throughout the development process.

- Sabre's VantagePoint lets corporate travel managers perform what-if scenarios with vendor contracts, travel services and travel expenses. American Express Interactive integrates a company's travel policies and automatically steers corporate users to reservations that comply with company policy while flagging plans that violate it.

Greater disclosure raises new issues about protection of the corporate database—issues that relate not to the technology but to what constitutes sensitive information. Company policies should be solidified before the data starts flowing.

WHEN THEY CAN READ YOU LIKE A BOOK

What's one of the most ironic examples of an open-book operation? The U.S. Central Intelligence Agency has put up a Web page for kids, complete with the sound of a dial lock opening, an area for trying on a disguise, and the "virtual guard dog" badge for their favorite CIA pooch.

The nation's secrets may not be at risk with the CIA for Kids site, but in the Net Future corporations may not be as fortunate. Many of the strategies and tactics of a company will be clearly visible to competitors that, with just a few clicks, can see what the company is selling and for how much. A few more clicks brings them to rich, detailed financial information.

While most large companies have organized business intelligence systems to track competition, not all are relying on the

Net as their most valuable source of information. With large companies leading the way in placing more emphasis on the Net to gather market data,[12] companies of all sizes still need people to sift through the sea of information that will become instantly, electronically accessible.

"The Net is a great starting point to locate the real human sources outside a company," says Bill Fiora of The Futures Group, a Connecticut business intelligence company. "And it totally changes the speed of gathering information." While there are companies that specialize in providing competitive intelligence, or CI, on the Net, Fuld & Company contains links to several hundred other sites, broken down by industry, to lead others through the maze. The Montague Institute provides a journal containing such subjects how to use the Net for competitive intelligence, and the Society of Competitive Intelligence Professionals has a listing of hundreds of CI experts and research papers.

Most corporations include on their Web sites their annual reports, company officers, lines of business, and product offerings. But if a person spends enough time at a corporation's Web site, plenty more can be learned about the company.

- Job openings—now a required listing at Web sites for most companies to remain competitive—frequently give clues to future corporate intentions. A company launching a new offensive in Europe may be found advertising openings for a marketing manager, support staff, and a variety of other positions—all based in London.

- Timing and content of company press releases can be tracked and archives easily viewed. And since not all press releases make it into newspapers and magazines, the archives can provide a wealth of unpublished company plans.

- Key executives within a company, including detailed contact information and background, can easily be located by competitors looking for new management talent. Many companies even provide handy organizational charts.

- Who are the company's business partners and best customers? No problem! Companies are understandably quite proud to list their best customers, often with testimonials and detailed case studies of how they are working together. Side benefit: some of the thinking of the best customers becomes apparent.

"Some companies aren't always the smartest in terms of what they put on the Net. Some person way down in the ranks who feeds the raw information has been told to give them everything, so he does, and it goes up on the Net," says Fiora.

Comparison pricing is a staple of such services as CompareNet, which compares manufacturers' list prices for seven categories of products: cars, electronics, sports/leisure, home/garden, software, services, and home office equipment. NECX, an online computer retailer, goes even further. It automatically retrieves prices from other retailers' Web sites and compares them with its own. Talk about opening your books to your competitors! NECX has electronic links between its 20,000 global suppliers and the more than 20 warehouses that supply its orders.

Is there a way around this? Not really, but it doesn't matter. The velocity of change in the Net Future is such that any intelligence gathered via the Net can easily be viewed as simply looking at what a company was doing. It also is reason for companies to keep nimble enough to move with the changing nature of the Net Future.

WHO'S IN THE DRIVER'S SEAT?

So, companies that always wanted to be consumer driven—or claimed to be—will have their chance by becoming a true, open-book corporation. As long as executives and managers can handle the idea that in an open-book corporation the customer really *is* in charge, they can sit back and let the customer do the work. And the smart company will, in fact, let the customer *drive* in the Net Future.

PRODUCTS BECOME COMMODITIES

In the Net Future, any person will be able to buy anything from anyone at any time from anywhere, as the Net environment turns the value proposition for the creation, distribution, and sale of products on its head. This dynamic will affect not only pricing but also the true value of products themselves.

The age-old saying, "What's a product worth? Whatever you can sell it for," doesn't fly in the Net Future. The new mantra more likely will be: "What's a product worth? Here's what I'll pay for it at this moment." Or: "That's not the best price." Or even: "Here's what I'll pay, take it or leave it." Or worse yet: "You want how much? I thought I was a valued customer."

No matter the mantra, the message is clear. When internal decisions can be made more quickly because of the Net, when the competition is only a mouse click away, when the public has access to more options than ever before, when information can be updated and made public on the fly, the value chain shifts dramatically.

The producer drove the traditional environment; the consumer drives the new one.

Webster's dictionary defines a commodity as "something useful or valuable." In business, however, the term can have a somewhat negative connotation. In the financial markets, commodities are items that are generally traded in bulk. Pricing is based less on the features of the product itself—it's difficult to differentiate between one farmer's wheat crop and another's—

than on external factors such as weather and availability. Pricing can fluctuate wildly on the basis of these external factors: bad weather or a Gulf war can create a scarcity of wheat or oil that drives up prices.

The negative connotation stems from the fact that marketing strategies cannot really be used to justify higher prices for commodities because the basic product is relatively so widespread and similar from producer to producer. Frank (and now Jim) Perdue's campaign featuring their chickens is one example of an effort to transform a commodity into a brand. The generic, black-and-white labels for cereal and canned vegetables popular a decade or so ago represented a movement away from brand and toward commoditization.

The commoditization of some products is the logical extension of the cybereconomy going Main Street, since it will be caused by many of the same factors. To the traditional external factors that have driven commodity pricing, companies must now add the Net consumer or E-consumer, who has access to more products and more information than ever before and can be aggregated in ways previously unimaginable. Only those who realize that in the Net environment the consumer has become another force of nature will be prepared to make the changes necessary to survive.

CORE ASSETS BECOME PERIPHERAL

Commoditization can affect just about any product, from hard to soft goods. The value chain involved in selling gravel demonstrates the point.[1] There is almost an unlimited amount of gravel in the natural ground. True gravel comprises a jumble of various-size grains, all the way from rocks down to fine sand. Before it is excavated from the ground, so-called bank gravel is nearly worthless. In its natural state, before trees and shrubs are cleared, that bank gravel costs about $1 for a cubic yard of what is basically dirt.

After the land is cleared, allowing access to the gravel, it is then worth $1.50 per cubic yard while it is still in the ground.

Gravel companies exist to increase the value of the gravel and create wealth by adding more and more value. Here are the basic economics:

Bank gravel	$1.00/yd
Grubbing (land clearing)	$ .50/yd
Loading	$ .50/yd
Crushing	$3.00/yd
Sifting/screening	$ .50/yd
Delivering 30 miles away	$2.00/yd
Delivering 60 miles away	$4.00/yd

Each process adds value, and you can buy value any way you want. You can buy bank gravel loaded into your truck at the gravel pit for $2 a cubic yard. You can buy crushed and screened gravel delivered 30 miles to your site for $7.50 a cubic yard. You can even be really cheap and buy bank gravel for $1 a cubic yard, but you need to work harder and bring in your own machinery to grub the land and load the gravel into your own truck, then crush it and screen it yourself.

In the same way, information sitting in a vacuum has little if any value. This includes huge amounts of information that sits in mainframe databases somewhere in the bowels of an organization. In the Net Future, many products considered valuable may be sold the same way that gravel is. For example:

- The core product of the *Journal of Commerce*, a 170-year-old newspaper owned by the Economist Group, was the listing of cargo ship schedules. When the Net came along, the paper's lead advertisers—such as Hanjin Shipping, Cosco Group, and P&O Nedlloyd—bypassed the venerable publication by posting the ship listings on their own Web sites and communicating directly with shippers electronically. The core product—the ship cargo schedules—became a commodity, since all the companies could just as easily post the ship listings. The *Journal of Commerce* restructured, laid off nearly 75 of its 450 employees, invested to hire other staffers for its Net effort, and looked to add archived stories and links to other cargo carriers' Web sites.

- Quote.com, a Mountain View, CA, company that provides 15- to 20-minute delayed stock quotes and other financial information on various financial sites, has garnered half its revenue from selling business information and financial tools to other companies for use on their Web sites. These fees help underwrite consumer subscription fees. Rather than the individual paying for the stock quote service, the sponsoring company pays. The stock quote gets commoditized—it would be impossible now to charge on the Web for delayed quotes— and the fee passes from the consumer to the sponsor!

- Product commoditization is beginning to touch real-time stock quotes, traditionally available only to brokers who were charged a stiff fee by the New York Stock Exchange. Real-time quotes are now distributed free by InfoSpace, *Money*, and Wall Street City; a year earlier, the standard fee for real-time quotes was $29.95 a month.

- Free E-mail has become a staple of Web sites that seek to attract and retain users.

- MLS real estate listings traditionally have been a valued asset for participating brokers. They're now available in abridged form on the Web at Cyberhomes.com in cities where the company is licensed to provide them. Owners.com allows buyers who want to sell their homes themselves to post a picture, property data, and price.

- Free computer space to host a small-scale Web site has become a standard offering for many Internet service providers. Icat, which makes software for online catalogs, offers a similar deal to companies that sell fewer than 10 items.

- Netcentives helps commoditize air travel when it offers frequent flier miles as rewards for consumers who shop at participating E-merchants. For each purchase, customers receive points that can be aggregated and exchanged one for one for frequent flier miles on six major airlines.

ASSETS AS LOSS LEADERS

What happens when products are commoditized, when "ground zero" is your profit margin? Companies must find other ways to provide something that people will be willing to pay for. In many cases, what used to be a company's core asset can become a loss leader, with peripheral products and services driving new revenue streams. The theory behind the 99-cent six-pack of soda that gets you into the store to buy $10 worth of groceries now is applied to a wide variety of products and services.

- On today's Net, Auto-by-Tel can get you a car for $500 over dealer cost. After purchase, an E-mail asks if you would like an insurance price quote from a particular company. In the Net Future, an insurance company might offer you the car at cost, if you agree to use that agency for insurance during the ownership period. The value of the car to the insurance company is barely an issue; the value is in the insurance and the potentially new customer relationship. What does this do to the car dealer network?

- To the real estate agent, the central real estate listing is the core asset. In the Net Future, realtors might give a local newspaper the rights to print and distribute the listings. The newspaper then could add context around the listing, such as information on local schools, demographics of the neighborhood, and distance to shopping centers. After the house is purchased, the real estate agency might offer the data on the individual to after-sale services, such as moving companies, lawn services, and insurance brokers. The real estate listing is commoditized, with the value shifting to after-sale transactions.

- Convenience in supplying travel arrangements was a core "product" for travel agencies. However, airlines and other companies practically eliminated that product by offering search services and superdiscounted tickets on the Net. They also reduced commissions to agents. The travel itself has become a commodity, and agents face the prospect of charging travelers for their services. Other companies offer aggregation of frequent flier miles. Aggregation will change the business model so that the value is not necessarily in the ticket sale, but rather in selling advertising to companies that want to reach frequent flyers. The added value is in the products and services that surround the ticket sale.

- Health information was traditionally something you went to the doctor for. Sapient Health Network furnishes a vast library of information aimed at people with chronic and serious illnesses—all for free. The Web site uses an individual patient's profile to provide a customized reference "bookshelf" containing information about the health issues most relevant to him or her; the site also includes message boards, live chats, online workshops with health experts, a medical dictionary, and a drug database. How can Sapient provide such a robust site for free? By aggregating the information provided by its users and supplying that research data to the health-care industry. Patient privacy is protected because individual profiles remain confidential, but the aggregated profiles are used by pharmaceutical companies to determine marketing strategy.

Part of the opportunity is to see where the core product or service can be leveraged for an unrelated—and often unexpected—product or service. When Southwest Airlines decided to expand its information technology department, the airline looked to its frequent fliers for help in hiring. The company offered vacations and free tickets for résumés, and gathered more than 1400 résumés. The airline also planned a referral bonus program for workers who came up with new technical job candidates. When you overlay the Net onto such ideas, they can become powerful.

In the Net Future, that new added value can come from either a product or service. Broadcast.com aggregates broadcast programming, including those of existing radio, TV, and cable stations, and repackages it not only for public consumption but also for corporate intranets. In doing so, it shifts the value from the information itself to how it is packaged and distributed. Corporations could buy the information directly from the original producer, but the service broadcast.com provides represents value. New York startup Root, which acts as an online valet for its customers by performing a variety of online services, also bases its business model on its service rather than the products it delivers. "Root is not for everybody," says CEO Seth Goldstein. "It values time above all else, and assumes that its members will pay for the privilege of more free time."

NEW GROUND RULES FOR BUYERS AND SELLERS

Commoditization of products has implications for how buyers and sellers interact. With a few exceptions, such as yard sales, flea markets, and shops you visit while on vacation, companies generally have sold their products at fixed prices. Company executives assess what they think a market will buy, create the process to acquire the goods to manufacture the product, then produce and distribute it.

The consumer dutifully shows up at a store and while "shopping," sees what appeals (or is sold) to him or her, then buys as many as needed. When the stock runs out, the shopper either does not see, and therefore does not buy, the product or, even more tediously, asks a willing salesperson to special-order just one more.

The ensuing process might entail the order going from the store to the distributor, to the warehouse (which is sold out), to the manufacturer, then back to the warehouse, the distributor, and to the store, and finally, perhaps days or weeks from the initial order, to the consumer. If by then the customer has changed his or her mind, no problem; the merchandise goes back on the shelf in hopes that another willing shopper will happen by.

That's basically the traditional, old-world approach. Granted, various parts of the process have been streamlined; demand can now be forecast on the basis of past sales and seasonality, and technology has been deployed to make the order-fulfillment process quicker. But for the most part, this environment comprises relatively fixed costs and charges all along the value chain.

On the consumption side, consumers rightfully assume that because the producer has offered an item for sale at a given price, they will always be able to find it at that price. A shopper barely gives a thought to special-ordering an item once a store runs out. The expectation is that the specially ordered, out-of-stock item will cost exactly the same amount as when it was in full supply.

On the production side, some products sell early while some linger. Those that sell quickly may be priced too low. Those that sell late, or never, are perhaps priced too high. In either case, plenty of money is left on the table.

Not very efficient, but what else can be done? Without the Net, not much!

DYNAMIC PRICING

In the Net Future, product pricing takes on a totally new dimension. The consumer will have an infinite selection of goods and places from which to acquire them. In such an environment it becomes increasingly difficult to distinguish one's product on the basis of the product alone. And that affects what a producer can charge for the product. Unless a producer can manage to supply a context for the product—great service, convenience, brand image, and so forth—the product itself becomes a commodity and can only be priced accordingly.

Pricing Dynamics

TRADITIONAL	NET FUTURE
Seller-determined	Buyer-determined
Fixed	Flexible
Based on supply	Based on demand
Based on previous sales	Based on this moment's sales
Based on product features	Based on product context
Price changes happen periodically via discounts or premiums	Price changes happen continuously

Not only will companies need to discover new ways to create value beyond their core products; they also will find themselves under increasing pressure to respond to market factors much more quickly than ever before. As a result, pricing for the Net Future's new commodities becomes far more fluid. In the Net Future, "fixed" pricing doesn't necessarily make the most sense.

POWER TO THE SELLER

The Net is the great equalizer when it comes to determining true supply and demand. In the traditional world, products are created and handed to a sales force to sell. Sales forces are customarily aimed at the "low-hanging fruit": those customers who seem obvious to management to be the most logical to buy first.

On the Net, products and their buyers meet more directly, with the buyer in the driver's seat. In the Net Future, this trend will be magnified as networked suppliers reach out to networked consumers.

One way of coping with commoditization of product is actually to become the commoditizer, aggregating supply of the product by creating a network of affiliations. Doing so allows companies, by virtue of the size and scope of their networks, to retain some measure of market clout in ways that might be difficult for a single producer to achieve in the Net environment. One approach is straightforward aggregation of supply:

- Garden Escape aggregates dozens of niche suppliers of gardening equipment all over the United States. In exchange for receiving a listing in the online catalog, each of the approximately 30 suppliers must agree to make Garden Escape its sole online outlet.

- Mergers and Acquisitions Marketplace aggregates people who want to sell businesses.[2] At any given time, roughly 3500 businesses are listed for sale; another 1000 listings describe what buyers are looking for. Listings are free, but finding out how to contact a buyer or seller requires paying for a $34.95 three-month membership. Bob Brauns, president and CEO of the company and a former president of the National Association of Business Brokers, says some businesses have been posted on a Friday and a sale closed the following Monday.

Another approach is comparison aggregation, which offers the ability to compare prices from many different producers. Here buyers can still drive down prices, but affiliates are willing to pay to be on their list for consideration.

- LifeQuote will compare prices on life insurance policies from approximately 50 different companies; about 17 percent of people who request the service end up as paying customers (compare that with the traditional conversion rate for direct mail of 1 to 2 percent). LifeQuote collects a commission of 50 percent of the first year's premium.
- CompareNet aggregates the collection of information about products, including prices. PriceScan does the same on computer equipment and software.
- BidFind automates the process of finding items for sale on the Web by indexing thousands of items up for bid at roughly 70 different auction sites daily.
- Bottom Dollar lets consumers pick a product category and enter a brand-name item. The shopping bot (short for "robot") automatically queries a number of online retailers and returns with the best price on the product, including a link to the retailer.
- At ShopFind, users can enter an item they're looking for and find out where it's being sold on the Net, whether it's available, and for what price.
- The shopping channel at the search engine Excite not only retrieves a list of item descriptions, shops, and prices but lets users sort the selections according to whichever criteria are most important to them.

But these are relatively static examples of supply aggregation. In the Net Future, individual companies also will make those comparisons automatically for the consumer, using systems that constantly monitor marketing environment factors such as competition and demand. These systems will automatically adjust prices to suit the moment, just as any good salesperson might do to close a sale. Some examples:

- Books.com and the books area of Cendant's netMarket compare their prices with those being charged by online booksellers Amazon.com and Barnes & Noble's Web site. The service not only shows the customer the comparison chart; it automatically drops any price that is higher than a competitor's. Acses compares prices, availability, and shipping costs at more than 20 online bookstores within seconds.
- PriceDrop.com drops the price on any product at the beginning of each hour until the product is sold.
- Time.com's banner ads on other sites include headlines that are updated in real time, opening the way for the same technology to be used to alter price promotions on the fly.

"WHAT AM I BID?"

The auction will emerge as the meeting place of choice for consumers and producers. Those who look at online auctions as simply electronic versions of flea markets and classified advertising are missing the point.

Online auctions are truly an extension of the fabric of the Web itself. People are allowed to organize, find items they want to buy, offer what they will pay, and check with others in the "community" about the trustworthiness of the selling entity. Companies organize products and product sets and, through volume discount from say, aggregating excess inventory from a supplier, can cover their downside while still offering great deals to online buyers. It is the ultimate in free enterprise, with the community monitoring itself. With hundreds of auction sites, consumers will be able to find almost any product they desire at any time.

One way to look at the online auction is as the location where buyers and sellers are organized or aggregated. Some companies aggregate buyers; some aggregate sellers or products. In this scenario, everyone wins. Buyers get great deals, sellers move products in larger quantities, and most important, monitoring buyer communities will allow sellers to determine what they should produce. Many people don't realize how big the online auction concept really is.

One of the largest and most successful of the early online auction companies was onsale.com.[3] The company, based in Menlo Park, CA, started by auctioning excess computers and related equipment. The profitable Internet start-up, which now handles offers from more than 10,000 bidders a day and tallies monthly sales in the millions of dollars, went public in 1997 and within months was valued at half a billion dollars. Says its founder and chief executive, Jerry Kaplan:

> There are two fundamental myths in retailing. One, that there is an infinite supply of goods and two, that they will be available at a fixed price. There is a poor feedback loop between the buyer and seller of goods. From a buyer's perspective, it's just take it or leave it. We are just a first step in the new direction, where pricing and availability can respond to the marketplace.
>
> The costs of production and distribution are not uniform against everything sold. The cost of the first item is different than the cost of those items produced and sold later. A good example is pricing of airline tickets where airlines try to maximize yield. Another example is event tickets, which is ridiculous now. All prices are fixed and the place is full or the place is empty. They're not maximizing the value and the seat is perishable. The event runs and the seat is gone.
>
> We've created a market for excess goods and have a mechanism where the price is set by a willing audience of buyers. The future will be more like the airline ticket model. Not everything will be sold by auction. We will be able to request and get a spot price for just about anything, when you want to make a purchase. It's almost as if you could hold a pricing card against the goods and ask what is the price for that item at this moment and get a dynamic quote for anything. That quote might be good for two hours or twenty-four hours.

> We find that supply is everything. When you have an ade-
> quate source of supply, the audience seems to aggregate
> itself. Car sites have been very effective at aggregating
> information and getting money on a referral fee. It's like a
> virtual store where you're aggregating information about
> goods. This is not a symmetrical process. A buyer is not the
> same as a seller. It's a forum for small merchants to access
> goods. The price is neither higher or lower on goods, it is a
> function of supply and demand. This is way ahead of the
> free market process. This is stereo and hi-fi when all you
> had was a little radio.

Onsale.com experimented with declining price models and
found that people made unrealistic offers, and though inquiries
were high, sales were low. It also found that the average person
posted 11 items for sale, and buyers averaged five purchases.
With more than 500,000 customers, the company plans to
expand its current markets as well as enter new arenas, such as
airline tickets, real estate, and timeshare properties.

The human dynamic also plays a great role in auction systems. At onsale.com, as the 48-hour auctions heat up, people
start bidding against one another not so much to get the product
as to beat someone else. Fittingly, the top screen of onsale.com
doesn't say "How to Buy." It reads "How to Play." And every time
they "play," onsale.com gets paid.

Onsale.com is hardly alone in the coming wave of dynamic
pricing models.

- At eBay, customers buying at auction can rate vendors and
  send in comments about the online deals. The company itself
  merely puts buyers in touch with sellers; it does not get
  involved with shipping or warehousing. It holds approximately 35,000 new auctions each day; beginning with a focus on
  computer hardware and software, buyers and sellers now
  exchange everything from Beanie Babies to sports memora-
  bilia. The company takes from 1.25 to 5 percent of each
  transaction. By early 1998, the number of users signing up
  for the site was growing by 25 percent a month. The company became profitable six months after it launched in 1995.

- Interactive Buyers Network International of Ventura, CA, decided to target procurement officers to make buying regular supplies—from copy paper and lumber to janitorial supplies and operations and maintenance parts—easier and cheaper. The company launched a network called Virtual Source, which allows buyers to send electronic requests for quotes for the item sought. Sellers respond with their best price. The reverse-auction approach, with buyers available before sellers, helped the company double its business every month, with $72 million annualized passing through the company in its first year. Companies pay less than $1000 a year to sign up.

- FairMarket hosts auctions of business-to-business sales of surplus computer equipment, electronic components, and chips. A seller with excess inventory ships the equipment to FedEx's warehouse, where FairMarket representatives inspect it. Once it passes inspection, it is posted on the Web site and bidders have three days to submit bids. The winning bidder wires payment and the merchandise is then shipped out.

- CityAuction lets sellers choose whether to auction their merchandise around the world or in their local area only. It also conducts Dutch auctions, in which all successful bidders pay the same price: the lowest bid that still qualifies.

Auctions have migrated beyond consumer goods. Take, for example, the municipal bonds issued by city and state governments to finance public works. In most cases, the issuer pays a large investment banking firm to underwrite the bonds and resell them to brokerage houses and institutional investors. In the past, bidders for municipal bonds had to submit a single bid for an entire bond issue. As a result, regional underwriters were regularly shut out of the process by the large national underwriters with deeper pockets. And there were no second chances; only one bid per bidder was allowed and all bids were opened at once, and the best bid won.

However, when Grant Street Advisors of Pittsburgh launched MuniAuction it took a different tack.[4] Auctions are conducted in real time in full view of any bidders who want to keep an eye on their desktop, and participants can improve their bid if they choose, creating a more competitive dynamic. Because bond issues can be bid on in smaller segments, maturity by maturity, smaller underwriters have a better shot at a piece of the pie. For the issuers, the auction system not only cuts the commissions paid to underwriters but can reduce the interest rate that governments must pay to borrow money. In its first five bond auctions for the city of Pittsburgh, the financial advisory firm sold $500 million worth of bonds over the Internet.

Myles Harrington, one of the cofounders of MuniAuction, contends that municipal bonds have to some extent been commoditized by the bond rating system; nearly 50 percent of all new bond issues are insured and rated Triple A by one of the major rating services. MuniAuction was designed to supply value to issuers by making the bond issuance process more convenient. In fact, he says one of the unexpected benefits of putting the process on the Web has been to attract more bidders. Instead of 3 bids for the entire $30 million issued by the city of Portland, OR, the city received 74 bids from 15 different firms. "We've had firms in Florida and Utah bidding on issues in Pennsylvania," Harrington says.

In this case, MuniAuction delivered power to the sellers by enabling them to attract more bidders for their bonds. It also has delivered power to the smaller buyers who previously were unable to compete.

THE AGGREGATION OF REAL-TIME DEMAND

Both aggregation of sellers and aggregation of buyers have distinct advantages. However, the future will belong to aggregators of buyers. The consumer-centric Net Future environment reorders the value chain. In the true 180-degree fashion of the Net Future, the concept of Supply and Demand becomes Demand and Supply.

In many ways, it's the reverse of what the antitrust laws are designed to prevent on the producer side. Producers are forbidden to create cartels and orchestrate price fixing. However, there is no regulation that says consumers can't get together and say, "This is how much we'll pay for this." It's reverse price fixing. And because the Net Future will allow it to happen in real time, products increasingly are likely to behave more as traditional commodities markets have done: volatile pricing, bulk purchases, split-second timing.

The consumer is the winner, and not only because of greater pricing clout. This new dynamic allows customers to do just-in-time buying. As prices become a truer reflection of customer demand, no longer do consumers have to buy an air conditioner in January to get a good price. Because greater consumer demand can now be leveraged to drive prices down instead of up, consumption can occur on the consumer's schedule rather than on the seller's.

Paradoxically, this consumer-centric environment enables these newly aggregated customers to do one-to-one buying. With one-to-one selling, a corporation is able to leverage internal and external resources to target an individual customer. The one-to-one consumer is able to join multiple groups with similar demands and leverage that greater buying power against a single company or product to better satisfy an individual need.

While the consumer comes out ahead with this new equation, the Netted corporation has opportunities to profit. This dynamic will spur the growth of new types of companies, whose mission is to organize the demand (the consumers) and leverage their collective buying power against the supply. And as companies find new ways to determine customers' needs and serve them in real time, focusing more closely on those customers will be a requirement, as we'll discuss in the next chapter.

PRICING ON THE FLY

Travel consolidators have traditionally sold last-minute, unused airline seats and hotel reservations at discount prices. Now Priceline.com allows consumers to bid directly on unsold airline tickets.[5] Want to visit your mother in Tennessee at the last minute? Simply go to Priceline.com and fill in your flight dates, your destination, the amount you'd be willing to pay, and your credit card number. Priceline will search its private fare database for flights. If an airline accepts your offer, Priceline will get back to you within an hour with a nonrefundable domestic ticket (the response time for international flights is 24 hours). In its first 10 weeks of operation, Priceline.com sold 20,000 tickets. The company hopes to expand to credit card debt, hotel rooms, rental cars, and home mortgages. The company is headed by Jay Walker:

> It looks like we aggregate buyers, but we don't. We are a demand collection system with substitutable range associated with it. We create substitutable demand to get buyers substitutable product. In the past, a union of buyers might be required to get a good price, but now the Net renders that model obsolete. The only requirement for this new model is that the demand must be certified up-front, usually by a credit card. A buyer transfers the proxy to us. We say to the seller, `I have one customer and here is the substitutable range.' The seller can choose whether to accept the offer. It's more like the stock market. We believe that buyer-driven commerce is the future.

Within months of launch, Priceline expanded its concept to cover new cars, taking a $25 referral fee from the buyer for finding a car at the buyer-specified price. The company also takes a $75 fee from the car dealers when the car is sold. Rather than the widely perceived threat of disintermediation, or elimination of the middleman or broker, Priceline is a classic example of what some have called re-mediation or re-intermediation made possible by the Net. Here is a Net-based company that placed itself in the middle of linking buyers and sellers together, providing a valuable service to both. The buyer gets the price desired, and the dealer receives an extremely qualified lead to presumably a car sale. What happens if the buyer reneges on the deal? The customer is charged a $200 good faith deposit, which goes to the dealer to cover costs of processing or removing a vehicle from inventory.

Just about anything that can be sold will be aggregated, and just about anyone who wants to buy anything can find an umbrella organization under which he or she can participate.

- Bionetwork, a site for biological scientists, not only offers information about scientific topics, but plans to start supplying products. Like many other niche sites with a highly focused audience, it could potentially leverage that small, aggregated universe of users and negotiate lower prices.

- Some companies are trying to aggregate demand by paying users to do things. For example, Intellipost's BonusMail service gives people who register directly with the service credits for reading and responding to targeted-advertising E-mail messages. The credits can be used for frequent flier miles and gift certificates to various retail stores and restaurants.

- LendingTree Inc. lets borrowers submit an online application for a loan. The application is sent to multiple lenders, who in effect bid against one another for the right to make the loan. LendingTree also helps prescreen borrowers so that applications are submitted to the lenders most likely to approve them, making the process more efficient for lenders. The borrower pays nothing to apply; lenders pay a startup fee and monthly maintenance fee. The service started with mortgages, lines of credit, and credit cards, and plans to include car and student loans.

- Barter will join auctions as a method of online exchange in the Net Future. Ubarter.com gives consumers the ability to swap electronics, vehicles, vacations, and home furnishings for things they'd rather have; other sites allow corporations to swap equipment.

"BUT I SENT MY MONEY . . ."

Once buyers and sellers have found each other, there will be new, third-party companies formed to act as escrow services or brokers to ensure that sellers get paid and buyers get what they bargained for. Some escrow companies will partner, as I-Escrow, Inc., of San Mateo, CA, did by teaming up with such auction sites as CityAuction and Haggle Online. Others will take a different route, as did Trade Direct of Tampa, FL, which promotes its service by advertising at various auction locations.

Trade Direct is a third-party clearinghouse for online transactions.[6] Once a buyer has a purchase in mind, the buyer notifies the seller—who can be anywhere on the Net—that he or she
wants to use the service. The buyer sends the purchase price to
Trade Direct, the seller sends the goods directly to the buyer, and
the buyer has two days to decide if the product purchase is as
advertised. If so, the funds are sent to the seller by Trade Direct,
and the buyer is charged a 5 percent fee. If not, the goods are
returned to the seller. "This gives the seller incentive to be honest," says Tony DiPollina, president of Trade Direct.

In the Net Future, new companies will continue to be created as fast as new market needs are identified. In the case of
online auctions, an obvious need arose out of the fear of total
strangers bartering almost anonymously, one hoping the product is as good as it looks, and the other hoping the buyer really
will send the money. Yet another opportunity was identified
inside the corporate walls, as companies looked to sell excess
inventory to customers.

THE COMPANY AUCTION

Based in San Francisco, Moai Technologies is a provider of
business-to-business, enterprise-level software applications for
electronic commerce.[7] Moai's products are aimed at manufacturers and distributors in the semiconductor and computer
industries. The company's first application was a Web-based
inventory auction system that automates inventory negotiation
processes in real time, providing a highly efficient alternative to
the traditional paper-based and telephone method.

Moai says its goal is to enable corporations to achieve higher revenues, improved control of their sales channel, increased
profitability, and reduced inventory overhead. Unlike online
auction services, Moai seeks to provide technology so that companies can establish their own electronic auction marketplace,
with the companies controlling the products auctioned, auction
times, minimum bids, and trading partners involved.

The concept behind Moai Technologies actually began in
1994 as part of a consulting project in the natural gas industry.

One of the Moai founders worked on a team that developed a system to allow customers to bid on natural gas, creating a spot market for excess capacity. When the commercial Net emerged, the founder decided to build software for electronic marketplaces that businesses themselves could deploy.

The company is headed by former Tandem executive Anne Perlman, who sees the customer attaining dramatically more control over pricing over time. In her words:

> Most commercial business has been conducted with buyers and sellers being separate, and the transaction almost being serial. The seller begins the sales process, starting with list price, and the buyer figures out what the value is and whether the negotiated price matches the perceived value.

> By contrast, a marketplace is an environment in which buyers and sellers come together, with sellers offering goods and buyers actively participating with the sellers. The Internet and its browsers give the sellers and buyers an electronic or virtual marketplace to meet easily. We allow bidders to buy quantities at "the right" prices evidenced by their bids. This is a dynamic pricing environment and also a place where supply and demand truly meet to determine price. This is obvious when one highest bidder buys the entire lot.

> In our experience, buyers come together to create demand in the marketplace. Prices are dynamically created, and the only semblance of fixed price is the minimum bid that was set by the seller. A lot comprised of a large quantity of the same good can have multiple winners at various prices if no single bidder buys all of the quantity at the highest price bid.

> For the top bidder, who gets all quantity desired by that bidder, the demand need is very strong. For the second winner, who may buy at the next highest price, demand is not quite as high and therefore price was a bit lower. For a third winner, who buys at the third highest price and may have only part of the quantity need fulfilled, demand was not strong enough to outbid the two top bidders, but sufficient to drive winning at least partial quantity fulfillment at a desired price.

Our customers use this in a very practical way today, typically selling excess and obsolete inventory. The auction environment yields them about a 15 percent price increment over their fixed prices, keeps their sales channels intact, leverages their brand identity, and allows these benefits at much lower administrative cost than the old method of phoning and faxing their trading partners.

At the same time they're seeing returns on investment of up to 100 percent in under three months from auctions. But they're also thinking proactively about the future. Will auctioning eliminate the middleman? How can auctioning be used not just for our inventory, but also as a service to help our competitors sell their inventory faster? How will dynamic pricing affect the negotiated contracts we have in place? At what stage shall we use auctions for all products rather than just part of our inventory?

As companies focus on shrinking margins, the thought of online auctions where buyers set pricing can be somewhat daunting. Moai found that rather than driving prices down, the online auctions tended to drive prices up, since true demand is measured by the marketplace. Says Perlman:

Ask a corporation about having the customers set the price, and the answer is typical. "Are you crazy? If we ask them what they'll pay, they'll say zero.' Some may, but most won't. The well-known precedent is enterprise software. Most large-scale software solutions sell by the "seat" or by the "user license." Most corporations could bootleg this across an enterprise, but few do. The practice would be short-sighted.

Most business customers actually would be happy to give constructive input on the price they pay. In fact, they want to pay a fair price. Sure, you'll always have those customers that want to squeeze every dollar out of a vendor, but the best long-term vendor-buyer relationships are mutually beneficial.

More and more, customers are demanding that vendors rationalize pricing. No longer satisfied with price sheets and catalogs, customers are looking to the full complement of goods in a particular space, and asking vendors to base their pricing on the market.

Leaving this dynamic to the good graces of sellers is a quaint notion, but naive. More appropriately, it's the collection of buyers, gathered in one place at one time with the expressed purpose of acquiring goods for a market set price, that is the more efficient way to achieve this balance. Customers don't want to go one on one with the vendor.

No one likes getting into a cubicle and haggling with a car salesman. The best buyers walk out of a car showroom content if they ground every penny out a dealer. But what if you had to buy again tomorrow? And the next day? Soon the dealer would go out of business, and then what? Simple grinding is not the answer. It is no surprise that the idea of dynamic pricing is one that is gaining steam.

What could happen if buyers could drive pricing? Let's look at it the other way around. If you put a small group of sellers in one room, and have them set prices, what do you have? A cartel, which is illegal in this country. But put buyers together in one room for the expressed purpose of determining price, and you have an efficient market. The aggregation of buyers gives them more power to determine what is the fairest price for a good.

Soon we're going to see the market come together for all types of products, following the model set by the financial industries. For only when all products are seen as commodities can true dynamic pricing really take effect. We're seeing this happen in the high-tech industry now. Innovation is making product differentiation difficult, particularly in hardware. As products become commodities, and differentiating factors fall away, we're left with price and supply.

With the proliferation of goods on the market, and a growing trend toward buyer aggregation, a key determining factor becomes supply. If you could buy all you want of something, you'd pay little for it. But if a company can lead you to believe there is only so much available, your desire would rise.

In the coming revolution of dynamic pricing, supply will play an enormous role in price, much more than ever before. Add to the list of customer buying criteria the question, "How much is left?" This has enormous potential of turning the tables on the entire market.

Let's take this another step further. You're a manufacturing manager at a computer company. Your products are being priced by the aggregation of buyers, who have near perfect information about you and your situation. How many do you make? The short answer is, "As many as the market wants." The real answer is: none.

What happens when customers get used to Web-based auctions and demand that their price be set by the market? What else can a good computer company do but make their products as people demand them? Dell's business model is a window into a future world where customers have the ultimate power, dictating a company's manufacturing schedule and pricing. All aspects of corporate structure are dictated by the demands of customers. We enter a pure age, where the voice of the customer truly saturates a corporation.

THE AUTOMATED HAGGLER

In the Net Future, shoppers may not even have to worry about negotiating prices for themselves. Automated shopping agents will not only do the comparison shopping but in some cases may even negotiate a price on behalf of the wired consumer. MIT's Media Laboratory Kasbah project allows users to create an intelligent agent that can seek out a potential buyer or seller and negotiate with them based on a strategy determined by the agent's creator.[8]

Kasbah works in much the same way as the stock market does for securities. Let's say you want to sell a book. You tell your Kasbah agent the price you want to sell the book for, as well as the lowest amount you will accept. You can view a tickertape that shows current ask, bid, and last sale prices for the types of goods sold to help you determine prices. You can also determine a selling strategy for your agent. You can instruct it to resist lowering the price as much as possible, or you can instruct it to make a deal quickly even if it has to lower the price.

Once you've briefed your agent, it goes into the marketplace and begins negotiating with any agents who are interested in buying your book. Once a price is agreed on by two agents, each goes back to its respective creator to describe the deal, which can be accepted or vetoed. Price limits or buying strategies can be altered at any time. In one Kasbah experiment, sellers began to tell their agents to drop prices rapidly because the experiment was drawing to a close, at which point the item would become worthless. Any deal became better than having nothing.

Kasbah is currently a simulation of how the virtual haggler marketplace will work. However, it demonstrates that the boundaries of flex pricing on the Net have only begun to be tested.

THE DEATH OF FIXED PRICING: CAUSE OR EFFECT?

The $64,000 question might be summed up as: "Is the death of fixed pricing the cause or the effect in the Net Future?" Think of the implications:

- Manufacturing moves to real time. As suppliers and distributors are mandated to become part of the process, manufacturers can respond immediately to consumer demand, as discussed in the last chapter. Manufacturers will be able to wait to distribute products until true demand is identified. And that true demand will not be market research but a person making a financial commitment or even actually ordering the product.

- Fewer salespeople are needed at the retail level as consumers purchase more goods directly online.

- All staples become commodities, since any consumer can buy any item at the lowest price at the moment—delivery included.

- Pricing becomes momentary: consumers can place their bids that execute when the first seller meets the price offered. Producers move to what I call "flex price" models.

- New aggregators corral willing buyers to use their combined buying strength to negotiate better pricing.

- Market research focuses less on the competition and more on the customer's competitive environment.

- In the Net Future, it will be increasingly difficult to use prices to forecast revenues.

LEAPFROG

Many adults can recall playing leapfrog as children. A child gets down on all fours, with hands and feet on the ground, as a player from behind jumps over the player in front. Then the jumper gets down on all fours, as a new player at the back of the line leaps over both to the front of the pack. The game doesn't seem to have much point, except that each person playing always gets to be in front, as well as in back. In the Net Future, companies will participate in a new version of leapfrog, as twists and turns in business models and human dynamics cause companies to go from the leapfrogger to the one being leapfrogged.

A leapfrogging mentality will allow companies to turn commodities back into products in the Net Future. One example is the Internet search engine business. Search engines, which nearly every Web user depends on to find information, quickly emerged as the starting off point, or portal, to the world of information. Because so many people rely on them, most of the traffic on the Internet flows through one of the major search engine companies: Yahoo!, InfoSeek, Excite, Lycos. Those companies have capitalized on the traffic, selling large amounts of advertising to companies that want to reach individuals searching the Web. In almost any listing of most-visited Web sites, the search engines are found at the top of the list.

Idealab devised a variant on the search engine business when it created GoTo.com. Though the search engine worked similarly to the others, the results were offered to advertisers that had to bid for the right to be "found." The thinking was that if an advertiser paid to have its product or service information first—and paid every time a user saw it—that information would, in fact, be the most relevant to the person conducting the search. So every time a user searches a particular word and a result is displayed, the advertiser is charged 10 cents. GoTo.com turned the commodity of a search into a revenue-producing "product."

Once a company gets over the shock that flex pricing will replace much of fixed pricing, it can start planning for the Net Future. Coupled with a wired workforce and an open-book corporation approach, the company can begin to use pricing as a barometer of customer demand. Because everything affects everything else in the Net Future, that real-time pricing allows the company to better leverage its internal and external resources to create the products the market wants, when it wants them.

C H A P T E R

S I X

THE CUSTOMER BECOMES DATA

In the Net Future, an infinite amount of information about customer desires and needs can be accumulated in real time. With the coming explosion in electronic commerce, that ability to capture customer information will drive demand to make greater use of the data being captured—and to do it quickly to keep up with the constant inflow of new data.

The combination of more information and more sophisticated use of it is about to give customers new and unprecedented power to get what they want, the way they want, when they want it. Companies also will be faced with new capabilities to satisfy those needs and desires, before a customer is even aware of them.

While companies have traditionally captured plenty of customer information, they haven't always been as good at integrating all that information about any one customer. Although a marketing executive might espouse being "customer-focused," many companies' information has been organized around products, services, or functions, not individual customers.

A company might have a lot of information about a customer, but part of it might be in a call center database. Another part might be in a billing database; still more might live somewhere in shipping—or in the company's Web server. And if the company has multiple divisions organized around products, each of these same kinds of information might reside in still more databases. In the Net Future the concept of being truly customer-centric will be totally re-defined.

THE SHADOW YOU

Many interactive computer games embrace the use of avatars, which allow players to adopt an electronic persona that represents them in the game. In the Net Future, a similar electronic re-creation of the individual—or more accurately, an individual's behavior—will exist in cyberspace. This alter ego—based on real behavior rather than a fictitious personality, and generally invisible to the user—will provide enough electronic "information" to companies to enable them to better target and serve specific needs and desires of each customer. I have termed this invisible alter ego the Shadow You.

Companies will re-create the essence of a person's behavior, with an eye toward picking people, products, services, and anything else that might logically appeal to the person who exhibits that behavior. This Shadow You, with its emphasis on re-creation and prediction of individual behavior rather than participation in some group profile or demographic, will be the seller's and marketer's target in the future.

"Cookies" technology, which essentially deposits a crumb of information on a person's computer that identifies where within a Web site that person has gone, became a relatively common practice as soon as Web traffic began to grow. Though most Net users either are not aware of this tracking or don't care, they can "refuse" the cookie (or at least easily see who is trailing them by searching their own computer for the word *cookies*.) That technology was just the precursor of what is to come in the Net environment as companies begin to deploy customer-analyzing technologies with names such as datamining, collaborative filtering, online analytical processing, and neural networks.

These and other technologies might be best classified as recommendation systems, since they make recommendations for future action to either a customer or a company. One of the earliest examples was a system called Firefly, which compared a music buyer with many other people who bought the same music; on the basis of what else those people liked, the system would "recommend" that the target buyer sample those other purchases. The approach is sort of like "the friend of my friend is a friend."

Since many companies already have captured information of one kind or another about their customers, the latest emphasis has been on organizing that data into massive data warehouses. These companies are positioned to use the Net to capture, aggregate, integrate, and disseminate customer information on an individual and group level in real time.

That on-the-fly feedback not only will allow marketers to deliver marketing messages at the most strategically timed moment, but also to forecast buying behavior on the basis of the preferences of other, similar customers. And new technologies will allow that information to be distributed to many more people than ever before.

The Road to Customer as Data

1. Capture the data.
2. Build a data warehouse by creating an information architecture, such as sales by store by item.
3. Aggregate customer information.
4. Integrate individual customer information.
5. Send forecasts to sales and marketing staffs in real time.
6. Electronically connect customer information with product information.
7. Predict behavior, buying patterns, product supply, and pricing.
8. Make recommendations to customers at the time of the transaction.
9. Make recommendations to customers in advance of the transaction.

In the Net Future, the time required for the flow of information from customer to information systems to management will be compressed to nothing. The dynamic of real-time feedback will allow more simultaneous interaction among those three segments.

As a result of all this gathering and processing of data, the value of customers in the Net Future will be more than simply the revenue they produce. They will become the data that helps drive future sales to other customers who may not yet be in a company's sights.

The information flowing into all those databases will become an increasingly important driver of decisions about which products the company chooses to produce and how it markets them. The technologies of datamining, collaborative filtering, and predictive modeling will increasingly alter the process of forecasting how consumers behave and what they want.

THE NEW WAY TO MARKET

Using computerized data to understand customers and buying patterns better has been done for years. However, datamining differs from traditional methods in three important ways:

1. Datamining is more open-ended in the way it searches the data. Traditionally, a company would query its database using a set of clearly defined assumptions and requirements. A typical query might be, "Do Californians or New Yorkers buy more consumer electronics products?"

A typical datamining request might be, "Give me a model that shows which characteristics of consumer electronics buyers are most likely to forecast future purchases." Traditional approaches build on assumptions based on past data; the new approach starts with both past and present information, and makes no assumptions that dictate how the data is explored.

The power of the less structured approach is its ability to turn up totally unexpected relationships—and potentially new ways of reaching customers. In our consumer electronics example, the person using datamining might discover that a parent of a teenage boy is likely to be a big buyer of stereo equipment. More important, it might reveal whether that factor is more important in predicting future purchases than where the buyer lives.

Or datamining might show that time of year is a more important factor in a buying decision than either parental status or geography—or that time of year is important in New York but not in California. That knowledge enables a company to develop a highly targeted marketing campaign aimed at its most likely customers.

Mining the Data Lingo

Way of Using Customer as Data	How It Works	Typical Query
Predictive modeling	Compares every transaction against every other transaction in real time and recommends next logical transaction.	"We know how you should behave. Might we suggest a Ford Mustang?"
Collaborative filtering	Compares actions of individuals against similar actions of other people and makes suggestions based on what else those others did.	"We know what people like you have bought. Might we suggest a Ford Mustang?"
Online analytical processing (OLAP)	Data analyst uses highly structured queries to compare specific pieces of data. Results are highly dependent on how the query is structured.	"Are more Midwesterners or Californians buying cars since we changed the price structure?"
Datamining	Uses open-ended questions and sophisticated algorithms to discover patterns in data and forecast customer behavior on the basis of those patterns.	"What is the most important factor in the decision to buy a car?"
Decision-support systems	Allows construction of what-if scenarios based on hypothetical changes in specific variables.	"What would happen to sales in the Midwest if we altered our pricing structure?"
Executive information system	An older technology that summarizes data within a company and allows executives to get greater detail on ongoing transactions.	"How many cars have we sold in the Midwest in the last three months?"

Understanding these unexpected relationships can help companies discover new products, services, or markets to develop—some of which might have otherwise been overlooked.

- A legal services company decided to explore new market segments by placing ads with Infoseek's Clickseek service, which uses datamining technology to profile people who respond to a given ad, and then adjusting the targeted audience in real time. The ability to focus on a specific client profile—single mothers—increased the clickthrough response to the ad from 7 percent, achieved by displaying ads only to people who clicked on a given keyword, to 10 percent.

- Using Merck-Medco's ExpeRx system, executives at the managed care system reviewed information about patients with gastrointestinal ailments to try to find out how cost-effective an existing treatment was. When they found that this was one of the most expensive drugs for their corporate clients, they went looking for an alternative drug that would be less costly. The new drug that was developed saved one Merck-Medco corporate client with 2 million employees about $10 million in prescription drug costs.

- Bank of America executives developed a new set of programs and promotions targeted to Hispanic customers, the fastest-growing sector of California's population. After datamining information about its existing customer base, the bank found that the Hispanic population was becoming more affluent and better educated. The finding contradicted stereotypes that argued against pursuing the Hispanic population.

- US West Communications found out through datamining that cheaper rates were not the sole factor in a customer's decision to go with a given telecommunications company. By offering non-price-related incentives, the company was able to reduce customer turnover by 45 percent.

2. Datamining lends itself to being used by a wider range of knowledge workers within the enterprise, making it better suited to the wired workforce of the Net Future. Because the open-

ended approach to exploring the database requires fewer analytical or statistical skills, queries can be done by people who are closest to the decisions being made and who have the best understanding of what information is needed. Linked through the corporate intranet and the proper password, executives in the Net Future may need only to be able to generate such straightforward requests as "Show me the factors that influence when Midwesterners buy cars." Like the Net itself, the technology can be used to push information-gathering ability out to the people who need it most.

It is the ability to disseminate knowledge that is leading Bank of America to make datamining accessible to large numbers of bank employees by embedding it in customized software that is tailored for specific uses within each department. Lenders in the field will be able to enter information on a potential loan deal and get up-to-the-minute data—on credit history, risk factors, debt-to-income loan ratios, and interest rates—that allows rapid processing of a loan application.

Merck-Medco expects that the kind of questioning that resulted in the alternative gastrointestinal treatment, now being done by roughly 400 analysts, ultimately will be done by all product marketers in the company to find similar cost savings.

3. In the most advanced uses, datamining technology relies on massive neural networks, technology that essentially mimics the human mind. Companies can analyze customer information in real time instead of grouping the information and having it wait to be processed at one time. By automating the number crunching, neural nets can continuously update feedback on customer buying behavior. Instead of seeing a snapshot of consumer behavior at a designated point in time, companies will be able to watch a running movie that shows ongoing customer behavior.

This minute-by-minute feedback has profound implications for marketing in the Net Future. Just as technicians have been able to monitor performance of their computer networks constantly, so marketers in the Net Future will begin to be able to adjust their strategies in real time.

Checking That Data

TRADITIONAL DATA ANALYSIS	DATAMINING
Done by core analysts (5 to 50 people)	Done by more end users (50 to 1000 people)
Applications-focused	Content-focused
Done by people who know where the info is	Done by people who don't know where the info is
Uses ad hoc queries	Uses standard vs. exception queries
Takes 1 to 4 hours a day	Takes less than 1 hour a week
Done by information producers	Done by information consumers
Done by people who understand analysis	Done by people who understand the business
Relies on information pulled by analysts	Enables pushing of information to users
Bases many forecasts on outdated historical information	Can base forecasts on current information
Provides view of customers at a single point in time	Provides ongoing view of customers over time

Previously, if a company sent out a direct-mail piece, it was on the hook for the cost of the entire mailing. The company could reduce risk by doing a test mailing, but that meant spending extra time to get the results and make a decision about whether to mail the rest. On the Net, companies now can adjust advertising campaigns on the fly, based on what's working and what isn't. For example, Stockpoint, owned by Neural Applications Corp., uses neural network technology to power its delivery not only of real-time stock market data but also of ad campaigns that actually adapt to customer behavior.

Let's say an advertiser has two different ads rotating throughout Stockpoint, delivered by the company's software. The system monitors how well each ad is doing at specific times of the day and in specific ad locations. If Ad A does well between 10 a.m. and 2 p.m. Monday through Friday but poorly on the weekend, the program will learn to serve Ad A more frequently then and substitute Ad B on the weekend, when it performs better. Or if Ad A pulls more viewers on Stockpoint's home page than it does on, say, a page of price charts, it will be delivered more frequently there. And if Ad B seems over time to draw visitors who gravitate to price charts and annual reports, the software will automatically begin to serve Ad B to new visitors who match that pattern of behavior—in other words, to the customers most likely to respond to it.

This use of recommendation systems in real time has many implications in relation to looking at the customer as data. Neural networks capable of refreshing the database constantly, automatically creating models that forecast consumer behavior and giving instantaneous feedback on the basis of that constantly updated information, empower companies to be highly personalized as well as instantly and interactively responsive to customers. Companies can even become proactive. When you consider the power of linking this capability in a customer-focused enterprise with the flex pricing capabilities previously discussed, the business model changes 180 degrees (the 180-degree effect!). Customer behavior can actually start to drive the business, as long as an organization is aligned to create and change products in real time.

MARKETING WHEN THE CUSTOMER BECOMES DATA

This rapid response means that in the Net Future, sales and customer service will merge. It also means that Netted companies can take advantage of three new marketing dynamics I have termed "distributed marketing," "preemptive marketing," and "dialogue marketing." Each will be driven by the interactive individual's desire for instant response and service as well as by a need for highly personalized information, products, and services.

DISTRIBUTED MARKETING

Chocolate is the quintessential impulse buy; an urge delayed is an urge denied. When Godiva Chocolatier wanted to develop a

Mother's Day Web advertising campaign that took advantage of that fact, it turned to "distributed marketing": the ability to convert its banner ads on the Web into both point-of-sale terminals and data collection agencies.

Godiva developed interactive ads that not only attracted attention by inspiring the appropriate level of Mom-related guilt but also gave the customer a choice of two Godiva candy assortments to send. Once the chocolate of choice is selected, the ad lets the customer enter a credit card number and delivery address for shipment. The system not only captures information about purchasing patterns but feeds the information directly into Godiva's existing systems. All that happens within the ad itself. However, if customers would rather shop the Godiva site, the ad also can link them there. AT&T and Citibank use the same technology, developed by Narrative Communications of Waltham, MA, to generate sales leads; L. L. Bean and Eddie Bauer use it to generate catalog sales.

Distributed marketing can shorten the purchasing cycle dramatically. It can move the customer from interest generation to decision to purchase to transaction almost instantaneously. It makes a banner ad the equivalent of that rack at the checkout stand of the grocery store, where you toss a magazine onto the conveyor belt because it caught your eye and you had your wallet out anyway.

Plus it can make your Mom happy.

PREEMPTIVE MARKETING

If distributed marketing makes the interaction between company and customer instantaneous, preemptive marketing makes it invisible. Because companies can use predictive modeling to match an individual customer's transaction or pattern of behavior—the Shadow You—against all other transactions or shadows, the interaction can take place even before the customer initiates anything. When statistical tools are based on predictive models and profiles, an individual customer's concerns can be addressed before the customer is even aware of them.

Let's say an E-commerce company wants to conduct an E-mail marketing campaign to its existing customers. A datamining server can compare an individual customer's profile against a computer model and automatically select the right offer to make based on what that individual is likely to do in the future. What information the computer retrieves depends on how the customer compares with a predictive statistical model.

That model can include not only demographic data and account history but business considerations as well. For example, the computer might generate an on the fly forecast of the customer's lifetime value to the company. Customers whose profiles match a "higher lifetime value" profile might get one offer— say, for a longer service contract. Those who don't might get another offer designed to upsell the customers to a more expensive service.

Or a recommendation system might suggest that a customer who buys patio furniture in the spring is more likely to buy a lawn mower next rather than a set of garden tools. A retailer could develop a targeted E-mail marketing campaign featuring lawn mowers and send it to new patio furniture buyers. And because recommendation systems learn from each transaction, the computer would take the purchasing behavior that resulted from that mailing and use those additional dimensions of the Shadow You to refine future forecasts.

If, for example, the computer found that customers who responded to the lawn mower campaign also bought seeds, that information would be taken into account. Because it is conducted electronically, the campaign could be modified on the fly to encourage seed sales as well.

Preemptive marketing becomes especially important in industries where the customer base is highly fluid, such as the cellular phone markets, or where companies are engaged in a market-share battle. If your competitor is out to steal your customers, the last thing you want is to give the customer a reason even to think about switching services. If you can use every contact with a customer to anticipate future needs, you've not only made a sale but reduced the odds of losing future sales.

DIALOGUE MARKETING

Real-time processing will mean greater immediate back-and-forth than ever before between customer and company. An individual will do something—say, click on a Web ad banner. The company will immediately respond to that in a way that prompts future action. That action will then induce additional response by the customer. Because of the power of neural networks, this dialogue between buyer and seller can occur in real time. Moreover, the dialogue is based not only on real-time interaction between the two but on the previous and ongoing interactions of millions of other customers as well.

Unlike many Internet start-ups, Thinking Media has been profitable from its beginnings in the late 1990s.[1] Its ActiveAds service is being used by IBM, BarnesandNoble.com, @Home Network, Tanqueray, CDNow, and CMP Publications. Managing Director Owen Davis says the secret is not only in the interaction between company and customer but in the database compiled as a result of aggregating the Shadow You of all those customers:

> In developing transactive ads, we wanted to be able to quantify the cost of a sales lead. At the same time, we wanted to be able to take the information about behavior that we obtained as a result of those interactions and use it to make all other interactions in the future more personalized. We developed a technology that would send a really, really small Java application to the viewer's computer when the ad is delivered. That application sends information back to a central database to tell it what information needs to be shipped to the computer next, whether it's streaming audio, product details, or a form for ordering or credit card information. All this information about that back-and-forth between customer and company is captured and analyzed in real time, so a company knows precisely how an ad campaign is working.
>
> More important, that same information is put into a database so that when that person returns, there is a record of what they've already seen and done. The content of future ads can be more precisely targeted to that person based on

how they've behaved in the past—even if that past is only a moment ago. For example, a computer company buys a keyword in a search engine so its ad will be delivered to someone searching on that word—let's say *laptops*. The ad that appears will have the word *laptops* already filled in so all the customer has to do is click it to search that manufacturer's catalog for a list of laptops.

Or let's say a customer of a wine retailer responds to a series of questions about his or her food preferences. The product offered at the end could be tailored to those preferences. If "steak" was checked instead of fish, it could suggest a nice Pinot Noir; if "fish" was chosen, a Sauvignon Blanc might be in order. If the customer saw the ad again, it might ask if he or she wanted another Pinot Noir or a Cabernet.

And because that behavioral information is aggregated in our database, it allows advertisers to do some pretty powerful things. For example, a BarnesandNoble.com might determine from online book orders done through its banner ad that Sidney Sheldon sold better online than books about Leonardo DiCaprio to people who visit travel sites. It could use that information to offer more Sidney Sheldon books in its ads on travel sites. The more advertisers use it, the more behavioral information is captured, and the more precise the tailoring becomes. That means that if a travel site then wanted to run a transactive ad, it would know that it might attract more of Sidney Sheldon's fans than Leo's.

There are all kinds of ways to capture and use customer data. Some companies do real-time online surveys, where customers fill out a series of questions within the banner. Others deliver real-time headlines or use the ads to actually sign up subscribers without the individual having to leave the site they're on. As a consumer you get only what you need when you need it.

One company that needed to predict its customer behavior or keep losing money on transactions is Orange plc, a British wireless communications company.[2] It was faced with the problem of customers wanting to upgrade the handsets they received as part of their service. Because the company subsidizes most of the handset's cost, it took Orange between 12 and 20 months to cover that cost.

However, the company found that customers were calling after about a year wanting a new handset for the same price. Orange wanted to find a way to meet the company's cost constraints yet prevent customers from considering switching to another service. Relationship development manager Stephen Boulton-Wallace decided to try a recommendation system experiment manually, without using any recommendation technology.

> We tried to predictively model who would be most likely to want a new handset. We called those customers and offered them free batteries and extra talk time in return for signing a six-month additional contract. Our data also showed that in 80 percent of cases, the old handset simply gets thrown away. If customers called in and said they wanted a new handset, customer service reps were instructed to offer them a discount on the new one if they would keep the old one in use, perhaps by giving it to a teenager or a spouse. That additional revenue would help offset the cost of the new handset.

> About 50 percent of the customers we spoke with took the offer; it was by far the highest conversion rate we've ever had. And that was with only one day of sales training for the customer service representatives we had asked to participate in the trial.

> We want to be able to automate the process to speed it up. Even where we have a predictive model, we still have to kick it off manually. If I have a hypothesis, I have to go to my data analyst, who has a queue of work and may say, "I can start on it in four days' time." He has to go away and use his skills to get data. Then he may come back to me with 60 percent of what I expected. Then I go back to him and say, "Can we do this and this?" and he comes back next time with 90 percent of what I want. Then we have to be able to get the lists of names to contact. And every time we run the model, we have to tell it what to look at. The process can take four weeks. It's also based on data that may be outdated by the time the campaign starts.

Once we automate the process, it will probably take about the same time to work out the propositions—what media we're going to use to contact the customer, designing the offer—but it will help us with reporting and analysis. Right now we've got to run through the entire list of names before we can analyze results. Automating the process will feed the information back to us in real time, so we can tell if something's not working much sooner. We can change it or stop it and do something different. Right now we have to wait until a campaign is finished to see if it worked.

We want to look at identifying the probability of certain characteristics of customers indicating whether they're likely to leave, and when. We're looking at how we can not only automate the datamining process itself, but have the system automatically produce the customer lists that meet those criteria, and output those lists to a dialing system or in the right format for a mailing house so we can schedule a mailing. It won't automate the proposition, but it will give us clues to what that proposition should be.

In all of these situations, we're in control of the customer contact. Looking further out, we'd like to be able to deal with situations where we're not in control, where the customer contacts us. Let's say we've worked out when a customer is likely to churn, or to request a new handset, and then that customer happens to call us about something else. We want to be able to alert the customer service representatives to that—and enable them to do something about it before the issue ever arises.

The advantage of some of the newer technology is that it "learns" as it goes. An online people-matching service, for example, could use a recommendation system from companies such as Net Perceptions or Aptex. The system could match individuals based on the personal preferences they enter at the start. As a person selects and rejects various other people and participates in online discussions and E-mails, the system could modify the Shadow You in real time.

The Shadow You becomes the essence of the person's behavior, which is continually updated, as are all others' shadows and all other parts of the "universe." What the company stores is not specific data on the individual, but rather a mathematical dimension of that person's behavior while at the Web site.

"In three to five years, enterprise personalization will be something every company of any import will use anyplace there is an interaction with a customer," says Michael Thiemann, president and CEO of San Diego-based software developer Aptex, a part of HNC.[3] "You use that knowledge to enhance the interaction."

DATA DRIVES THE ENTERPRISE

The customer-as-data model will prompt changes in areas beyond marketing. A practical application of technology that sounds somewhat blue-sky is in simple E-mail.

Aptex saw E-mail support as an explosive area for large companies as they expand their Web sites to include more online forms and options to send E-mails back to the company. Sensing that E-mail support would start to supplant and replace costly customer service representatives, the company created an automated system to filter the deluge.

"It's like credit cards were," says Thiemann. "A human being used to look at every transaction. Now there's no way this could be done with a human being. Now, when an E-mail comes in to a company, there's a hyperlink directly into the data resource itself. If the program is confident, it responds directly to the sender. If it is not confident, it can route the E-mail to the person most likely to be able to answer the question. The program also E-mails the sender, telling who the message was sent to for a response." The system can analyze and process 20 messages per second.

- Qualcomm, which gets thousands of E-mails a day, uses the Aptex content mining technology to answer E-mails automatically. The system "reads" each E-mail, analyzes all the text to decipher the question, selects the appropriate answer from a database, and responds to the sender automatically if it feels the query is properly understood. About a third of all E-mails fit the bill, saving human intervention.

- When Charles Schwab & Company faced a surge in online trading, E-mail started pouring in at the rate of 3000 to 5000 a week.[4] "We had one time that we received 15,000 E-mails in one day," says Mary Kelly, vice president at Schwab. "There's no way humans can handle that." The company installed automatic E-mail "reading" software. "The system categorizes two-thirds of incoming E-mails, selects a response, and sends it back to the sender. It even selects from the FAQs [frequently asked questions] database," says Kelly. "This is an exciting time. We're going to move to more customized, electronic delivery, like newsletters that trickle download with a publication date feature. Then you can use full-motion video and drill down into advertising and customize subscriptions for each subscriber to it." Such automation will help the Web and E-mail grow to handling 31 percent of all Schwab's customer service inquiries by the year 2000.[5]

- As deregulation and new competitive pressures face public utilities in many areas of the United States, any statistical analysis based on a captive audience may not be relevant when customers can change their supplier. To cope, some utilities are using real-time datamining to forecast future usage on the basis of constantly updated information. Data about current usage, current weather patterns, and weather predictions is sent to a Web server that analyzes the information and returns a forecast. Because information about the customer base will no longer necessarily be static, constant updating of information is necessary.

- Movie studios are now using the Hollywood Stock Exchange to make marketing decisions about film promotion. The HSX is an L.A. version of "rotisserie baseball," except that instead of managing virtual teams, players invest in films and individual stars. The 90,000 participants get a fantasy $2 million when they begin, and can buy and sell MovieStocks or StarBonds. The action is said to be used by Hollywood moguls to help determine how positive the advance "buzz" is about a given movie and hence how much they should invest—for real—in promoting it. The HSX is said, for example, to have forecast the unexpected success of *Men in Black* and the disappointing returns of *The Lost World.*

- By analyzing data about customer interaction with its call center, ADP learned that it had been training its call center staff exactly backward. Reps had traditionally received detailed training about a narrow range of products and had specialized in answering calls about that area. However, the analysis showed that customer calls got a lot shorter if reps were trained more broadly before receiving specialized training in a particular area.

- Canadian Imperial Bank of Commerce had assumed that people who were chronically late payers would be most likely to become seriously delinquent. In fact, datamining showed that people who usually paid their bills on time but who missed a payment were most likely to delay payment even further; the problems that caused a normally responsible customer to miss a payment were usually serious enough to lead to greater delinquency.

- By mining its database of asthma patients, Foundation Health Systems of California found that only 18 percent of the people it treated used a device that measures how efficiently their lungs function, even though many more owned such a device. Even if supplied in the aggregate to protect patients' privacy, this information could be extremely valuable to companies marketing the devices. It not only suggests further research on whether rethinking the device might improve usage, but could encourage the health-care organization to set up targeted educational programs.

- Eddie Bauer, a subsidiary of Spiegel, Inc., established a Web-based gift registry at each of its 29 Eddie Bauer Home stores. Customers can register a wish list by roaming the store and running a handheld scanner over the tags of the items they want; the resulting list can then be used by well-wishers who can tailor their purchases to a recipient's desires. In addition to providing convenience for last-minute shoppers, the system captures a tremendous amount of information about customer behavior on the part of both the giver and the recipient. That information can then potentially be used to suggest product line expansions.

ARE YOU READY TO MINE YOUR DATA?

How many of the following statements can you make?

1. *"My company's data has been reviewed, cleaned up, and put into a data warehouse that is capable of responding quickly to a lot of simultaneous queries."* You may not be ready to do datamining because the databases underlying the system are either incomplete or very inconsistent. Consider doing a small-scale datamining trial to see where the problems are and what information you'll need before developing a data warehouse. A well-constructed data warehouse is key to any datamining efforts. If you're just getting into customer transactions on the Net, think about what types of information you'll want for datamining when designing your E-commerce system. In fact, because you may still be in the midst of developing the E-commerce side of your business, it may be the perfect place to explore your entire datamining strategy.

2. *"My company has a well thought-out policy about access to the system."* You will need to consider the impact of giving your workforce greater ability to discover information. Consider how it is likely to be used and which information is most critical to have when thinking about supplying more widespread access.

3. *"I'm counting on datamining to reduce the overall workload of my IT department."* Datamining is not a panacea for an overworked IT staff. If that's your only reason for adopting datamining, think again.

4. *"I'm prepared to train my managers on how to use the system."* Though datamining may allow users with less data analysis expertise to obtain information, that doesn't mean they'll be able simply to flip a switch and start using datamining. Count on needing at least some training on the system's capabilities

and the types of information available. And make sure you do user testing with any system you're considering; datamining is valuable only if people use it.

Like the commercial Internet, datamining is still in its infancy. Companies are only beginning to integrate multiple databases—including Web-based systems—into large data warehouses that can be accessed by datamining systems. But as datamining companies develop ways to return speedier results from those large data warehouses and easier ways for users to ask questions of the database, marketers will begin to learn things about their customers that they never would have expected.

THE CUSTOMER BECOMES THE PRODUCT

In the Net Future, the customer will not only buy products, but will also create or add value. When Lotus 1-2-3 was launched in the 1980s, the buyer would plunk down several hundred dollars for a large box that contained volumes of documentation and several disks comprising the program. After loading, the buyer was faced with a blank screen or an empty spreadsheet. The user actually added value by building the spreadsheet. Lotus was a big winner, having provided the capability to millions of people who instantly saw the value that *they* could create using this new tool.

In the case of recommendation systems, the customer constantly adds value by simply doing things. Every action continues to build the Shadow You. Net-based technologies such as datamining and collaborative filtering make the customer more profitable—not only for the immediate sale but for the information the customer-as-data can provide to help drive future sales.

WHAT'S A CUSTOMER WORTH?

In the Net Future, customers who demand proportionately more of the company's resources than others might be considered as valuable as a new customer who spends more money, simply because their demands and fickle attitudes may offer a greater amount of data about customer behavior. This is contrary to traditional models, where profitable customers are determined by their spending levels.

In the Net Future, there is a new way to determine customer value:

$$\text{Net Customer Value} = \text{Current Sale} + \text{Lifetime Value} + \text{Predictive Value}$$

For Cendant, looking at the customer as data is the company's strength.[6] Cendant was formed in 1997 from CUC International and Hospitality Franchise Systems Inc. (HFS), two companies that made a specialty of owning as little as possible in the physical world.

CUC International began as a shopping club that offered members steep discounts on purchases in exchange for a yearly membership fee. Members used phone and mail to buy from a database of a quarter-million products, which were shipped directly from the manufacturer to the buyer. Because the company made its money from the membership fee rather than taking a percentage of the sale price, the discounts were dramatic. Essentially, it made money from putting buyers in touch with sellers.

The other company, HFS, owned several large franchise operations: Days' Inn, Ramada, Howard Johnson, Coldwell Banker, Century 21, ERA. The company also bought Avis and took the company public.

The merged company owned information about CUC's club members, information about an additional 100 million consumers in HFS's databases, a computer network, and recognizable brand names—precisely the sorts of assets designed to make the most of the Net environment.

Cendant's NetMarket service is the ultimate commoditizer of product as well as the ultimate example of getting value from the customer as data. Taking advantage of the distribution efficiencies of the Net allows the company's rock-bottom pricing strategy to flourish. Members can buy at the company's regular discount prices or participate in scheduled auctions, where they may be able to get even lower prices.

In many ways, Cendant is the epitome of looking at the customer as data. Its entire business is aimed at aggregating customers under one umbrella. Demonstrating the approach to marketing in the Net Future, it truly views products as commodities.

THE TOOLS OF THE TIMES

Another way that customers create value is by enhancing what a company sells. For example, companies are using collaborative filtering to suggest products to the customers most likely to purchase them. In many ways this is the flip side of datamining. Rather than breaking a huge customer database into smaller chunks and trying to find relationships among them, collaborative filtering starts with the preferences of one user and develops a totally new grouping based on a synthesis of the preferences of similar users.

With collaborative filtering, customers themselves are enhancing the product. All those who reveal their prefer-

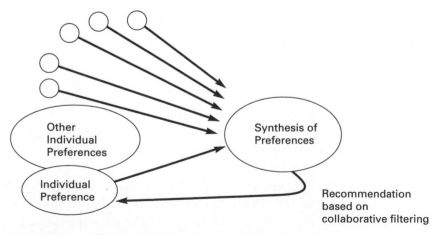

FIGURE 6.1   How collaborative filtering works

ences—whether they answer a questionnaire or simply click on what they like—provide information that makes the system better at providing predictions for everyone else.

TotalE!, the online arm of direct-marketing giant Columbia House, has given the recommendation agent that knows your musical genetic code a brand: EDNA (for Entertainment DNA). EDNA not only can make suggestions but can warn you about CDs you're least likely to enjoy (though chances are you already know Guy Lombardo is not for you).

EDNA represents the next step for collaborative filtering: the ability to integrate real-time behavior with the information a company already has about you from any previous interactions as well as interactions with others like you. If you've ever bought anything from Columbia House's mail-order operation, EDNA can use that information to make recommendations from the first time you log in. Rather than requiring you to fill out a questionnaire about your preferences, or rate a couple of dozen CDs so the computer can get to know your preferences, the technology is able to draw from previously existing databases to forecast what you'd like to see on the Web site.

Combining datamined information about your previous purchasing behavior with your behavior on the Web site with the buying behavior of others who have demonstrated similar interests (collaborative filtering) enhances the chances that you'll find something you like and buy it.

One might think that such systems would lead to greater homogenization of tastes. However, the reverse is true. Net Perceptions' recommendation system—the technology behind such leading consumer services as Moviefinder.com, Amazon.com, and Starwave—often suggests older, more obscure titles that may not have gotten wide attention but that have a small cult following. A generalist's inquiry about a movie or book may result in exposure to titles he or she might never have known about otherwise.

Collaborative filtering also can help companies offer instant community-based experience. For example, search engine Lycos' Web Guides provide categories of information—travel, politics, and so on—and list related Web sites ranked in order of how highly they were rated by others visiting the subject area.

By personalizing the user's experience, collaborative filtering technology has the ability to convert first-time users to loyal customers. Almost two-thirds of Amazon.com's customers are repeat business. As in other companies that use collaborative filtering, the customer-as-data actually becomes part of the product. Amazon.com is not simply selling books; it's selling the online book-buying experience. And a big part of that experience—that product—is the opportunity to utilize the experiences of all those other customers-as-data.

COLLABORATIVE MIGRATION

Collaborative filtering is one of the first technologies born and bred on the Net to affect a broader arena. The Net demands response within milliseconds; collaborative filtering was developed with those constraints in mind. That emphasis on operating in real time will have a profound impact on the way companies do business. Overnight batch processing of customer information will increasingly seem cumbersome and slow as the capabilities and requirements of the Net Future permeate the culture. And as companies begin to match live customers in real time to previous customers, service in a variety of areas will become increasingly tailored to provide what seems most likely to suit the individual.

Consider this scenario of how a hypothetical large department store chain could use collaborative filtering to get customers to visit its local store more often:

> Like StoreChain's typical customer, Linda McGregor usually goes to StoreChain about once every three weeks. Today she had to get diapers for baby Ian, but she also ended up buying a dog leash and a pair of running shoes (on sale) for herself. As she unloads the items from her shopping cart, they are scanned into the StoreChain computer, which is generating a Shadow Linda based on her purchases.

While the clerk is packaging Linda's purchases, the system is comparing her shopping profile with those of others who have also bought diapers, a dog leash, and running shoes. It finds that other customers who bought that combination also tended to buy baby clothes on their next visit. When Linda gets her receipt, the register automatically generates a coupon for 20 percent off on any item of babywear. Because the coupon expires in two weeks, it gives Linda an incentive to come back to StoreChain sooner than she normally would.

By focusing on the products that customers like Linda indicate she is likely to need in the future, the system increases the chance of her making another purchase. Putting a time limit on the coupon improves the odds that the return visit will happen sooner. And getting even 1 percent of its customers back into the store more often would generate a substantial increase in annual sales.

In the future, these recommendations will appear in real time, electronically. Online customers can be presented with coupons and buying opportunities that expire in minutes, not days. This call to action can be very powerful, especially on items that a company "knows" the customer will like.

These new methods of forecasting individual buying behavior on the basis of behavior by similar individuals are increasingly migrating from use by consumer retailers, which were early adopters, to broader use in the corporate organization. A few examples:

- As with datamining, call centers can take advantage of collaborative filtering to help companies sort the hundreds of incoming calls they receive daily. For example, when you call a telephone company to establish new service, the company might want to sell you additional services such as call waiting or caller ID. By looking at information such as area code or street address and matching it against the results of a collaborative filter of others with similar characteristics, the company could learn which services you're most likely to be interested in.

- A company could use the same technique with service complaints to determine which of many different solutions—rebates, additional free services—is most likely to satisfy an irate customer. To return to the case of Orange plc, which relies on datamining to forecast customer complaints, collaborative filtering might help the company discover in advance which offer is most likely to satisfy those customers.

- A major U.S. airline is putting together a system that uses collaborative filtering to improve service for their best customers. When someone calls the airline's toll-free reservations number, the system uses caller ID and collaborative filtering to determine if he or she has bought tickets directly from the airline before or is likely to do so. If there's a match, the call is automatically routed to the top of the phone queue so it will be answered more quickly. Because a ticket bought directly from the airline represents a greater profit margin, the additional value that these customers bring to the airline is rewarded with better service.

Open standards are emerging that will permit the capture of information from a customer from multiple sites. The process of capturing information and making recommendations is becoming more transparent. Some systems, rather than requiring a user to fill out a questionnaire or list preferences, instead serve up information based on what a user has previously explored. For example, eGenie from Open Sesame automatically shows information about categories you have previously explored on a site. Similar technology is being used to automatically suggest new leads for sales representatives based on previous success rates.

Other companies are streamlining customer service and technical support by providing representatives with a system that supplies information based on how frequently a given piece of information is used. For example, if the highest percentage of a financial services company's calls deal with one line on an enrollment form, the system learns from the fact that representatives accessed that information more than any other. It would then supply the information to a representative first; moreover, it can generate a report that lets managers know which line on the enrollment form is a problem.

CUSTOMER DATA AS BUSINESS FUEL

Because of its ability to channel the tidal wave of information that flows through corporations, collaborative filtering will become useful not only in customer relationships but for knowledge management inside the enterprise as well. Intranets coupled with collaborative filtering will increasingly automate the process of letting workers receive information that their peers feel is important, and share information themselves.

- Bay Networks is using collaborative filtering in its online forums for members of its supply chain. Members can rate information supplied to the forum; for example, a news article that indicates strong demand for the company's products six months in the future might alert the company to gear up. The system helps executives cope with the cyclic nature of the business and makes them less dependent on retailers' sales forces.

- When J. Walter Thompson wanted to test an ad campaign for Ford Motors, it used collaborative filtering to develop an online focus group. To figure out how to position a new truck, the agency put samples of suggested ad copy online and tracked the demographics of people who responded to it. The collaborative filtering mechanism enabled marketers to see what else interested the kind of person who was attracted to the ad, thus giving marketers clues on how and where to promote the truck.

NEW CUSTOMERS

As discussed in Chapter Two, some companies are concerned about commerce on the Web cannibalizing their existing business. However, the Web's ability to measure customer information has helped alleviate those fears in many cases. Web marketers in traditional media are finding that far from cannibalizing existing businesses, their Web businesses are attracting a new audience. Consider:

- The *Wall Street Journal Interactive Edition* found that about two-thirds of its online subscribers are new readers; only one-third also subscribe to the print version. And there has not been a dramatic drop in the number of readers who cancel paper subscriptions to go online. The same pattern is true of online editions of the *New York Times*, with 50 percent new readers, and *Playboy*, with 75 percent of online subscriptions new ones.

- The ability to provide information in smaller slices has meant new customers for West Group, which publishes legal information. More than half its sales on the Web have come from nontraditional customers, including some consumers who want general information on a very specific legal topic.

THE 3D CUSTOMER

This new ability to tap information means that companies will have an increasingly well-rounded relationship with their customers. Netted companies will be able to link information obtained over the Net with information already in the company's data warehouses.

They will be truly customer-centric, able to develop and maintain a unique relationship with each customer. Such relationships will be especially important in high-touch industries with a lot of direct interaction with customers: banking, insurance, telecommunications, catalog sales. The customer representatives who deal directly with the customer will have at their fingertips a fuller portrait of the whole customer, and that portrait will be available no matter whether the customer contacts the company in person, on the phone, over the Net, or through the mail. The customer portrait will change just as the customer's needs and concerns change—in real time.

Perhaps in no other realm is real-time customer data more critical than on Wall Street, where a 15-minute delay can mean the loss of millions of dollars to traders and their institutional clients. Traditionally, investment banks have been organized around product—equity investments, bonds, emerging markets, and so on—rather than around their customers: large institutional investors such as mutual fund portfolio managers. However, in an era when massive amounts of information are available to anyone who can install a Reuters or Bloomberg terminal on a desk, people who sell to money managers must figure out how to cut through the infoglut to make themselves valuable to those customers.

Organizing around the customer is the only way for the Bankers Trusts and Morgan Stanleys of the world to do that.[7] Alexis Kopikis and his two cofounders of WorldStreet were salespeople at ING Baring Securities until they decided to start a company that would address the information needs of institutional securities sales reps like themselves. They are developing a browser-based system that organizes and tracks all information a company has about each client and matches that customer profile to information about specific investments, regions, sectors, and market events—all in the split-second time frame that can make or break a mega-investor. Says cofounder Kopikis:

> Ten or 15 years ago as an institutional salesman I could call and tell you what a security's selling for and make a sale. Nowadays everyone has access to the same data. The industry has become more service-oriented. The way they try to differentiate themselves is by who can give the ideas that are the most relevant to the portfolio managers. We have access to a world of data, but we don't know what's relevant to what client when. I used to cover 200 securities in Latin America alone. The large institutions are trading all day long in securities all around the world. There's no way to know what's most important to whom; there are too many variables to match up.
>
> I used to call somebody and say, "How about this stock?" Half the time they'd say, "How many times do I have to tell

you guys I'm not in that sector anymore" or "Why are you calling me? I just sold 50 million of it. Talk to your trader in Brazil." Everybody in Wall Street calls you to buy; nobody calls you to sell, because nobody remembers what they sold you. Ordinary pipeline management tools don't work in this environment; on the trading floor, my pipeline is measured in minutes, even seconds.

It's not only salesmen who are involved in selling to these guys; it's traders, research analysts, other salespeople. When you're selling as a team, it's important that everybody's pitching from the same book. Imagine if you went to a car dealership and one person said, "Buy the blue car." You came back a second time and another person said, "Buy the red car." And then when you went to pick it up, someone said, "Why did you buy that? The green one's the way to go." Your perception of a broker changes rapidly when that occurs. Institutional salesmen need to know in real time what interactions their entire company has had with this client, and they need to be able to share investment picks with one another.

The focus in automating the process in the past has not been on the customer. It has been on the trader—on doing trades faster, handling larger trades, doing more sophisticated risk assessment. Salespeople need to map in real time the sources of incoming data to client profiles made up of their current interests, holdings, trade histories, and real-time activities.

As an institutional salesman, you care most about the clients that are going to give you the trade. And that doesn't necessarily mean your big clients. If I have a client whose trading activity is triggered by certain events in the market—when recommendations are changed, when an earnings estimate gets revised, when earnings come out—I need to be able to know instantly who to call when I see that happening. Right now the salesperson doesn't know, so what does he do? He calls Fidelity on absolutely everything; the poor portfolio manager at Fidelity is getting every call, including multiple calls from people at the same organization.

And if somebody on the buy side calls to ask about what's going on in Ecuador, or to check on three different industries, I as a salesman have to say, "Let me check and I'll call you back." I need to be able to organize all the sources of information I have quickly around that one subject, to put context to that data. Reuters, Bloomberg, Thomson Financial—they've all created services designed to give you more and more information. There's so much data now that it actually makes your life as a salesperson more complicated; it's a hurdle you have to go over to provide value to your clients.

Some of our clients are already beginning to use their extranets to capture customer information in real time. If their customers are clicking around on their extranet—let's say they're clicking around reading about U.S. steel companies—that activity on the Web site automatically updates their profile in real time. It's real-time client management instead of sitting there figuring out when to do a marketing campaign. This kind of real-time customer interaction is a change we're seeing in other industries as well.

Another company that is exploring how to make the best of the customer as data is the Chrysler Corp.[8] Richard Everett, Director Strategic Technologies, Sales and Marketing Operations, heads Chrysler's online efforts:

The big investment will be in data. Where are the customer preferences kept? Companies will need to be able to lock into that information. At any point in time, I may need to know everything about that customer, since customer service is everything and I will need that data when that customer wants service. The real, unmined value nobody talks about is customer relation management. Once you understand the 220 attributes you have per customer, you can get away from mass advertising and target directly. That very targeted advantage will come from knowing exactly who the customers are.

We have 47 million records in our database. We separate people by the categories of bought new, bought used, bought new/still own, and bought used/still own, which is the biggest opportunity along with bought new/don't still have.

The car dealer network isn't going away. People still want to trade and want positive reinforcement that they're buying the right thing. It's a personification of their personality. And an automobile is still a periodic purchase, since the average person only does this once every six years. In the car business, you've got the switchers, the loyalists, the utilitarians and the newbies; that's it. The people who come through the dealership door who have used the Net know exactly what they want.

By October, we've committed materials for November and December. If we miss the number, between two-doors and four-doors, cloth and leather, we have six months of a model year to work ourselves out of. If we knew up front what the public wanted, we could take an immense amount of money out of the cost in the system.

In addition, we should be able to say we just had a management meeting and decided on a $500 rebate on a certain car. We then would automatically find the 17,000 people in the database and send them an E-mail, so that all the people who had an interest in the particular vehicle would get a note saying, "Here's a rebate offer that really matters to you." We'd automatically check the address and identify the closest dealer, then check that dealer's inventory of cars for availability and even color and then add that information into the E-mail to the customer. The customer's E-mail says "Here's the closest dealer to you and here's what he has in inventory of that particular car." The dealer also would automatically get a copy of the E-mail. We can get a person approved for finance now in about three minutes. Think of what that does when you tie all that together.

Everett sees enormous opportunity in capturing customer data and then mining that data to streamline the manufacturing process. "People can configure a car on the Net and we'll be able to check, geographically, which markets might want a certain color and body type. We then can make those kinds of cars for specific markets. We then can reduce the inventory on the lots, which impacts the real estate needed by the dealers. If you can predictively understand what people are going to buy, it will drive a tremendous amount of excess out of inventory. We're gathering information and understanding of what people are doing out there. This is real-time research."

As is typical in the 180-degree effect in the Net Future, Chrysler's online investment might appear to be aimed simply at stimulating car sales; in reality, its true return will come from streamlining its entire manufacturing and delivery operations based on real-time customer data. This is another example of how true E-business requires end-to-end networking, driven by the consumer.

The customer as data can drive not only a company's own internal processes, but also those of its customers. Maytag is the third largest manufacturer of large appliances in the U.S. and owns such well-known consumer brands as Jenn-Air, Magic Chef, Hoover, Admiral, Norge—not to mention the Maytag name itself. The common view of Maytag was created by a popular advertising campaign featuring the Maytag repairman just sitting around with nothing to do, implying that Maytag appliances never broke. But Maytag has become more than just a washing machine manufacturer. It is the leading U.S. manufacturer of soft drink can and bottle vending machines.

Much of the vision of how the company executes in the Net Future is driven by Edward Wojciechowski, Vice President of Information Technology.

"IT falls into the trap of trying to be perfect and there is no such thing," says Wojciechowski. "We implemented the 80-20 rule, which means IT functionality will reach 80 percent, not 100 percent perfection. This allows us to deliver faster and have a much clearer vision. We don't drop quality or key features. This is a much faster way to drive the business forward."

Vending machine companies already are experimenting with networking machines to enable price modifications in real time. For example, when the outside temperature at a Coke machine location in Dallas reaches 98 degrees, the price of a can might be raised 25 cents to capitalize on greater demand, or lowered 25 cents on a winter day. This glitzy use of networking technology might catch the public's eye, but—as is typical in the Net Future—there is a different kind of revolution behind the scenes.

"The vending machine has enormous potential to provide food products, such as really good meals, through a vending process," says Wojciechowski. "What about breakfast or fresh fruit? Money is heavy. If you made smaller machines and used smart cards, the Net could enable dynamic inventory assessment. Then you just take up the products you need. You can monitor the device itself and change the quality of the products." This would allow pricing on the fly. If eggs or fruit were within two days of expiration, for example, the price might drop 50 percent.

Think of the implications. If machines were smaller, they could be distributed to more places. Fewer or smaller trucks might be needed. Inventory can be kept to a minimum. And, as we discussed in the last chapter, real-time consumer demand truly drives what is supplied.

LEVERAGING CUSTOMER KNOWLEDGE

As with the auction-based sales environments previously discussed, true consumer-centric marketing and the instantaneous nature of customer feedback will put pressure on the enterprise to move ever more quickly on the operational end. There are profound implications for how a company is organized to take advantage of this new customer knowledge:

- Sales staffs will need to become more familiar with customer service. As the customer takes greater control and more products become commodities, service will become more important as a product differentiator. And customer service representatives will increasingly be equipped with customer knowledge that enables them to cross-sell and upsell appropriate products.
- Manufacturing systems will have to be designed for even greater flexibility. Rapid changes in marketing strategy will require greater ability to adapt manufacturing schedules more quickly.
- Product design will need to become more modular to allow both greater mass customization and quicker adaptation of

designs. The advent of computer add-ons that allow consumers to record their own CDs will be complemented by the ability to search large databases of individual music files from multiple sources onto a CD. Customers of N2K might eventually download an individual song from the *Titanic* soundtrack, a sea chanty from a folk album, and a recording of "Happy Birthday," then package them on one CD that could be given as a personalized gift to a sailing buddy; other companies are racing to offer the same service. The type of music selected could provide information about both the buyer and the person receiving the gift. Information based on those combinations could be used by collaborative filters to help future customers design their own "albums."

- Companies will need to think "out of the box" about what the customer really wants. Wells Fargo is exploring offering access to outside financial services as part of its Web site to enhance the chances of the customer viewing the bank as a one-stop center for their financial lives.

- Companies that continue to organize around products will find a greater need to focus on knowledge transfer within the organization. The less customer-centric a corporate structure, the more a company may need to spend on ensuring that information is readily available across divisional lines. For example, a company's internal network might need to be especially robust compared with that of a customer-centric organization that routinely puts employees from different functional areas together.

TREATING THE SHADOW RIGHT

With this increasingly sophisticated use of the customer as data, will privacy on the Internet become a greater issue for consumer worry than it is already? Those involved with it say no. They contend that as long as companies create and adhere to a publicly stated policy about how customer information will be used, the customer is free to decide whether to supply the information. Companies are hiring third-party auditors to veri-

Marketing to Customer as Data

Product-Centric	Customer-Centric
Focuses on getting more customers	Finds out which customers are most likely to buy
Focuses on getting customers to buy more	Focuses on which customers are most profitable
Focuses on price competition	Focuses on meeting customer needs
Acts on policy or predetermined responses	Acts on real-time feedback
Relies on sales forces to sell and customer service representatives to resolve complaints	Intertwines sales and service
Obtains revenue and sales data from each sale	Obtains revenue and customer data from each sale
Provides what the company wants to sell	Provides what the customer needs

fy that their use of customer data conforms to their stated privacy policy.

And though datamining in its most sophisticated form may create the Shadow You, it is a shadow based on behavioral patterns, not specific data points. Think of the Shadow You as a "behavior brand." Just as a product's brand image is not its substance, so your behavior brand—your Shadow You—is not you as an individual. No matter how strong the shadow's outline, it cannot capture the rich nuance that makes up an individual's total personality or the quirks that fit into no perceived pattern.

Still, if marketers are to supply customers with the information, products, and services desired, they must start somewhere. In the past, that has meant focusing on finding better ways to convince people to buy what they produce. In the Net Future, marketers will be more able to focus on listening to what people want—sometimes even before they want it—and creating and delivering it.

EXPERIENCE COMMUNITIES ARISE

In the Net Future, cheap global communications will accelerate the pace of human interaction in both the personal and professional realms. As the price of worldwide contact via the Net drops and people master instant, global communication, knowledge will get aggregated in real time, speeding the pace of discussion and decisions.

Collaborative thinking will create instant human networks that develop and dissolve as the need arises. In the Net Future, thinking becomes global and simultaneous, not local and linear. Human information processing will increasingly resemble parallel processing in the computer world, in which multiple processors attack parts of a problem simultaneously to solve complex calculations in a fraction of the time that traditional computing takes. But in the Net Future, human problems can be attacked by people.

AGGREGATED EXPERIENCES BECOME EXPERTISE

Knowledge has traditionally been thought of as something captured and put on a page. That expertise, accumulated over time, was updated periodically when enough new information had been gathered to make an update worthwhile—a new edition of a textbook, for example, or a periodically refreshed database.

The Net gives people not only faster access to all information but also access to the aggregated knowledge of populations who, collectively, have experienced almost everything. Those experiences can be collected and used in real time to supplement or in some cases replace the more traditional forms of expertise. I have termed these aggregated pools of knowledge, where individuals can be aggregated and can even self-aggregate, "experience communities."

As the credibility of many traditional institutions—government, science, the news media, the professions—has diminished with large segments of the population over recent years, individuals have become more reliant on the word of others. The popularity of talk radio, reality-based TV shows, and memoirs attests to an increased desire to learn from others' successes or failures at coping with the same issues that we face.

Rightly or wrongly, people increasingly see the advice of someone they know—or even someone they don't know but who they perceive to understand their situation—as valuable, in some cases more valuable than that of so-called authorities.

Consider this comment from a forum for nursing mothers, rebuking a man who had criticized some of the online discussion:

> You are just about as "supportive" as the doctors who claim to be very pro-breast-feeding and then advise a new mom to supplement with formula at the first little thing. If you would like to become supportive, then listening a little bit more to women and respecting our collective experiences—that many times pediatricians give advice that is poor advice and that sabotages breast-feeding—and being a little less inclined to criticize the advice given from hard-earned experience by one nursing mother to another would be a great place to start.

In the Net Future, online experience communities will add an extra dimension by allowing real-time aggregation of collective experience. As the pace of change becomes increasingly swift, the longer it takes to aggregate experience, the more out-of-date the earliest information collected may be. An E-mail broadcast to dozens of people asking their advice may not yield a better decision. It will, however, provide a broader and possibly more current base of information on which to make that decision.

In the Net Future, companies will need to leverage experience communities if they are to acquire and maintain credibility. Companies struggling to cope with the challenges posed by the Net Future are prime examples of experience communities. One executive said of his desire to form a community of customers of a particular automated procurement system, "No one knows the rules on how to implement this stuff; it's helpful to talk to people who are actually doing it."

Many companies already monitor discussion groups for mention of their organization or products. By keeping tabs on keywords that crop up in discussion groups and bulletin boards, a company called WordOfNet can tell an enterprise what experience communities have to say about it.

SPREADING THE WORD!

Word of mouth has always been important to corporate image, of course. But never has word of mouth been able to spread so rapidly or so far. As an example of the potential impact of experience communities on business, consider this voice from the Net Future, taken from a newsgroup that deals with Volkswagens:

> Even though there exists at least 2 sides of every argument...I don't mind reading of someone's bad experiences with a vendor...[it] may save me money and time invested. There's simply too many vendors in this industry where I could take my business. Let free-market forces...with help from the collective experiences in this newsgroup decide who has superb service...and those who don't. A bad reputation travels faster than a good one...as it should.

Experience communities may be based on business or personal interests. They may be ongoing or fleeting. They may be as intimate as a one-to-one conversation or as global as the Net itself. But whatever the form or subject, they will shape the way everyone processes information in the Net Future.

QUICK, INSTANT-MESSAGE COMMUNITIES

Because the Net is really a communications medium, it will facilitate the creation of new, real-time "communicating" communities. Among the various forms of communities are what I call "instant-message communities," which may concern a narrow but timely topic. They may involve as few as two people or, as in the case of Merrill Lynch, a company's entire brokerage clientele. When the stock market plunged in October 1997, the head of Merrill Lynch fielded questions and addressed issues from worried investors in a chat session that included more than 500 people. This kind of up-to-the-minute, open, interactive communication would have been impossible before the Net unless it was done through an intermediary, such as the news media.

Instant messaging allows people to send messages to others who are using the Net and reach them in real time. Unlike an E-mail message, which is typed, then sent, then viewed when the recipient gets around to it, the instant message is just that: instant. America Online members have been using the feature for several years; the company even allows members to create "buddy lists" so a person can instantly check on whether any friends or associates are online at the moment. It's sort of like knowing that a person is home before you place the phone call. And you get the same result: the person may be home but choose not to answer the phone. The person at the other end of the Net connection may be connected, but away from the computer getting a cup of coffee.

ICQ is an abbreviated way to say "I Seek You." Developed by Tel Aviv-based Mirabilis, the free program has become a popular way to find anyone on the Web; it offers not only instant messaging but real-time chat. In the 18 months following the

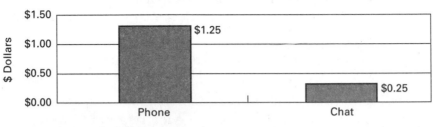

What's Servicing a Customer Cost?

Source: Jupiter Communications

FIGURE 7.1

launch of ICQ, Mirabilis acquired 11 million registrations. The company estimates that 6 million of those were active and have developed 5000 interest lists and 13,000 active chat rooms. And the ICQ metacommunity has the ability to grow itself; by clicking on a button, members can E-mail a friend the URL for downloading the program themselves. It's community growth by "word of mouse." And how was the company going to make money? It didn't really know, until AOL stepped in and bought it. The price? Up-front cash of $287 million, with potentially another $100 million based on future performance!

CHAT GOES CORPORATE

Instant messaging may have begun as a cool trick for consumers, but it will increasingly be adopted in the business world as a way to stay close to customers and colleagues.

- When Charles O. Holliday, CEO of E.I. duPont de Nemours, needs to communicate quickly with duPont executives in Europe, the group uses chat software to set up an instant virtual conference room. There they not only talk but share Web pages, transfer files, and save a transcript of the session.
- An internal chat room at Fore Systems allows its 1500 employees to get answers to questions in real time. The net-

working products company uses a virtual reality environment such as the company cafeteria and photos of "guides" to answer questions such as "Where's Conference Room 2?" Questions and answers can be stored in a database and retrieved when another user needs the information.

- Computer software company Symantec in California initially used an internal online chat system in its telephone customer support area that let customer service representatives ask a supervisor questions without putting customers on hold.[1] The company realized that online customers could substitute chat for the phone to get their questions answered, and that the company could offer it as a for-fee service after a customer's initial free tech support period expired. The use of ChatNow has been about what the company expected, says Symantec's Mike Gelardi, and the company now is looking at using chat in other ways, such as conducting seminars for developers using the company's products.

- To better service its customers, online software retailer Egghead, Inc. decided to allow customers to chat with a "sales egg" as they shop, and with other customers at the company's virtual lounge.

The ability to contact a company directly and immediately on the Web will prove especially important as the cybereconomy goes Main Street. "I think a year from now people will not shop at a Web site that doesn't provide the ability to answer questions online instantly," says P. V. Kannan, CEO of Business Evolution.[2] The Princeton, NJ company developed a software program called @Once Service Center, on which Symantec's ChatNow is based. "Studies show that 98 percent of people who put items in their shopping cart abandon the transaction before completing it. One of our customers found that sales were 40 percent fewer than they could have been because people couldn't get answers to their questions."

Companies often look at chat as a way to deal with the volume of customer inquiries. "They often express their problem as 'I get a lot of E-mail and I want to get rid of it.' We ask them whether solving their E-mail problem is their real concern, or whether it's providing effective customer service."

The true power of instant customer interaction is its ability to shorten the purchasing cycle. Giving customers the information they need, whether that information is simple reassurance about online security or factual data, encourages them to complete the purchase. As on-the-fly pricing becomes more widespread (See Chapter Five) and promotions entice customers with discounts if they buy within the next 15 minutes, a customer who has to wait 24 hours for an E-mail response is a customer lost. And that ad campaign to stimulate impulse buying? Wasted.

However, implementing instant messaging for customer service requires some thought. The natural tendency is to assume that online customer service is essentially the same as phone service. "The reality is that text-based interaction requires a somewhat different skill set—easy with technology, good written language skills," says Kannan.

In the Net Future, the capability will be integrated into a variety of programs so that anyone can reach anyone at any time.

LET'S CHAT

Experience communities are at the heart of the Net. After all, the Net itself began as an experience community of U.S. Defense Department researchers who wanted to exchange notes about their work. Other researchers at universities soon joined those early communities. Though these efforts did not involve sophisticated chat capabilities, they nonetheless demonstrated the Net's power to aggregate like-minded people in a way previously unimagined.

The precursor to chat was bulletin board systems that allowed people to post written messages to a predefined group such as California-based The WELL (Whole Earth Lectronic Link). These emerged in the mid-1980s and used the phone network rather than the Net as the connection.

Chat took the bulletin board concept one step further by allowing participants to type messages back and forth in real time. Its power was demonstrated by the emergence of America Online as perhaps the most well-known provider of Internet service. In contrast to Prodigy, another early online service that concentrated on providing rich content, AOL built its base of users by promoting chat as a cornerstone of the online experience. Because its revenues were based on usage per hour, it was to AOL's advantage to keep users online as much as possible, and chat proved to be an excellent way to do that. Parents who may have been thrilled to connect with New Zealand or Brazil on ham radios in their youth watched as their children carried on the same kinds of global communication in a different medium.

As more people go online and become accustomed to the idea that they can communicate with anyone, anytime, anywhere, they will begin to be more discriminating about where they spend their time. Communities will need to evolve to accommodate that increasing sophistication. For example, Tripod began as a community for 20-somethings, with funky names for its communities (called "pods"). After being acquired by search engine Lycos for $58 million, it revamped its community categories with names that were a bit more sedate—not enough to offend its core users, but mainstream enough to accommodate a wider range of interests.

Tripod also suggests how chat and online communities will increasingly be integrated into mainstream life. Using collaborative filtering—which in a sense creates an instant community itself—Lycos integrates Tripod community members' content with its search results. When a user searches on a keyword, Lycos not only returns listings of Web pages, but highlights Tripod members' personal home pages that deal with that subject.

The next step for chat in the Net Future is to become established in the corporate arena as a way of sharing knowledge, which we discuss later in this chapter.

A TALE OF THREE CITIES

With the explosion of communications capabilities, there will be many opportunities for people to "move in" to communities and find others like themselves with whom they can share experiences. In the Net Future, part of the challenge for an individual will be to select the appropriate neighborhood, because, as in the real world, it is not that easy to move.

Granted, on the Net it takes only a click of a mouse to jump to another community, but it's difficult to take along electronic friendships, some of which are the reasons for belonging to a specific community in the first place. Following is a look at the different approaches of three communities. One has moved from a general community to one that is aimed primarily at women and that tries to organize experience to help members solve problems. The second focuses on heavy discussion. The third essentially encourages members of the community to govern themselves.

THE WOMEN'S NETWORK

One of the oldest and best known of the people organizing groups on the Net is iVillage. The Silicon Alley company is headed by Candice Carpenter, a former president at Q2; longtime friend Nancy Evans, former editor of *Family Life*; and Robert Levitan.[3]

When the company started, it focused on fostering a sense of community among its users, now mostly women. After garnering major investments from firms ranging from cable giant TCI to Silicon Valley's premiere venture capital firm Kleiner-Perkins, the company evolved into a women's online network.

"We view ourselves as an aggregator of eyeballs," says Carpenter. "Community is really one of the main ways we can serve our audience. The deliverable is the utility and the problem solving. We are a community with a problem-solving objective. For example, foreign adoptions are difficult. You might come in and the community will help you move forward toward a solution."

"We're trying to find a way to index people's experiences," Carpenter says. "We use home pages as the indexing of the problem-solving aspects, and now we're starting to get into knowledge transfer. At first, it was about leisure, but now it's really about getting your life done. Someone might come in and say, 'I was just diagnosed with breast cancer and I have two small kids.' People immediately lend a hand."

Once people have been helped in any way by the iVillage community, they in turn commit to it to help others. "If you get life-saving help from a community, your impulse is to be of service to other people. The Net is secondary here. We're upgrading their neighbors, in a way. We think of every issue a woman might face. My goal is to wake up in the morning and whatever issue I might face that day know that iVillage members will be there to help. You can come here and find anyone who has had the experience you need, from the sublime to the mundane. It's a woman's network, and it provides a layer of perceived safety to women. Our research showed that there's no safe feeling place on the Net."

The company's success points to the strength of its mission. IVillage was looking to finish 1998 with more than a million members, doubling each year for the next few years, with more than 2 million different visitors each month. How much do these women look at in a month? By mid-1998, with more than 70 million pages of people-created "content," iVillage was the seventh largest pure content site online.

"We hope we will be used as a primary resource for women to get through their day," says Carpenter.

And as companies borne out of the Net environment find, as their online communities or businesses grow, there is much behind the scenes that has to change. When iVillage decided to reassess how its production and technology departments should work within its organization, it brought in a Net-savvy strategic consulting company to review workflow and systems infrastructure. It showed that iVillage needed a more scaleable approach to meet the demands of the growing and constantly evolving business.

To rapidly implement interactive content, IVillage and the consultants developed multiple production units. A separate IT organization now maintains network infrastructure and provides the systems tools that enable production and technology to execute their creative vision. Technology relationship managers ensure that the systems tools are meeting the needs of editorial, production, and the other business units. And a full-scale internal help desk routes technical issues to the right resource.

Typical of companies in the Net Future, iVillage took a proactive stance in changing its organization and systems infrastructure to prepare for future growth in the online market.

ALL IN THE FAMILY

While iVillage: the Women's Network targets women, another company 3000 miles away focuses on communities of families. The California-based LiveWorld Productions, Inc, which grew out of Apple Computer's unsuccessful online services venture eWorld, named its community Talk City.[4]

With more than 1 million active participants, the company quickly became one of the largest community builders in the Net, chalking up more than 3 million hours of chat per month and 500,000 home pages posted in its first three months. LiveWorld raised $10 million for the community and within two years of launch was logging about 4 million hours of chat per month, including 36,000 that are moderated. More than 5 million people have come through Talk City and more than a million a month are regulars, averaging 20 minutes per month for some, and three hours for the regular visitors.

"They believe they're members of Talk City," says LiveWorld CEO Peter Friedman. "They perceive themselves as belonging to it." Since Talk City's launch, 800 million screens of "chat" and other community interactions have been viewed by its members. "In the future, it will be about time spent, not pages viewed," says Friedman. "We established a large, loyal following by doing chat. Then we went to channels, and the biggest are family, teens, and college. We have about 3000 college students regularly coming in here and 50 percent of the audience is female.

"Most of our growth is by word of mouth. People don't want to be part of, say, just a sports community, but they belong to multiple communities within Talk City. People will find the community they relate with and identify with and it will be the

center of gravity on the Net for them. The community-switch-
ing barriers are high, but a community has to have a culture to
grow in the first place."

One-third of all discussions in Talk City neighborhoods are
moderated, meaning that one of 700 moderators leads an order-
ly online discussion in which anyone can participate. Groups
that are not moderated are self-policed, so that anyone can,
with one click, call a "city standards adviser" to deal with any
offending culprit.

Talk City is busiest between 3 p.m. and 10 p.m., and 60 percent of its members are 25 to 50 years old. The company has
found that access to its members is of high value to other companies, mainly for research purposes. Talk City recruits members for online focus groups for such companies as NBC,
Sprint, Microsoft, Cisco, and US West. "People talk more in an
online focus group," says Friedman.

The company lets people set up home pages at the Talk City
neighborhood—what Friedman calls "home pages for the mass-
es." All the pages are integrated into Talk City's neighborhood
structure.

"We created a structured environment, a clean, well-lighted
family-oriented place," says Friedman. "We think that community is the most distinguishable aspect of the Net, more than
any other media form. People interact and build relationships.
It's much different from looking at content or searching,
because it allows people to interact with people. It speaks to a
fundamental human need and condition, to communicate with
each other. It's not an isolated Net experience. We find a great
many of the people who use the service to be families."

The Talk City approach allows people on the Net to form a
chat room at the Talk City site, then embed the site into their
own home pages. For example, if Rose and Agnes Theriault, sis-
ters who live in different cities, want to create a family chat room,
they can fill out a few forms at Talk City, then notify other family members of the Web location. Theriault family members could
then "chat" with one another without stopping other work they
might be doing at their computers. Within a short time after Talk
City was launched, 35,000 groups had joined the neighborhood.

"People have found long-lost family members here," says Friedman. "Community is the differentiating experience on the Internet."

POWER TO THE PEOPLE

Theglobe.com was founded in 1994 by Todd Krizelman and Stephan Paternot while they were students at Cornell University.[5]

"We saw the opportunity to create an online audience," says 24-year-old Krizelman. "We put together a small business plan and ultimately raised $15,000 from friends and family," says Paternot. By 1995, Krizelman and Paternot had launched a community Web site, and over the next two years they raised $2 million. It was then that they bumped into Alamo Rent-A-Car owner Michael Egan. He met the pair, saw the plan, and bought in, to the tune of $20 million!

By 1998, theglobe.com had 1.5 million members, growing by 150,000 a month. Eventually, it added news, stock feeds, and even car sales to bolster the community experience.

What was so appealing about this type of community was that rather than trying to determine where people should go for discussions and community, the duo decided on a strategy of allowing the community members to define the communities themselves.

"People create their own communities," says Paternot. "We created a system so people can create their own microcommunities, districts, and cities. Instead of us trying to figure it out, we created an infrastructure for people to do it themselves. We've had weddings, religious sects, and other things we never would have thought of creating as communities."

"We try to mimic the real world as much as possible," says Paternot. "We wanted to make people band together first, then surround themselves with others who have like interests. In New York City, what makes one bar different from another? They all serve the same alcohol. The difference is in who goes there. Where is your circle of friends?"

"It was important to create an image," says Krizelman. "We bet the future of the company that there is an image and a brand that will be necessary to have people relate to you. No one yet has any brand recognition." The company put an $8 million television ad campaign against its idea, to establish the globe.com as the hip, cool place to go.

The pair view their community as a government, of sorts, complete with rules and residents. The community comprises 50 percent 18- to 34-year-olds, more than half of whom are males. And just how democratic is it? At theglobe.com, anyone can suggest a group. If 15 others agree, by voting, that they are interested and say they also will participate, the group is created. The group may grow to a large number, but if interest dwindles it is "purged" from the community. The community interest defines the subcommunities.

"We have themes and then cities," says Krizelman. "Within Romance, you might have a city called 'City of Love,' and eventually you get down to a specific interest group. It's completely organic so people always have a place to go."

The Silicon Alley company allows people to have discussions about any topics that interest them, and offers software so that people can create their own home pages. "People really like to publish information about themselves or their interests," says Krizelman.

"If someone is interested in community, the likelihood of finding a group of friends here is high, and then it becomes tough to leave," says Paternot. "Over the next three to five years there's the opportunity to get customers; then it will be tougher. People will be less likely to move if their friends are there."

What surprised the company were the types of subjects that its electronic residents wanted to include. "Spirituality and religion are huge," says Paternot. "We get a lot of Bible Belt users who want a clear, well-controlled environment, so we created a profanity filter that each user can turn on or off. Everything is user-driven and we're passive to everything that is going on."

When the company conducted focus groups of its audience, it found that community members reflected the mass consumer audience. "They said that society was no longer fulfilling their need to connect to other people. People also said the image of the community was important."

The average resident of theglobe.com spends about 30 minutes a month "conversing." True to the company's name, 40 percent of the traffic is from outside the United States, mostly Japan, Australia, the United Kingdom, and Germany. A major attraction for these non-U.S. visitors is that they are allowed to publish and communicate in their own languages. And after hundreds of marriages developed through the electronic community, theglobe.com created a "cyberchapel" for couples to exchange vows. To fuel the online community's growth, theglobe.com filed for an IPO to raise an additional $50 million.

YOUR NETWORK IS THE NETWORK

Being able to access a wide network simultaneously is like casting with a net—or the Net—instead of fly fishing. More information is acquired more quickly. For individuals, this means greater access to a broader range of expertise in a shorter time frame. For companies, it can mean creating communities of customers—buyer-seller communities—through an extranet, and making more effective use of the collective knowledge of employees. The approach can be used to keep a wired workforce happy, by giving people a sense of belonging to the "community" of the company.

THE BUSINESS COMMUNITY

COLLEAGUE-COLLEAGUE

It's Monday, and Bob Kleinrath sits down at his computer to start planning how to test a new polymer that The Gillette Co. might use in developing its next generation of toiletries products.[6] He remembers that one of his colleagues had an interesting idea last week when they ran into each other in the hallway and stopped to talk. He wants to not only refresh his memory but also review his own notes and get a couple of his colleagues involved in the discussion.

In a few minutes, Bob sets up an area on the company's intranet where all these people plus other people working on the polymer development can collaborate during the test planning. He decides who will have access to which sections of the area he's setting up—an area that will be replaced in a couple of weeks by a new project area covering the overall product development. He also puts in the area a folder with his notes, dragging the folder from his desktop to the browser-based area. He then E-mails the five people he wants involved in a discussion about the testing process to notify them he's set up the area and to ask if they can be available online tomorrow for a brief discussion of the process.

The next morning, Bob's computer alerts him that someone's already put some new information in one of the folders. When the group gathers online and starts communicating about the test, someone suggests that they get the manufacturing facility in Chicago involved. Bob quickly gives the manufacturing representative access to the area and updates her by E-mail on what's going on. After developing several possible test procedures, the group agrees to review them offline and then vote on which makes the most sense. The system being used for the collaborative effort will automatically tally the votes and record the result for everyone to see. Once the testing procedure is set up, all notes from the discussion will be available for reference later.

"Most of our customers started out as grassroots efforts," says Jeffrey Beir, president and CEO of Instinctive Technology, whose company makes the product used by Kleinrath's group and four others within Gillette.[7] The company was founded after Beir discovered there was one big problem with groupware and document management systems: employees often didn't use them. Why? The systems took too long to set up. They required too much support from a company's information technology department. Employees had to learn a sophisticated application to use them. And the systems often were deployed companywide as a major corporate effort with all the bureaucracy and unwieldiness that implies.

Despite their ability to facilitate collaboration, such highly structured applications simply don't fit the Netted business world. That world requires the ability to pull teams together quickly across organizational and geographic boundaries (and often outside them) and manage projects that come and go. It is a world in which the wired workforce is able to create communities spontaneously when they are needed and maintain them only as long as they are needed.

Beir decided to launch e-Room, which uses a Web browser to enable nontechnical workers to set up their own communities with internal and external colleagues. Within six months after the product was launched, 200 companies were using it for everything from managing complex ongoing projects to pulling together an adhoc team that involved 15 separate companies to develop a joint business proposal in two weeks.

"Groupware was mostly targeted at applications developers. We wanted something that people could deploy themselves, that would be easy enough to get up and running that there wouldn't be a barrier to people starting discussion groups when they needed them," says Beir. "There are two types of IT departments: enlightened and unenlightened. Most of them are enlightened; as long as they see it doesn't create a data management nightmare, a support nightmare, they tend to say, 'This is fine with us.' They want something that will let them not have to worry about the data and go back to laying the pipes and developing the corporate infrastructure."

Kleinrath's group has experienced some unexpected benefits from collaborating electronically: "One person in the group is an excellent researcher, but sometimes it's been difficult to get information. She's really taken to it, and a lot of ideas have come out that we might not have gotten otherwise."

PEER-PEER

As discussed in Chapter Three, occupation-based work communities will become just as important as company-based communities:

- Knowledge Ecology Fair, an online conference, attracted people interested in the development of shared learning environments. During the month-long conference, 375 participants from 17 countries registered for the various scheduled sessions and ongoing discussions. "Somehow, being in a virtual community makes my internal processes visible to me, perhaps because I have not yet learned to put them aside, as I do so adeptly in face-to-face situations. I invite you to bring who you really are to the wonderful conversations you are creating in this temporary, man-made, extraordinary world," said one participant.

- Not all talk is cheap. When the Pristine Real Time Trading Room started, the intent was to connect swing traders so that buy and sell instructions could be communicated in real time. This would allow subscribers to cash in on fluctuations in stock prices. Membership in the community was $525 per month, and more than 400 people from around the globe joined.

- AOL's business channel has forums on a wide number of specific industries.

- Some communities get better with size. PlanetAll is a database of personal information that recognizes and tracks connections within the community. The community-based service reached a million members less than two years after launch, at a growth rate of between 5000 and 10,000 members a day.

SUPERVISOR-ASSOCIATES

In a wired workforce, communities can enable more widespread discussion of issues within a corporation by involving more people throughout the hierarchy. Rather than calling a huge company meeting or limiting discussion to as few as possible in order to make a meeting workable, instant communities can serve as a middle ground.

When executives at Trans-Canada Pipelines, a Fortune 100-sized energy company, wanted to plan future scenarios, officials decided to open up the discussion beyond the 15 top officers previously involved in the process. However, convening 200 high-level managers from the company was logistically impossible. The Meta Network was hired to set up 30 online conference spaces accessible via the Web. The strategic discussion groups provided real-time discussions among the managers. The conference was opened and closed with all participants present, but the results also were retained and accessible at the click of a button. Said one official, "Finally I can know what is on the minds of my colleagues on a day-to-day basis." Participants said that instead of talking about the weather when they bumped into peers in the office, they were able to bring up subjects that had appeared in the conference's Open Space.

The true value of the conference was demonstrated dramatically two days after it opened. One of the company's pipelines burst in a rural area and caused a lot of physical damage to the environment. Previously, when such incidents had happened, a small group at the top had been charged with handling the problem and the response to the media; there was no opportunity for discussion within the organization. This time, 200 of the top officers of the company were able to discuss why the break had happened as well as respond to technical questions about how the pipe was made.

In 36 hours, the climate in the company changed from one of defensiveness to embracing a deeper sense of social concern and identification with the country where the accident occurred. The event became a way to raise larger issues about the company's responsibilities and mission.

Another example: The Department of Defense is using a combination of real-time conversation and bulletin boards to plan what the military healthcare system will look like between now and the year 2020. The planning was kicked off with a face-to-face meeting of 240 participants that was continued in ongoing forums.

SIZING THE OPPORTUNITY

Companies in the Net Future will be faced with creating their own networked communities of employees, suppliers, distributors, or customers. Once a company makes this leap in thinking, it can become more than simply a seller of products to buyers. It can become an organizer of communities where buyers congregate and, while buying products, provide ongoing intelligence that can help the company define its future products and business.

One company that espouses the virtues of electronic communities for companies is the Mining Company, an Internet startup comprising hundreds of digital homesteaders who run sites devoted to specific interests. The Mining Company finds guides to run the groups and pays them to create content and discussion that is valuable enough to attract others interested in that subject. Citibank commissioned the company to develop a community of people around its banking services. Says Mining Company CEO and Net veteran Scott Kurnit:

> Big companies are busy building big, sprawling brochure-ware Web sites, even though big sites are unwieldy, expensive and hard to scale—not to mention difficult for users to navigate. Businesses will do a better job using multiple approaches to provide engaging experiences for specific user groups. Companies will get closer to users—and let users get closer to each other—to maximize customer involvement and increase the Net's productivity for sales and service.

> Big sprawling sites will become the first dinosaurs of the Internet Age because a single large company site, no matter how elegantly designed, so often ends up seeming cold and impersonal. On the Net, smaller is better; one size does not fit all. And communities need to be small to be effective. Large communities are not communities; they are cities. People with questions stop by day and night, but no one's ever home. Companies eventually will abandon these sprawling, top-down sites in favor of bottom-up company networks made up of smaller, more specialized sites—each focused on a particular aspect of the company's business.

> The human touch will be provided by actual human beings, responsive company representatives who greet visitors on arrival, provide real answers, keep users involved and up-to-date, and facilitate the growth of trust and loyalty around the company's products and services. These people

Future as community organizers encourage their members to support the companies that support the group.

DEVELOP EXPERIENCE COMMUNITIES
AMONG EMPLOYEES

When the general manager of Buckman Laboratories' Singapore office was preparing a proposal for a multi-million dollar contract from an Indonesian paper mill, he needed information about ways to control the amount of pitch in paper pulp.[10] He posted a notice on K'Netix, the Memphis-based chemical manufacturing company's internal network. Within 48 hours he had 12 responses from Buckman associates in six different countries, all offering advice from their experiences dealing with the problem in their areas. The proposal based on that information won the contract, and the company awarding it indicated that Buckman's ability to gather so much information in such a short period of time was influential in its decision.

"Eighty-six percent of our people are outside the office and in any one of 90 different countries," says Robert Buckman, chairman and CEO, who envisioned the K'Netix system as a way of keeping his staff closer to the customer at all times. "Tacit knowledge is 90 percent of the knowledge in the organization; it's the knowledge that's walking around in people's heads. Most companies concentrate on the explicit knowledge that's written down. That's where things are beginning to change. By the time the information is written down, it's usually too late. If it's six months old, its part of the historical baggage. In the current world, you can't wait for it to be written down.

"The challenge is: How do you get the tacit knowledge shared on an as-needed basis? Sharing knowledge when there's no need is a nice intellectual exercise, but it has no economic value. We want what we do to have economic value."

K'Netix includes electronic forums, bulletin boards, virtual conference rooms, and libraries as well as E-mail; videoconferencing is out because the company's global nature would create scheduling difficulties. The Buckman culture insists that instantaneous experience communities be used as the way its more than 1200 associates do business. Since the network's development, products are delivered roughly 50 percent faster than before. Sales of new products, which would logically require proportionately more information exchange, have risen from an average of 22 percent of total sales to 33 percent. Says Buckman:

> Knowledge sharing is cultural. We've been taught from the time we entered school not to share, to hoard knowledge. To try to do things collectively and collaboratively, you've got to learn to give away knowledge to get ahead. There are some people who react very well to this type of environment and some who are scared to death. To achieve what we want to achieve, to get the best we can out of the systems that are in place involves culture change. A very small part of it is technology; 90 percent is culture change.

> The type of people we hire are different. Some of the best sharers out there are teachers. We're more interested in people who are natural teachers. There are certain questions you can ask to find out if people will do well. For instance, if individuals don't care about their family, they won't do well with us. We don't want lone rangers; it just doesn't work in our culture.

> The old command-and-control structure breaks down because it's too slow. The speed of our response to customers has gone from days and weeks to hours. It's all about people helping people to succeed. When I asked [one of our people] what knowledge sharing meant to them, she said, "Communications is human nature. Knowledge sharing is human nature."

The company is enhancing learning through experience communities with an online learning center where employees take company-approved for-credit courses and even degree programs at company expense. It is working with universities in Brazil, South America, the United Kingdom, and the Netherlands, among others, to include multicultural programs. Since the learning center was inaugurated, one-fourth of the company's workforce has taken at least one course. Buckman wants to expand the program to allow children and possibly spouses of employees to take courses through the center.

"If you want to be helped in the future," says Buckman, "you have to help somebody else now."

THE PERSONAL COMMUNITY

FRIENDS—FRIENDS

Experience communities can forge powerful bonds among people who already know one another. They also can provide a source of support from people one would never have come in contact with in real life. Online experience communities provide what I call the "credibility of anonymity"—for better or worse. As noted above, in some cases communications in experience communities carry weight with members precisely because the speaker may be perceived as having no reason to volunteer extremely personal, often intensely emotional information.

That information can be as frivolous or as serious as life itself. Consider this exchange from an iVillage forum:

> I have two children, 6 and 6 months, I have recently separated from my husband of 9 years. I currently am the sole support of my family. I live in a state where the rent is minimum $750 for the basic two-bedroom apartment. Add utilities on top of that and I am in trouble. I make $19,000 a year. My husband does not send any support money at all and I have the costs for my oldest in clothing as well as clothing for my work where I have to dress real professional. I do not know what to do. I do not have a car either and the city where I work is a very high-rent area. Please send some suggestions on what avenues there are to alleviate some of my financial woes.
>
> *Re: Single Mother with low wage and high debt.*
> God bless you, sweetie. I used to be where you are. It's now 20 years later, my daughter is grown and I have a marvelous husband I thank God for every day. First things first. Call

your local District Attorney's office to see if they have a Family Services Division. They do a good job of tracking down deadbeat dads and forcing them to support the children they have brought into the world. If they don't have such a service, they may be able to direct you to a source that can help you. Don't start feeling sorry for the guy if he cries to you that he can't afford the support payments. He isn't taking care of two children, so he has plenty of time to take on an extra job and give you the proceeds. Also, if you have a supportive family, that can be a great help. If not, seek out a co-op of some sort where you can trade babysitting, clothing, etc. Lots of luck!

Re: Single Mother with low wage and high debt.

Been where you are. Now, 10 years later, we're living a decent standard of living and all is well. I agree completely with all the previous posts. Plus, check into area job training programs—sometimes you will qualify for incredible training in this situation. If someone you talk to doesn't have the answer or shrugs and says, "I don't know," ask them who you can contact who might know—or ask for their supervisor. You'll make it. I agree about going after the dad for child support. Whatever you do, do not assume he will stick to his word if he promises he'll do the right thing. Get it in writing. In the divorce decree, don't undersell yourself and your situation or let him off the hook. You'll regret that later. Very sad to say, but it is very common for a parent to promise they'll co-parent and pay child support, right after the separation—and then slowly drift away. Trust me, I never dreamed it would happen to me, but it did. Prepare now by getting all the legal help you can to make him pay. Good luck. You'll make it. Life can be very good on down the road—it is for us! I'm single, have two teens, a decent paying job, and even own my own home— and believe me, I had no money 10 years ago. Believe in yourself and your ability to pull it off!

Re: Single Mother with low wage and high debt

I love these message boards because we can really connect and empathize with each other! My sister has the same problem. Two kids, low income, works all day, babysitting is always a challenge. She lives in NYC and earns about $200 per week. How far can that possibly go? Especially when she gets no help whatsoever. I think the suggestions offered by all of you who responded were great. Especially creative was that of getting a roommate-mom. My sister lives in public housing. The area isn't great, but it's the only possible solution for her right now. She got to know her neighbors, other single moms, and they watch out for each other. And you can't beat the rent, which is adjusted according to your income. I don't know what the area is like where you live, but you may want to look into the public housing in your area. I would certainly recommend training or education to better your opportunities in the job market. Keep us posted. I'd like to know what happens.

As much as human nature loves connection, it also loves getting something free. Imagine, then, the power of the business strategy of Tribal Voice, which has gotten more than 2 million people to develop 4000 communities using its PowWow software. By making PowWow readily available on the Net at no charge, Tribal Voice hopes to develop a large enough base of users to make it the de facto standard for community-building and chat, for both personal and—perhaps more significant—corporate use.

Successful communities also create an experience so compelling that people want to connect and share a communal response to it.

- Origin Systems, Inc., a division of Electronic Arts, employed this strategy. Within three days of its introduction, the company's fantasy role-playing computer game Ultima Online sold 50,000 copies of the CD-ROM startup program, at $59.95 each. The buyers then signed up for the Ultima Online Network, at $9.95 a month. A pre-release test version of the program drew a community of 25,000. The network connects communities of 2500 players in nine "worlds" at a time, with a total of about 25,000 players simultaneously using the multiplayer game. The best gamers can even have their chance to be in the spotlight. When the Professional Gamers' League (PGL), founded by Net gaming service Total Entertainment Network, opened its second season, it offered players an opportunity to win $45,000. But the 1500 video game fans who entered the championship were not just competing for fame and fortune. They were competing to become the focal point of this new community. Celebrity status can count for a lot in certain communities.

- A freelance Web site designer named Jennifer Ringley has built a worldwide community around the experience of being Jenni-watchers. Cameras in her apartment take photos every few minutes of Jenni being, well, Jenni; the photos are then automatically posted on her Web site. Ringley now charges a subscription fee for access to the Jennicam.

THE HOMESTEADERS OF SERIOUS LIFE

The growth in community that results from the ease of connecting people through the Net will lead to the birth of a new industry of community builders. Just as there are homebuilders in the physical world, so too will there be home—or community—builders in the Net Future.

One of the pioneers in allowing people to create their own digital communities was GeoCities. The company created a frontier for "homesteaders" who move into one of several virtual neighborhoods and set up Web sites that can be as elaborate as the resident desires. GeoCities develops its wide-ranging services by encouraging residents to create engaging content that will in turn attract meaningful communities; it provides incentives to do so by splitting ad revenues with those voluntary content developers.

GeoCities also incorporates interest channels that link to other Internet content and commerce services. The intent is to capitalize on the homesteader community's ability to attract visitors by giving those visitors additional places to explore in the community. After all, a community usually has a commercial district too.

Perhaps the most literal interpretation of community is the Virtual Berkeley Community project. Sponsored by a number of local high-tech companies and the University of California at Berkeley, it aims to provide a Web-based version of the city. Proposed features include:

- Interactive classrooms where children of the inner city schools of the East Bay can be taught by top faculty and work with other children from diverse backgrounds and skill levels.
- Areas where people can send feedback directly to local government and have direct access to community information.
- Local shops online.
- Periodic videoconferences that can be accessed from free public terminals located throughout the city.

DIGITAL WATERING HOLES

Chat   A method of simultaneous communication among a large number of users. The communication is generally written but may also include videoconferencing. The discussion is generally not archived for future reference. Chats may be monitored and comments screened by a moderator.

Bulletin Board   The posting of comments by a large number of users to a common area where comments are archived and accessible to all users. Discussions are usually grouped into topics.

Forum   Same as chat, really.

Threaded Discussion   Similar to bulletin boards, with communications organized according to the order of response to a comment, called a *post*. The organization allows users to follow the sequence of responses, called a *thread*.

Buddy List   Tells you who among your pre-designated associates is online at the moment.

THE 10 RULES OF THE NET FUTURE FOR CREATING COMMUNITY

1. *Nurture a core group that sets values.* Though online communities tend to be fairly democratic, there needs to be a sense of community values that influences how the group's members behave and share information online. The most successful groups have a few individuals who seem to set the example for others and gently enforce the community's code of conduct. They may be cheerleaders, monitors, or simply active participants, but this core group will set the pace for the others and give the community a sense of continuity.

2. *Develop a community personality.* Tripod has lured 20-something users by maintaining a resolutely irreverent tone in its editorial offerings and corporate information. It's not for everyone, but that's the point. It fits the community that Tripod targeted from the outset.

3. *Be clear about the group's reason for being.* A community with only a vague bond among members isn't likely to remain a community for long.

4. *Be responsive to members.* Interaction is at the heart of community. If questions about technical problems or anything else go unanswered for very long, the community risks seeming like a one-way conversation.

5. *Constantly recruit new members.* Just as having a core group gives a community stability, new members give it spontaneity and fresh life. A mix of the novel and the familiar keeps a community from hearing the same voices on the same topics.

6. *Encourage an atmosphere of trust among members.* Buckman Labs has a 10-point code of ethics that governs the way its online community members interact. Sharing information requires that participants trust their fellow members to adhere to whatever values the group shares.

7. *Combine individuality with community.* Communities are groups of individuals. The opportunity to post home pages

or individual profiles as part of a community gives members the opportunity to share not only opinions but themselves.

8. *Stay flexible.* Real-world communities evolve over time as people move in or out. So will your online community.

9. *Be clear about how the group works.* Community is great; the Tower of Babel isn't. New members should have access to guidelines that help them understand what group members already know and expect. It's an introduction that will make expanding the community easier for everyone. A little protocol about how to ask questions or post messages is like posting street signs in the community; it helps keep everyone from bumping into one another.

10. *Make topics easy to find.* Users like to be able to sort information quickly to find what's most relevant to them. Community is no substitute for convenience.

HERE COME THE NEW COMMUNITIES

The Net will continue to include regular communities that are not true experience communities. With Net traffic doubling every 100 days, creating communities became almost a technology feature of several companies. Search engines, a jumping-off point for large numbers of Web users, will increasingly integrate that broad reach with the ability to keep those users around rather than simply waving at them as they pass through on their way to somewhere else. Incorporating them into communities is one way to do that. Lycos' investment in Tripod is one example.

The reverse is true as well: content-heavy services need large audiences to attract the advertising needed to pay for that content. That accounts for the integration between search engines and media companies. America Online bought Mirabilis not for its technology but for the community of millions of users it represents.

When Internet search engine company Yahoo!, which already had one of the most visited sites on the Net, felt it needed to participate in the "community" arena, it purchased a minority interest in community organizer GeoCities for $5 million. It also partnered with Gist Communications, a Silicon Alley company that creates customized TV listings on the web for 11,000 cable channels and 35,000 zip codes. The search company created a new service called Yahoo! TV.

Gist collected names, E-mail addresses, and zip codes of thousands of people in thousands of communities, now re-created into digital communities of TV watchers. However, unlike publications such as *TV Guide,* which captures only a person's address (and subscription revenue), Gist also captures E-mail addresses and specific programming content preferences by offering free, individually tailored TV listings. That information offers the potential to connect those people later with others who have similar preferences.

Publishers generally have been both information providers and community voice—particularly in the case of local newspapers with their editorial pages. However, in the Net economy, consumers demand and expect unprecedented depth and breadth in the one-to-one information they consume. Publishers will be challenged and even hard-pressed to fulfill each person's needs. Moreover, with the Net, the community now has its own direct voice, its own ability to comment, communicate, and exchange information through E-mail, chat, and ultimately real-time audio-video. Publishers will need to figure out how they can fit into and facilitate that exchange and become more deeply involved in a community—or more likely, multiple communities—rather than simply delivering information or news.

- The Thompson Publishing Group, a $7 billion-plus publisher of daily newspapers, health, education and legal information, and reference works, expects that by the year 2000, 80 percent of its revenue could come from specialized or custom publishing. In its quest to ensure that its content was properly aligned for the digital future, it developed its own digital asset management software to give various subsidiaries access to company archives and provide group data sharing.

In preparing for its own digital future, the company ultimately realized that other owners of intellectual property could use the platform tool kit it created. Thompson formed a group called Thompson Editorial Asset Management Solutions. The group created a commercial version of the software to allow content management by Net users, on the theory that highly customized content will be of high value in the digital future. Thompson saw an opportunity to be the creator of the platform, rather than simply a content provider. Thompson targeted not only other publishing companies but aerospace, government and medical organizations, as well as film and television companies.

- The Australian Provincial Newspapers Holdings Ltd, in Sydney, Australia, views the move to the Net as a great opportunity to become a gateway for its consumers. "This is not defensive; this is a great way to grow our business," says chief executive Cameron O'Reilly.[11] " Sixty to seventy percent of adults read us every day. We could be the gateway for all E-commerce in our community. Who else is going to tell you all about the Net? There are no limits to where we could go."

- Knight-Ridder newspapers are exploiting the opportunity to be a community's collective memory by opening their archives of newspaper stories on a pay-per-view basis. Users can search for information by community or by topic.

- Clarin, a major newspaper in Buenos Aires, launched Digital Cities, an online community-based service that positions the newspaper as the community organizer.

- New Century Network, a joint venture of many newspapers across the country, fell apart when individual chains and papers decided that it offered no compelling advantage over developing their own services. In its wake have emerged online efforts such as nationwide services that provide local information on many major cities (CitySearch, Microsoft Sidewalk). In addition, services such as the *New York Times'* New York Today or the *Boston Globe's* Boston.com provide in-depth local information on a single geographic area.

As more and more people spend more time on the Net, and away from traditional media, publishers will have to move into this new role of community organizer to protect their "time-share."

THE SOUND-BYTE GENERATION

With information at everyone's fingertips—whether by pager, wireless phone, fax, or TV—information will be the commodity, and instant, person-to-person reaction to that information the value. This instant access to information all the time, combined with the ability to contact anyone anywhere in real time with any of this information, will usher in what I refer to as the "sound-byte generation."

Kids will become accustomed to processing large amounts of information simultaneously. Already, parents are beginning to see their children do online gaming with music playing in the background, while watching TV and doing homework. With so much input streaming in constantly, information increasingly will have to be delivered in a short, easily digested format that can be absorbed quickly. The Net will do for information what the remote control did for television: train people to move on quickly to another of any number of alternatives if they don't get what they want immediately. And with the growth of the Net, digital communities will have even more relevance. It is fast becoming a case of "so many people, so many interests, so little time."

While virtual communities won't soon supplant the need for neighbors, meetings, conversations and ski clubs, they will supplement these kinds of social gatherings. In the physical world, you can't easily look at a database of people and find a match of your unique interests and theirs. Finding people with similar interests within your geographic sphere is often a matter of chance or helpful acquaintances. However, in the Net Future, you can not only locate different people in each of your interest areas; you can also communicate directly with them on your own terms and at your leisure.

LEARNING GOES REAL TIME, ALL THE TIME

Go to school? No, school will go to you in the Net Future—if you're motivated to learn. New technologies will create classrooms in which the students may be in 100 different locations, all different from that of the teacher. Whether in colleges or corporations, whether used to gain a degree or new technical skills, online education will become an increasingly popular way to help students and workers get the education they need to remain competitive in a rapidly changing world.

There are several key drivers in the growth of online education.

1. *The rapid change in skill sets required.* With the growth of the knowledge economy, more and more corporate assets are developed, maintained, warehoused, managed, and distributed using information technology. The need for IT professionals is expected to double by 2006, according to the Information Technology Association of America. That new emphasis, plus changes in the technology itself—the rapid inroads of the Internet foremost among them—is driving a tremendous increase in the need for corporate training. U.S. companies spend $60 billion a year on training. The amount spent on Web-based training and education of just IT professionals will grow to nearly $2 billion by the year 2000.[1] And more than half of

adult education participants have some portion of their tuition reimbursed by their employers.[2]

2. *The cost of training.* About 70 percent of a company's training costs are tied up in getting people to classes: transportation, meals, lodging, and instructors. The Net has the power to eliminate those costs. Web-based training also makes the process more efficient. Rather than having to hold multiple sessions over a long period of time, corporations will find that doing at least part of the training on the Web means that less time is needed in the classroom. Qualcomm, which makes E-mail software, finds that online preparation for classroom courses reduces butts-in-seat time by 40 percent. That is a critical factor in the highly competitive Net Future, where being slow in getting a sales force up to speed can give a competitor precious time to gain market advantage.

3. *Employee recruitment and retention.* Recognizing that they can no longer guarantee long-term employment—and that the workforce is increasingly mobile—companies have discovered that training programs can act as an effective employee retention tool. Both entry-level and more experienced information technology professionals say that the opportunity to improve their skills is a better perk than flextime or additional compensation; for IT managers, it ranks third.[3]

When employees at CSX Technology check out job openings on the company's Intranet Career Mapping program, they learn more than simply what's available within the company. If the employee's skills don't match the position desired, the person can search the Intranet for available training and even take an online course from the company. The career-mapping center is the only place where employees can find the total picture of openings at CSX. More important, it helps define a career path within the company—an aid in retaining the knowledge that people have already gained at CSX.

4. *The explosion in adult learners.* Roughly 40 percent of all people pursuing degrees today are over 40. Unfortunately, these adult learners often find traditional educational schedules difficult to meet. Enter Net U, where learning adapts to the student's schedule rather than the other way around. The *Chronicle of Higher Education,* the bible of academic life, estimates that every institution will be teaching online by the year 2000.

As bandwidth increases and standards for Web content creation become better defined in the next few years, companies will be able to migrate much of the multimedia training delivered a few years ago via CD-ROM. Such training was regarded as a huge leap forward because of its ability to provide instruction on demand as well as rich animation and graphics.

In the Net Future, those digital assets will be delivered via the Net. And because the Net lends itself to alternative ways of interacting with others, new ways of learning and teaching will emerge. At least one study of online education has shown that students in a virtual classroom can learn as well as or better than their counterparts in a traditional classroom.[4]

ANYTIME LEARNING

With Net-based virtual learning centers, school will become something you do, not someplace you go. Online classrooms can include not only lectures and other materials posted by the teacher, but E-mail exchanges (teacher/student and student/student), bulletin boards or chat rooms for class discussions, and tests. Using the Net, education no longer will need to have students gather at one time in one physical location unless being there serves a specific purpose.

University College at the University of Maryland is one of several colleges that have established full undergraduate or graduate degree programs online. About 4000 students have enrolled in the school, and 1500 have graduated.

In the Net Future, there will be a blurring of the lines between the 18- to 21-year-old student body that higher education has traditionally catered to and an adult population that will be pursuing degrees in nontraditional ways, seeking professional certification or getting training to improve job skills. At SUNY, 80 percent of all students also have jobs. Those students need greater flexibility if they are to be able to handle course work at the same time.

In the Net Future, students will be buying not only an education but the convenience of how they get it. In some cases, institutions have been able to charge higher prices for online instruction than they have for campus classes; students are willing to pay tuition that is as much as four to five times higher, because online simply makes their lives easier. Convenience is the key reason students cite for taking courses online—the ability to attend "class" at midnight on Tuesdays and Thursdays instead of 8 a.m. Monday, Wednesday and Friday, or to do homework whenever it makes the most sense.

The same is true in the corporate training arena, where companies want to reduce the time and money employees spend physically going to training sessions. Fidelity Institutional Retirement Services Company, which administers corporate 401(k) programs, used to offer 90-minute seminars on retirement planning that were broadcast via satellite to employees at multiple sites around the world. Using live phone hookups that allowed employees to ask questions directly of the experts and hear questions from all the other sites, the seminars were intended to dramatically cut the time needed to make presentations to a large, geographically dispersed workforce.

The seminars were designed to reduce the number of Fidelity employees who had to spend time on the road briefing their clients' employees on their retirement plan. However, the broadcast process proved too cumbersome and expensive for most clients. Fidelity found that even clients that had established their own internal broadcast systems were beginning to substitute Intranet-based information, which required no set schedule.

WELCOME TO NET U!

When UOL Publishing began offering distance education courses in 1984, its name was University On Line.[5] However, when the company went public in 1996, its name was changed to reflect the fact that 80-90 percent of its customers now are corporations. Of the 700 courses in the catalog, data communications, telecommunications, and information technology are the three biggest instructional areas; there even are courses for teachers and trainers on how to develop a Web-based curriculum. The demand for online corporate training over the Internet increased the company's revenues tenfold almost overnight from $1 million in 1996 to $10.1 million in 1997.

Individuals can sign up for instruction on the company's Vcampus (or Virtual Campus), but most of its marketing efforts are directed toward corporations. The company's courses, which can become part of a company's intranet, can track course performance and crucial return-on-investment figures down to the individual student. Executive Vice President Scott M. Kline previously worked for a company that delivered distance learning via satellite broadcast:

> We've learned to trade some of the sizzle for convenience. While satellite was growing quickly, people would reach a point after six to eight months that they'd say, "If we only could do more of this from home or at 11 at night after we've put the kids to bed." We have one program that includes a telephone conference call every month with well-known business leaders plus a slide presentation downloaded over the Net. We've delivered the same course over interactive television; we use the same content, the same presenters, but reaction to the Internet combination has been much more favorable. People seem to get more of a feeling of closeness to someone that they're interacting with over the phone than over TV, even though the TV version was actually more interactive than what we're doing now. I'm consistently amazed that people would pay the same amount to do an Internet program as a satellite version. People are becoming less impressed with the technology. I don't think companies that have internal satellite networks are abandoning them; I just don't see them expanding. Once we can get reasonably good video to the desktop, I think satellite is in serious trouble.

> Bad Internet learning has simply been online page turning. What our clients are looking for in the next few years is a

mix of technologies used with an Internet backbone. A lot of what we're developing are courses where 80 percent of the instruction is done over the Internet, with the rest maybe video or some sort of synchronous interaction device.

There are certain obstacles that simply don't exist with the Internet. It allows us to develop instruction that is much more customized for the individual learner. Learner segmentation theory shows that some people learn best by reading, others from watching videos, others from interacting with people. With the Internet, we can do online pretesting of a company's workforce and then customize a program to fit individuals' learning styles. In the past this has been a very expensive proposition that could only be done in very large consulting environments; for a company it could represent anywhere from a $250,000 to a $2 million piece of business. With the Internet we can develop programs that are customized for the 4 to 5 most prevalent learning behaviors and deliver education to a company's workforce in multiple learning paths. There's enough of a database now that we can identify learning behaviors by asking 15 to 20 questions online and get a sense of which learning paths work best with a given company's workforce.

When I worked in this area two or three years ago, Fortune 500 companies were saying, "Everything has to be created here." Now we have those companies coming to us because of our course catalog. And they not only want our catalog, but they're saying, "If someone is teaching a proprietary course in an area that's not our core competency, see if they'll license the course and let us use it." If a company has a small data communications component but that's not the focus of what they do, they may go to one of our current customers and see if they'd be willing to do the training.

I do think there will continue to be issues with motivating students and keeping them engaged. You are making it very easy for people to get into a course, and also very easy to get out of it. You will get some people who are impulse buyers and may change their minds. Convenience is a double-edged sword.

THE NET CAMPUS

Adult learners have traditionally been thought of as the market for distance learning. However, universities are finding that many of their online students are not in fact adults who live too far from campus to go to class. They are students who are already enrolled in campus classrooms. To cite only one example, the University of Colorado at Denver had 609 students enrolled in online courses in the spring of 1998. Of those students, 500 were also taking classes on campus.

Even high schools where students obviously live in the same geographic neighborhood are going online. For example, the entire science curriculum for the Plymouth, MA, school district is available online. At the opposite end of the spectrum, the Virtual High School offers 29 online courses from 30 different public high schools in 13 states. One of the participants is an Alaskan school district that did not have a geometry teacher; students there are learning geometry from a North Carolina teacher, whose class also includes students in Germany and Jordan.

If convenience is important for students when it comes to their education, think how important it is for administrative tasks. Real Education Inc., based in Denver, CO, tries to make online education convenient not only for students but for the educational institutions providing it.[6] The company promises that once it gets the okay, it can have a 20-course online campus up and running in 60 days. In the first two years after it launched the service, 32 colleges and universities used Real Education to implement online programs. The company offers not only design and hosting of the virtual campus; it also supplies course material or helps professors convert existing materials, provides technical support for both faculty and students, and handles back-office administrative work. Says Real Education CEO Rob Helmick:

> "Everything we do is based on three principles. First, every traditional "brick and mortar" service should be provided online; students who learn online also want to be able to

enroll for courses, buy textbooks and supplies, check on financial aid, and take care of other aspects of campus life as easily as they can check class assignments. Two, hardware costs for students should be kept at a minimum and software provided for free. Finally, sites should be easy to navigate and all pages should load in 8 seconds or less using a 28.8 modem.

Our online coordinators work with professors to help them plan the best way to develop their course online. We also work with Simon & Schuster, which can supply professors with pre-developed course content and textbooks developed for the online environment. Simon & Schuster's Distributed Learning Group has a database of questions that professors can use on tests to augment their own questions. However, if teachers want to use their own materials—text, sound, videos, whatever—that's fine too; we'll put whatever they want in the course materials. They can also sign up for our Internet-based course on how to build an online course.

Some professors find that they get better evaluations online than they do in campus classes; if they're not as strong on presentation, that may not be a problem online. We also provide tools that help professors track class activity—how often students visit the class, how long they stay—and create, administer, and grade exams, which can include audio and video components.

Real Education can put an entire campus online, including registration, admissions, academic advising, bookstore, library, and all of the courses needed for a degree for only $30,000. We only charge $120 per student, which is less than half what it costs a very efficient university to deliver a student course online.

In addition to course materials, online students have access to E-mail, a searchable online library and database of course-related Web sites, a record of their grades, an electronic notebook where they can keep all their class notes, and their own home page. They can buy books from the online campus bookstore and return books for credit at the end of the semester using an overnight delivery service.

We've found that online students are relatively price-insensitive; they're willing to pay for the convenience. For example, at the University of Colorado, students who live in Denver order more books online than other students, even though it costs $25 to return the books when they could do it for free at the bookstore on campus. Online students are interested in accredited degree programs more than just taking a course here and there.

Ninety percent of the programs we're involved with market themselves as asynchronous, but the best are cohort-based, meaning you have a group of students starting a course at the same time. Assignments are given on a regular schedule, but students can do the work at any time within a given time period.

Right now education on the Web is Pong. What's coming is not only Nintendo but Nintendo 64.

JUST-IN-TIME LEARNING

In the Net Future, "learn anywhere anytime" will be joined by "just-in-time learning." Corporations often need to train a lot of employees, business partners, and customers at one time, and that time is usually *right now*. When Chrysler Financial rolls out a new product, it wants to make sure everyone has the same information about it.[7] However, with the shortened product development cycles in the Net Future, the company also doesn't want to spend six months developing a product and have to wait two more months while people are being trained on it before launch.

Simply putting product information up on the corporate intranet or extranet and letting employees get to it when they need it won't do. Scheduled, instructor-led product briefings over its intranet have cut the amount of time Chrysler Financial needs to train a large workforce.

However, the process of deploying the training has taught its own lessons. The company had initially envisioned having people learn at their desks whenever it was convenient for them rather than having them travel to attend briefings; that would have meant deploying it to all 2800 desktops. A middle ground actually proved to be the best solution, says Karen Cowan, who managed the program's development.

"People need to be able to get away from their desks a little," says Cowan. "Our zone offices have a lot of calls coming in from customers, from dealers. If someone is at their desk, they may put up a sign saying 'Learning taking place,' but the phone will still ring constantly, people will still get interrupted. It's not really conducive to learning." At the same time, the company wanted to avoid having to take people out of the office simultaneously, which in some cases meant shutting down either an office or a specific function in that office altogether.

On the basis of an initial pilot, the company decided to create learning centers in each of its 25 zone offices in the United States. Each center will have between three and eight computers that are dedicated to training and are equipped with a system that integrates audioconferencing, multimedia, Web-based courses, and shared software applications.

Cowan sees the online system as enabling more focused learning in shorter bursts. "If you take people out of the office, it's not feasible to take them out just for an hour's training, so you wind up grouping things together. Then what was a vital piece of information that they need at a specific time gets lost among everything else, and may get delayed until you can put together a day-long program that can justify their being out of the office for a day." With the more distributed learning centers, people can leave their job for an hour, whenever it's most convenient for them, and go to the learning center. Says Cowan, "One person off the job for an hour is a feasible thing."

Chrysler Financial also learned that interactivity is essential in the online environment: "You can't do a 10-minute lecture; people will play on their computers. Information needs to be in short bites; you've got to get them involved, to have activities."

Real-time online training over the Net means shorter training times. Shorter training times means shorter product development cycles. Shorter development cycles means more products. In the Net Future, "just-in-time learning" becomes more than just a way to cut travel costs. It becomes a competitive advantage.

As video and audio begin to stream more smoothly over the Net, online instructors will be able to hold scheduled classes with live real-time video of both teachers and students when that interaction seems necessary—and use nonscheduled training when that is appropriate. For example, a live product rollout using an audioconferencing system might be accompanied by an ongoing bulletin board where salespeople can supply customer reaction on the product or ask questions they didn't think of during the introduction.

Just-in-time learning also will include the ability to train using multiple technologies simultaneously. When a large insurance company trains its employees in how to use a new software system for processing claims, it uses technology that allows trainees to view the actual software they'll be using at the same time they are using online course materials and interacting with the instructor live. A software company is planning to use the same technology to revamp its sales conferences. Instead of devoting the conferences to product introductions, it plans to use just-in-time learning to train the sales force throughout the year, freeing up the conference time to be spent on building relationships with customers and the selling process itself.

VIRTUAL, SELF-STARTING LEARNERS

The Net Future way of learning has implications for both teachers and students. The flip side of "learn when you want, where you want" is that the student must be motivated to learn.

When the virtual classroom is open 24 hours, 7 days a week, self-motivation will be needed to get the student in front of the computer and into class. There are things teachers can do to help structure classes to encourage participation, of course, and students have always needed motivation to get something out of an education. But the nature of Net Future learning indicates that the ability to set one's own routines and organize one's time effectively will become even more important for students who want to get the most from their education.

What will the Net Future student body with its increased proportion of adult learners look like?

- They will have greater self-esteem and be more willing to take risks than offline students. University of Phoenix online students consistently scored higher in these areas than on-campus students, both on entry into a degree program and on graduation.

- They will expect instruction to have practical value. Degrees and certification that help them advance professionally will be increasingly important.

- They will have more real-world experience before joining a class. They will therefore have a broader base of experience to share with their fellow students and are more likely to benefit from others' experiences as well.

- They will have more time pressures than the average student today and therefore more difficulty gathering in one place at one time unless the gathering is online.

- They will be accustomed to managing their schedules to balance online and offline priorities.

AUTOMOTIVE U

Though online education does demand initiative and discipline of its students, that does not mean that corporations will leave employees without guidance; many are finding that the concepts of employee self-service and career planning mesh well online. General Motors has a clear vision of how it wants to use its intranet to tie together multiple pieces of its human resources strategy for managing 650,000 people around the globe, says Mark Hillman, director of human resources information management:[8]

> We put online part of the ability for employees to do self-enrollment and planning of their own training in terms of

individual growth strategies and personal planning of their careers. As you identify career places you want to go, skills you want to develop, we've begun to enable employees to set those up online. GM University is both a physical and a virtual place; we have campuses with training facilities, but we also use other companies and suppliers. That's where we are today.

Where we're heading is helping people identify what's involved in various career paths. We've started to build job profiles that include the skills that are needed in a particular job, the tasks that people filling it would be responsible for. Those would ultimately be available online. We want to tie those to a training program that might have various levels—apprentice, master, and so on—some sort of a tiering structure. We want to be able to illustrate for people "This is the career path you want; this is the type of training that's involved."

We also want to be able ultimately to tie that development to our macro-level planning. We might have a vehicle program that could have 10,000 to 20,000 people on it. Getting the right people at the right place at the right time is critical. One of the variables is the current resource base you have. We want to be able to tie together our macro level planning with our capacity to deliver training and education. That's one of the pieces we're just starting on.

COLLABORATIVE LEARNING

Net-based virtual learning centers will create new ways of teaching in which exchanges among students are as important as the exchange with the teacher. Just as corporate employees will learn to work in more collaborative ways, so instruction in many cases will take on a new teamwork approach.

Because the nature of the medium lends itself to interaction with others, either in real-time or in delayed-response, students will learn from one another just as they learn from the instructor. Kids brought up in the era of chat rooms will find it natural to participate in an online discussion of Dickens. And as bandwidth expands and audio and video begin to stream more smoothly across the Net, the virtual classroom will begin to replicate more closely the bricks-and-mortar experience.

Collaborative learning is key at the University of Phoenix, a regionally accredited, for-profit institution with 65 campuses and learning centers in 12 states.[9] With nearly 50,000 students, the institution is one of the largest private universities in the United States and offers a glimpse of the direction in which education in the Net Future will move.

Students must be at least 23 years old and employed to enroll. The university employs a small number of full-time faculty who oversee curriculum and instruction, but most faculty members are part-time, and many were hired specifically to teach online. It is a leader in course work over the Internet. The university runs roughly 400 undergraduate and graduate distance learning classes in business, management, and technology. Online education represents 10 percent of its students, according to Terri Hedegaard-Bishop, vice president of distance learning:

> There are some demographic differences between our online and our regular adult students—online students are a little older, have a little more experience—but I don't think there will be a lot of difference in the future. As online education becomes more widespread, more available to adults, those differences will disappear. When we began teaching online, our percentage of female online students was about 3 percent. Now it's 35 percent and growing every year. The same trend is true of income; our online students' income is still higher than that of our campus students, but it's beginning to level out.
>
> Our university focuses heavily on the measurement of learning outcomes. All students who enter a degree program take a proctored exam to assess their subject matter knowledge prior to entry; we test them again upon graduation. This enables us to assess the gain they have made; it also provides the students with feedback on their academic strengths and weaknesses. Years of data have proven again and again that the online students perform as well as their campus peers on these tests of cognitive achievement.

Our courses are not self-paced but they are self-scheduling. The course work has defined time limits, assignment deadlines and participation requirements, but students can do the work when and where it is convenient for them. You don't necessarily do adult students a favor by making classes open-ended. Studies show that adult learners need some structure, too. All of our online courses are taught using asynchronous communication, which works much like an Internet newsgroup; messages are posted and responses are received at a later time. Our students are from time zones all over the world; it would be too difficult to coordinate having students online at the same time. In addition, online discussions tend to be richer and more compelling when students have time to think about what they want to say.

The best way to teach adults online is to form learning communities, to get students working together in collaborative groups. This capitalizes on the strength of the technology. Collaboration is designed into our classes. Our faculty members use short lectures and require a lot of reading and homework, but they also will initiate class discussion by posting open-ended questions that are centered around the topic. The discussion isn't an option; it is a requirement. Every student must participate; no one can "sit in the back of the class without speaking." We don't consider questions that are strictly between students and faculty an interactive environment. The real learning comes from adults sharing their ideas and perspectives about the subject matter.

Distance learning is traditionally notorious for high dropout rates. I think it's because not enough distance learning programs really engage the students and get them working together. It's a lot more interesting to communicate with other people and to network with them as a learning team than it is to work on prefabricated coursework all alone, with only occasional feedback from your instructor. About 93 percent of our students complete the courses they begin, and about 60 percent of them will continue online for the time it takes them to finish their degree program.

Distance learning is not for everyone, and it is not likely to replace traditional education completely. But with the pace of technology moving so rapidly, adults must continue to upgrade their skills in whatever manner is available to them. They need more flexible educational options and that's what distance learning provides.

As in other areas, giving away knowledge will equal power in the Net Future model of education. Students will be graded not only on how much they know, but on how much value they can impart to the rest of the class through discussion.

One component of Real Education's courses is the Webliography: a database of Web sites organized by subject matter that can be automatically linked to an individual class's Web site. Professors are encouraged to have students submit via E-mail the names of 3 Web sites relevant to that course's subject matter. The student who first submits an appropriate URL gets credit toward his or her grade. In doing so, the students themselves help the professor compile resources for the course. It also builds the total database available to all other colleges that use Real Education's resource material.

FUTURE TRAINERS

What will the Net Future classroom mean for teachers? Plenty. At the moment, faculty members who use the Web are doing so largely because they are simply interested in it; they may also receive an additional stipend to develop the courses. However, as institutions continue to look for ways to achieve economies, faculty will increasingly be under pressure to utilize the Web in some form.

Clayton College and State University, a nonresidential campus in Morrow, GA, has transformed itself into a "notebook university." All 9000 faculty members and students (including those of nearby Floyd College) are issued identical notebook computers, believed to be the largest single deployment of notebooks in an academic setting. A $200 fee added to students' quarterly tuition covers not only the computers but Internet access at home as well as on campus. Faculty members have a special area on campus complete with a designer of online instruction where they can develop online materials for their courses and learn to communicate with students. In the School of Health Management, a degree program for nurses is available using on-demand learning.

The program required initial funding of $24 million. How could an institution the size of CCSU afford such an expenditure on new technology? College president Richard Skinner convinced the Board of Regents for the Georgia University System that the program could actually fund itself after three years. The school accrues money from the $200 fees over the three-year cycle. At that point, the accrued money is used to replace the computers. At least two other public universities have notebook computer programs, and roughly 10 private universities supply notebooks to some students.

IS YOUR CLASSROOM A NET FUTURE CLASSROOM?

1. Do you focus on whether students meet clearly defined learning objectives, rather than on traditional metrics such as time spent in class?

2. Do you think in modular fashion when developing course materials? Small individual units—single questions, charts, exercises—can be combined in different ways online than they have been in a traditional classroom.

3. Do you think facilitation instead of lecture? Interaction among students increases their interest level, and group projects provide external pressure to keep up.

4. Do you use essay questions for discussion and grade on students' online participation? Online, it's important to gauge a student's ability to think, not just check off answers that can be looked up.

5. Is the length of time you allow for a group assignment matched to the forum for completing it? Unless students

are using live chat, assign fewer, more complex projects but give students longer to work on them. Flexible schedules can increase the time it takes to collaborate on a project.

6. How quickly do you give online feedback? "In a classroom a student can feel validated just by a nod or smile," says Terri Hedegaard-Bishop of the University of Phoenix. "Online, if a student puts up something and doesn't get a response fairly soon, he or she can be very anxious."

7. Do you use the Net to get prework out of the way before students attend a physical classroom? That way, you won't have to spend time making sure everyone's starting at the same level.

8. Do you use E-mail to explain students' grades?

9. Do you automatically assume online classes can handle more students? Class size depends on how the course is structured; the more interaction among students, the smaller the class size should be.

10. Do you have adequate tech support? Without it, students will get frustrated and become electronic dropouts.

EDUCATION ON THE SIDE

Because online makes education more accessible, students are finding ways to integrate learning with their regular jobs. And teachers are beginning to use the Net to learn how to teach online themselves.

- Duke University's Global Executive MBA is an online, electronic MBA program targeted to making it easier for working executives to get an MBA without taking months off from their jobs. After lectures delivered via CD-ROM, students collaborate through online bulletin boards, E-mail, and online chat. Although the program costs more than $80,000, companies line up to send their valuable managers.

- The University of Tennessee offers a physician's MBA program that is taught online. Doctors log on every Saturday morning for a lecture by an expert from the business world.

- Springhouse Corporation offers nurses the ability to earn continuing education credits online by reviewing materials and taking an online test, which can be charged with a credit card. Veterinarians also can get continuing education credits online.

- The Institute for Educational Studies, part of Vermont College of Norwich University, offers an MA· degree in integrative education. The program has enrolled teachers from around the world. Teachers take online courses, develop collaborative online research projects, use online library services, and have conversations in community "journals."

- More than 4000 elementary, middle, and high school teachers have participated in PBS Mathline, a professional development program for teachers that combines video lessons and online communications.

- The Department of Defense Dependents' School, which operates 200 K-12 schools around the globe, uses the Web to train the teachers of the children of military personnel on far-flung bases. All classes require the teachers to work on developing Web-based projects that use file attachments, graphic displays, and links. The technology automatically tracks attendance to ensure that teachers comply with the requirements.

The Net Future will bring opportunities for colleges and universities. It will enable them to draw on a wider geographic base, and offer the ability to collaborate more effectively. California colleges and universities have multiple campuses spread across the state. Some of the courses are redundant; by offering such courses online, California Virtual University reduces the costs of replicating similar materials on many different campuses. At the opposite end of the spectrum, a course that might not attract enough students if given on campus can draw from a much larger student population online, thereby making it cost-effective to deliver.

However, there also will be challenges that are the flip side of online's opportunities. Colleges may be able to increase their geographic draw—but so can every other college. Some lessons for higher education in the Net Future:

- *Play well with others.* Accrediting agencies, which are responsible for granting professional certification for doctors, lawyers, CPAs, and the like, will be faced with the dilemma of how to handle online courses relative to campus-based courses. They will need to cooperate more on issues such as how online college course credits are aggregated into a degree program.

- *Learn to share.* What happens if a student who is studying for a degree is offered a job across the country? In the past, the situation might have required either refusing the job to get the degree or transferring to an institution in the new location. The Net Future offers a third option: moving, but finishing the degree online. Colleges that in the past have been very demanding when deciding whether to award credit for courses taken elsewhere may need to become more lenient if they are to attract students who aren't limited by geographic proximity.

- *Try it; you might like it.* Educational institutions will need to be more flexible in how and where they offer courses to an adult population. When Qualcomm engineers wanted to take a graduate engineering course offered by the University of California San Diego via broadcast, only 12 said they were interested in enrolling for credit. The class size increased to 60 when the option of auditing the course was offered. The course is now broadcast to Qualcomm's site, only a few miles away from the UCSD campus. Qualcomm pays a flat fee for the broadcast, creating an unlimited learning opportunity for all Qualcomm engineers.

- *Do your best.* With an increased amount of education taking place online, educational institutions will need to think carefully about just what will induce students to attend bricks-and-mortar classes. If the socialization process for new high school graduates becomes the primary reason for students to attend class in person, what does that mean for how those classes need to be conducted? What will an institution need to offer in the physical world to make students willing to forgo the convenience of online study?

A U FOR ALL SEASONS

FINANCE U

- Individual Investor University, sponsored by Individual Investor Magazine, is developing online courses for serious investors in collaboration with the American Association of Individual Investors.

TECH TRAINING U

- Software Training University's online courses include additional software that allows students to run sophisticated multimedia displays.

- Intel Corporation has reduced the 8 to 12 hours of classroom time it used to spend training employees on new software applications to an estimated 1 to 2 hours. How? By embedding "anytime learning" within the software itself. Users of a new application can click on an icon to begin going through a training module on how to use the software. Unlike online help, the training module allows learners to manipulate the actual software at the same time they're getting instruction.

- Scholars.com offers true self-paced learning. Students can start courses at any time and study at their own pace. A team of learning advisers is available via chat rooms 12 hours a day, 7 days a week to assist students with academic questions. Courses are designed to prepare students for technical certification.

CORPORATE U

- Teamscape's Learning Junction offers corporations the ability to design their own courses to be offered over an intranet, as does SyberWorks.

- Fifteen educational and business organizations in Canada are using Virtual-U, which began as a research project at Simon Fraser University in British Columbia, to offer Web-based courses.

CONSUMER U

- For $5 per month, ZD University offers a menu of technology-related online courses accessible to anyone with an Internet browser. Students pay extra for any books required as course materials, but the cost of the course itself is minimal.
- LearnItOnline, another Ziff-Davis service, provides training for popular consumer software packages such as Microsoft Office. The service charges an annual subscription fee for courses that replicate online the experience of actually working on the software that students are trying to learn.
- Coach University trains people to coach other people in achieving their goals in life—personal and professional. Founded by a former financial planner, Coach U charges roughly $2500 for a two-year course that includes teleclasses held by conference call, training and reference materials, shareware that demonstrates models of coaching concepts, the student's own Web page, a listing in a referral service, and certification.
- DigitalThink offers primarily computer-based courses that include audio clips and live chats. Courses range from $40 to $300 and some include multimedia.
- The Altos Education Network is a totally Web-based institution that offers courses in entrepreneurship and intrapreneurship.

ONLINE TRAINING U

- The Educational Development Resource Centre offers resources for instructors trying to develop online education.
- Internet University does not offer courses but has an index of online educational resources, including articles about online education and a list of more than 2440 online courses.

GRADUATE U

- The Graduate School of America offers master of science and doctor of philosophy degrees.
- Athabasca University in Alberta, Canada offers 4 graduate programs, 13 undergraduate degrees and 15 certificate programs online.

The Net Future does not require that all education happen online. Some will still happen in the classroom, certainly until bandwidth problems are solved to the point that video can stream smoothly over the Net. However, many programs are finding ways to integrate online education with more traditional means.

- Real Education is launching virtual classrooms for Chinese schools because Asian students often want to attend three years of school in their own country and then do their fourth year in the United States.
- College students may take some courses in their degree program online, others on campus.
- Still others may take courses in which one class per week is held in physical space and the other two in cyberspace.
- Instructors are combining online instruction with proctored exams given in Internet-equipped libraries.
- The classroom where Wharton Business School professor Jeremy Siegal teaches students about the movements of the stock market is equipped with one of the same Bloomberg terminals that are on stockbrokers' desks at every trading firm in the country. Students can view in real-time what they're studying.
- The Graduate Center at Marlboro College offers a master of science degree in Internet strategy management as well as a master of arts in teaching with Internet technologies. Though much of the program is conducted online, students still have to travel to Brattleboro, VT every other weekend to attend classes.

NET FUTURE U

As a wired generation enters the workforce, schools and students everywhere will accept technology at increasingly young ages as children collaborate in various digital learning projects. At North Hampton School, where 500 children of the small New Hampshire town are educated in grades K through 8, Net technology is anything but novel.[10] In a one-week, five-hour daily summer computer camp co-sponsored by the school and the town's recreation department, students in grades 2 through 5 were given the challenge of replicating their favorite parts of town on the Net.

On Monday, the children, digital cameras and portable keyboards in hand, photographed local buildings and put the images onto the school's local network. They typed in the addresses and signs for the buildings they captured. Using a software package to generate patterns for individual buildings, complete with architectural details, they printed out the patterns and pasted them together to create 3D color scale models of the buildings. On Tuesday, they collected the individual buildings and made a paper-based tabletop version of the community. That afternoon they learned how to scan photos to convert them into digital images; in one hour, they learned how to import graphics and fonts. Wednesday morning they learned how to design and build a Web page that includes links to other Web pages. By Thursday, each child had selected favorite buildings to put on his or her page. By Friday, the children's pages were on the Web, along with links to other school content and their other favorite sites.

In one week, without reading directions, the children easily learned how to capture and digitize their version of their home town and re-create it on the Net for all to see. Says teacher Holly Doe: "We're using the Net and technology as a tool to gather information and share it with the world. It was really powerful to see how quickly they picked up skills they had never used. Because of their age and interest in technology, they were ready to go."

In the Net Future, there will be very few barriers to learning; teaching can happen in any location. Using the concept of experience communities, educators also can tap into real-time knowledge from any number of experts at any moment. And true to form in the environment, it will be the recipient—the person who wants to learn—who can benefit most.

THE BEST AND WORST OF THE NET FUTURE

The E-business revolution will have a wide-ranging impact on both business and personal life. But not all the effects will be earth-shattering. As with anything else, there are good things and some not-so-good things about the Net Future. In true Net Future fashion, the following lists were compiled not only from personal experience but through the use of momentary, experience communities of others knowledgeable about what the Net Future might bring.

This is a glimpse of the kinds of issues raised when technology turns the way we work, play, and live inside out.

BUSINESS RULES OF THE NET FUTURE

- Make sure you're as Netted as your customers.
- If you're in the middle—in your company's hierarchy, in your market, between buyers and sellers—you're a target.
- The Net creates the 180-degree effect, so get used to thinking differently.
- Connection allows customers to drive the company.
- The more information you share, the greater your return on that information.
- Anyone can find anyone or anything at any time.
- Content is important, but context and service are the value.

- Your network is the network.
- Aggregate or isolate.
- Every interaction on the Web is a one-to-one transaction and an opportunity to learn from your customer.
- Every customer on the Web is different, so treat each one differently.
- The winners in the Net Future will be those that are smart enough to constantly challenge their assumptions and gutsy enough to do something about it.
- Internet time means you can be obsolete by lunch.
- The opportunities are endless if you truly think out of the box.
- If you're standing still, you're already someone's lunch.

NET FUTURE SPEAK

Chief knowledge officer: Person responsible for developing and implementing systems for knowledge transfer within an organization

Collaborative filtering: The process of comparing an individual's behavior or preferences with those of other individuals who match a similar profile to predict what additional information might be relevant to that individual.

Datamining: The ability to do open-ended queries of customer data and other information sources in real time and to automate the process of constructing predictive models of consumer behavior.

Dialogue marketing: Marketing that adjusts the information delivered to the customer based on real-time interaction between the customer and the company. Dialogue marketing employs sophisticated predictive modeling and datamining techniques to enable a more personalized "dialogue" with customers in real time.

Two Sides of the Net Future

BEST	WORST
1. As a member of the wired workforce, you have separate phone lines for your phone, fax, and computer at home.	1. Your teenager can access a 900-number phone sex line from any of them.
2. You don't have to wake up early to get to an online class.	2. You have to do your online class assignments at 1 a.m. because that's the only time you have free.
3. You're free not to go to your online class if you don't want to.	3. You're free not to go to your online class if you don't want to.
4. Collaborative filters suggest CDs by artists that other people like you have enjoyed.	4. Their recommendations include The Captain and Tennille's "Muskrat Love."
5. Distributed marketing and ads that can also handle transactions make purchasing easier than ever.	5. "I was busy" is no longer an excuse for forgetting to get an anniversary present for your spouse.
6. Standards for online training systems emerge that allow companies to use multiple vendors' products on their intranets.	6. Modular components of digital training programs are endlessly reused without regard for the appropriate context.
7. Collaborative filtering becomes a part of the browser to make operation seamless for users.	7. A company misuses profile information submitted by users, and consumer concern over privacy issues has a chilling effect on effective personalization of services.
8. The Net delivers on its ability to offer an alternative way of learning and provides diverse groups of people with opportunities for collaboration and debate.	8. Instructors simply replicate a lecture-driven teaching style on the Net.
9. Companies use the Net to reduce employee travel expenses.	9. So much for junkets.
10. Flex pricing becomes widespread, and products are treated as commodities.	10. Budget season becomes a *major* nightmare.

(Continued)

Two Sides of the Net Future   (*Continued*)

BEST	WORST
11. Anyone can contact you anywhere.	11. E-mail addresses don't get integrated and begin to multiply like rabbits.
12. E-commerce makes it easy to find the best price on an SUV.	12. You still can't afford one.
13. Everyone knows how to operate a PC.	13. No one knows how to play a violin.
14. Suppliers enable their customers to automate ordering.	14. Customers' ability to switch vendors is reduced because changing the electronic ordering process would be too disruptive.
15. Experience communities provide alternative sources of expertise and support.	15. That hot stock that everyone was touting online tanks.
16. Instant messaging lets you stay in touch with people without requiring a major time commitment.	16. You get interrupted every two minutes while you're trying to concentrate.
17. Home and work become seamless.	17. You forget what your family looks like.
18. You can E-mail large numbers of people simultaneously and get help.	18. You can E-mail the wrong thing to large numbers of people simultaneously and get humiliated.

Distributed marketing: Reaching individuals through banner ads placed on multiple Web sites that serve as both point-of-sale terminals and data collection agencies.

E-business: The electronic integration of a company's internal and external interactions with customers, employees, suppliers, distributors, and business partners.

E-consumers: Online buyers who use the Internet extensively for either pre-purchase research or online buying.

Experience communities: Aggregated pools of knowledge based on the collective experience of many people. Experience communities may be momentary communities or ongoing, large or small.

Explicit knowledge: Documented information that can be accessed at any time by anyone who needs it.

Extranet: A company's online communications mechanism for linking customers and suppliers' to a company's internal databases and/or networks.

Flex pricing: The means by which prices will increasingly be determined in the Net Future. Flex pricing is based on real-time feedback about the pricing environment, including customer demand, available supply, and competitors' prices.

Intranet: A company's internal online communications network.

Netted companies: Companies that utilize the Net to transform their businesses end-to-end.

Nextroverts: Companies that use intranets and extranets to leverage external forces, such as their suppliers and customers, as much as possible to reach their business goals.

Preemptive marketing: The use of predictive modeling based on customers' electronic behavior profile to market products or services that eliminate future consumer decision points that might lead to loss of business.

Pullcasting: The Internet model of content delivery, in which a user not only determines which information will be received but may help create that content.

Relationship Age: The era in which companies create pipelines to customers for free exchange of information that is to their mutual benefit.

Tacit knowledge: Undocumented information that employees carry around in their heads and that often is most valuable to a company.

The Shadow You: An electronic re-creation of the essence of a person's behavior. This electronic alter-ego provides information to companies to enable them to better target and serve specific needs and desires of both that individual and other customers.

The sound-byte generation: The generation of people growing up accustomed to instant communication with anyone, anywhere, at any time.

QUOTES THAT SHOW YOU GET IT

- Great idea! He's always sharing information like that; that's why he got that big bonus last month.
- Hits on the Web site are fine, but let's talk about how people reach customer service online.
- Just call this number. If I'm not there, the system will try my office and then my pager. And here are both my E-mail addresses, just in case.
- We don't want to be part of a supplier's extranet. We want our suppliers to be part of our extranet.
- As long as we've got automated spending guidelines for online procurement, who cares if an employee orders an extra package of legal pads?
- We can't just rely on our technology.
- We can't just rely on marketing.
- I think I'll post something on our internal bulletin board (when said by the CEO).
- We can't afford not to do E-commerce.
- We'll help our distributors figure out how they fit into our E-commerce plans.
- How do we really add value?
- Do we really need a spinning logo that takes a minute to download?

- On the Internet small can be big, big can be small, and you can make it what you want to make it.
- What else can we tell the customer about our relationship?
- How do we get the most relevant information to an employee's desktop without their having to ask for it?

QUOTES THAT SHOW YOU DON'T

- Of course I use E-mail. My secretary prints it out, I write a response, she goes back, types it in and sends it. I'm totally wired!
- Wonder if CDNow has any BeeGees albums? (Sure…it stocks them with the Betamax videos.)
- We can't tell our employees that! (They probably already know.)
- The way we've always done it is just fine.
- Our customers don't care about price.
- Our Web site is a real success. We're getting lots of hits.
- Sure, our online sales training is effective. All our product brochures are on our intranet.
- Our online business is like any other store, just without the real estate.
- People don't want to be individually served.
- Now where did I put that carbon paper?
- Hey, they're having a big sale on 14.4 modems—time to upgrade!
- Is Yahoo! that chocolate drink?
- Why is everybody ordering books from the Amazon?
- What does that "E" in front of "E-mail" mean?
- Yesterday my 12-year-old came home from school talking about this Web thing and I thought she was talking about some science experiment.

- Most of this Internet stuff is just smoke and mirrors anyway; let's sit back and see what develops.

FACTORS THAT COULD CHANGE EVERYTHING

- If CEOs used technology as much as their workforce
- If the market crashed
- If the Year 2000 problem were solved overnight
- If every house were connected via the bandwidth of @Home
- If marketers and engineers spoke the same language
- If E-mail weren't free
- If video on the Net didn't look like an old Mack Sennett movie
- If we could spread 10 different electronic files on the floor and view them simultaneously
- If Microsoft could buy the Internet
- If automatic translation really worked
- If somebody really could beam you up, Scotty
- If search engines really knew what you were looking for
- If a large comet really did hit the planet
- If men and women spoke the same language
- If digital money was for real
- If you could send 100,000 volts to everyone who spams you
- If Internet stock valuations matched the S&P's

EXECUTIVE PREP FOR THE NET FUTURE

- Listen to the 24-year-olds.
- Learn to use a computer.
- Surf the Net.

- Prepare for the opposite of what you expect—just in case.
- Practice saying, "Let me send you some information that might help you…"
- Respond to all communications within 24 hours.
- Learn how to filter E-mails automatically.
- Memorize this phrase: "I've got to go now. I'm having dinner with my kids." Use it often.
- Clean up and integrate your corporate databases to get ready to do datamining.
- Use E-mail as a primary communications medium.

PERSONAL PREP FOR THE NET FUTURE

- Buy something online.
- Create your own home page.
- Pick a house/office site with real bandwidth.
- Acquire your own domain name.
- Get another phone line installed and make sure it doesn't have call waiting.
- Get a bigger hard drive.
- Set up a savings account for your newborn children and as soon as they start to crawl, buy 'em a computer.
- Set up a personal account at Office Depot online.
- Participate in an online auction, either as buyer or as seller.
- Join an experience community.

15 THINGS THE NET WON'T REPLACE

- Family and friends
- Body language
- Intuition

- Desktop toys
- A week in Provence
- Biobreaks
- Common sense
- *War and Peace*
- Creativity
- Chocolate
- A motivated workforce
- Situps
- Watching a movie in a theater
- A great martini
- Home-grown tomatoes

INDUSTRIES AND POSITIONS AT RISK

Entertainment

Media

Software retailers

Any kind of broker (real estate, mortgage/lending, stock, collectibles)

U.S. Postal Service

Traditional classified advertising

Specialized print media (especially in technology)

Travel agents

Retail stores

Traditional gaming

Phone companies

Banks

Insurance agents

Yours

CHAPTER

TEN

COMPLETING THE CIRCLE

Getting to the sweet spot in the Net Future is what it's all about. It's not just about transforming a company. The Net Future is about re-thinking how business itself is conducted. It's about evaluating what your business actually will be in the future.

The Netted company is like the Net itself. The seven cybertrends and the transformations they require are so tightly interconnected that it is difficult to address one without affecting the others. These issues cannot be viewed in isolation. To do so is to risk creating or maintaining a silo mentality, and developing elaborate infrastructures in different parts of the organization that can't be leveraged for economies of scale.

The seven cybertrends are a way of creating some structure for a sprawling, messy process. There's no question that a business can't be turned inside out overnight. But to succeed, every company must at least consider how each of these trends will affect its organization and operation.

The first step is to stay informed about what other companies are doing—and not just the companies in your industry. It's no secret that the rapid pace of change is putting new pressures on everyone. A company in a very different business might have found a solution to supply chain management or E-commerce that with a bit of tinkering would work for your company. In the Net Future, people and companies will have to live in the fast lane. The changes that can blindside a company come more quickly, and a constant stream of information is critical to staying competitive.

Technological advancements will play a significant role, as processing power and bandwidth continue to increase, allowing more networked devices to be linked to more networked devices. Individuals and companies will continue to innovate.

- Technology to scan faces is being deployed by Miros, a bio-metrics company in Wellesley, MA. A person walks up to a camera and in three-quarters of a second a face is captured digitally; in another three-quarters of a second it is encoded and within two milliseconds is matched to the face in the database. The technology, called TrueFace, could be used at airports to spot terrorists or at ATM machines to eliminate typing PIN numbers. The next step for Miros is to deploy the technology to the Internet so that a person could access a Web page simply by looking at a PC-based camera with the image being sent to the Web site owner and having it automatically compared to authorized entrants. The process would take one and a half seconds, says founder and CEO Michael Kuperstein. "This will be the way of transactions in the future."

- (Wireless communications tags made by Arial Systems allow employees to roam through their buildings without fear of ever missing a phone call. With sensors placed throughout the building, phone calls are automatically routed to the phone nearest the employee at the moment.

- The @Home Network, a high-speed information service that uses the cable television infrastructure, offered two-way transmission capability to 7.9 million homes in 31 markets within two years after its launch; about 150,000 homes had subscribed by mid-1998. The greater bandwidth of cable television wiring allows @Home not only to integrate Internet service with cable programming but also to deliver multimedia entertainment that is prohibitively slow over phone lines.

- Wearable computers will venture out of the labs into the workplace, disposable chips will allow appliances to communicate with each other, and more networked devices will continue to be linked to more networked devices.

But make no mistake, this is a people-based and business-based revolution being enabled by technology. The Net Future will involve changing expectations, delivery methods, and industries. The revolution involves everyone from the ground up, and will transform how we all live, play, and conduct business in an internetworked world.

The challenges of E-business transformation are different at every level. CEOs and senior executives are charged with the difficult task of harnessing all seven of these cybertrends to help their companies grow and prosper. Managers are on the front lines, keeping their superiors aware of how the seven cybertrends affect their respective areas and handling the day-to-day realities of a changing world. And workers must take on the responsibility of understanding how the seven cybertrends affect their work and personal lives, and how they can manage both successfully.

Here are some first easy steps to take when you're thinking about how to help your company become an E-business:

THE CYBERECONOMY GOES MAIN STREET

With the new ways of buying and selling and well-informed consumers whose expectations increasingly will be shaped by the Net, businesses must find ways to simultaneously enter the new arena and assess its impact on the old.

- Buy something online. It doesn't even matter what it is. You need to experience firsthand what consumers are discovering—both good and bad—about buying online. Even if your company is business-to-business, your company will sooner or later be faced with buying or selling something online, even if it's only office supplies. If you don't know how, ask a youngster to show you.

- Ask yourself what business you're really in. It's an old lesson, but one that will be increasingly important in the Net Future as industries begin to invade one another's territories.

- Reexamine your product line. Net Future economics mean that products that traditionally haven't been profitable could now help the company enter new markets or serve old ones more efficiently. Look particularly at whether customers would be willing to pay more for less (for example, for information that is targeted at a very specific or immediate need) and at how existing products can be chopped up into smaller pieces.

- Develop a worst-case scenario and plan what you would do if it happened. With the Net Future's 180-degree effect, you just never know. Another 180-degree effect: companies will have to decide not just what businesses they are in, but also what business they are not in.

THE WIRED WORKFORCE TAKES OVER

As more information is available electronically and work can be done anywhere at any time, companies must reorganize around their empowered workers.

- Include employee attraction and retention in calculating the ROI of an intranet.

- Be open to easing the division between home and work. Companies that expect employees to be flexible in their hours must be flexible with theirs.

- Before the company leases or builds one more office, make sure its space planning team includes some telecommuting expertise.

- Ask yourself what information you can share to increase your co-workers' ability to do their jobs.

THE OPEN-BOOK CORPORATION EMERGES

Companies will become a collection of constituencies as their operations become more tightly intertwined with those of their business partners and customers—the customer being the most important.

- Rethink low-margin markets. As with specific products, the economics of the Net can transform a previously neglected market into a stronger piece of the company's business.

- Find out what your customers hate about doing business with you, and see whether they would rather do some of those things for themselves.
- Provide information before others get it elsewhere.

Products Become Commodities

Net economics requires re-examining a company's value proposition and pricing to cope with a market environment that changes moment by moment.

- Think about every element that goes into the pricing of your products. Are there components of the pricing that could be eliminated or reduced if they were created, marketed or delivered over the Net?
- Think about your customers' businesses. Are there aspects of what they do that you could service over the Net?
- Think about what business you're really in, and what your value proposition would be if your product were suddenly available everywhere from anybody at far less than you can supply it.
- If you have no experience with flexible pricing, experiment with auctioning surplus inventory or a low-margin product to see what you learn about its impact on your operations or marketing strategy.

The Customer Becomes Data

Real-time customer feedback and technology to help employees make better use of that information will enable companies to become truly customer-centric.

- Cross-train sales and customer service. In the Net environment, they're part of the same process.
- Look at what's involved in integrating customer data sources so that your company is organized around individual customers instead of around products.

- Think of your customers as assets. What information or expertise can they offer one another that would enhance your service or product?

EXPERIENCE COMMUNITIES ARISE

In the Net Future, collective experience and instant, global communications will play a greater role in individual and corporate decisions.

- Participate regularly in an online community, internal or external.
- Create an incentive system that recognizes and rewards effective sharing of knowledge as highly as individual effort.
- Think about how you could speed time-to-market cycles by implementing instant messaging technology.
- Can your customers be leveraged as an experience community—or attracted through one?

LEARNING MOVES TO REAL-TIME, ALL-THE-TIME

As online instruction becomes more prevalent, learning will be an ongoing process, and self-motivation will be key.

- Make ongoing worker employability—not employment—as significant a benefit as any other. The more sure workers are of being able to further their careers elsewhere if necessary, the more likely you are to recruit them in the first place.
- Incorporate student experience as part of online instruction.
- Test online instruction in a variety of settings and situations before implementing an expensive system. This can help pinpoint when it's appropriate and when it's not.
- Is online training part of the service you provide your customers? For your company to become an open-book corporation, should it be?

Constantly challenge yourself and those around you with "what-if" scenarios. "What if we changed..." or "What if X happened?" Chances are the immediate response will be intended to show why the proposal won't work, or why the scenario will never happen. Respond with, "But what if it did?" Keep asking until you get an answer.

Becoming an E-business is about changing the behavior and habits of employees, business partners, consumers, suppliers, and distributors. It's about the 180-degree effect and challenging everything. It's about moving at breakneck speed and it's about being prepared for the next generation, a workforce that will expect to be wired.

Everyone is understandably most concerned with the area of business they're responsible for. But the Net Future manager will always remember that in an E-business, everything is connected. A company's Net strategies must be coherent, so that the Internet, intranet, and extranet efforts work in harmony. E-business means organizing not just technology but people, so that all understand the ramifications of not being totally connected.

When acting on any of the seven cybertrends, companies and individuals should consider the impact of their plans in light of the other cybertrends. Will developing a strong internal product training program also enable the company to become an open-book corporation for its distributors and take advantage of experience communities? Will reorganizing the company around the customer facilitate collection and dissemination of information to a wired workforce?

When it comes to making the tough decisions about which projects to propose or approve, here's a question to ask yourself: How many of the cybertrends does this project take advantage of? The more trends a project plays into, the more it promotes end-to-end E-business, and the stronger the argument for its implementation.

Managers and employees must know that they are in a company that "gets it." Their help is critical in any transformation into an E-business. Besides, with the wired workforce, companies really don't have any choice but to enlist their help.

And where is the sweet spot in the Net Future? It's the center of a circle, in which sits the consumer. Surrounding the consumer is an organization that helps and serves. That organization is connected, end to end, all the way to the consumer. When the consumer speaks, the company listens. The company listens even before the consumer has thought of speaking.

And when the consumer does speak, the company is electronically mobilized so that product desires will flow through the value chain of the organization, to the product creators, to the suppliers, to the employees, and back to the customer, in cyclical fashion.

These seven cybertrends of the Net Future need to be viewed together, like a circle. Companies that capitalize on these trends of the Net economy can electronically organize themselves into E-businesses in a circle around the customer. Those organizations will be the winners because in the Net Future, the circle will be complete.

NOTES

CHAPTER 1

1. The Digital Estate (New York: McGraw-Hill, 1996), Chapter 2: The Birth of the Digital Estate.

CHAPTER 2

1. "The Web in Perspective: A Comprehensive Review of Web Usage," Media Metrix.
2. Based on a study by Forrester Research.
3. WebCensus study by LinkExchange and Hambrecht & Quist.
4. International Data Group.
5. Relevant Knowledge, between August 1997 and January 1998.
6. "Internet Shopping" report by the National Retail Federation and Ernst & Young.
7. Based on information provided by Net Perceptions, which works with N2K.
8. Based on information from Relevant Knowledge.
9. Based on information from Relevant Knowledge.
10. "Internet Shopping" report by the National Retail Federation and Ernst & Young.
11. The following is based on the author's interviews with Bob Lessin.
12. Based on report by Forrester Research.
13. American Banking Association statistics.
14. Presentation at March 1998 Internet Commerce Expo.
15. Presentation at March 1998 Internet Commerce Expo.
16. Presentation at May 1998 @d:tech Chicago conference, chaired by the author.
17. Presentation at March 1998 Internet Commerce Expo.

18. The Travel Industry Association of America.
19. Presentation at January 1998 @d:tech Los Angeles conference, chaired by the author.
20. Presentation at March 1998 Internet Commerce Expo.

CHAPTER 3

1. International Data Corporation report.
2. "The Intranet: Slashing the Cost of Business," Ian Campbell, director, collaborative and intranet computing, International Data Corporation.
3. Survey of 466 firms worldwide by Watson Wyatt, 1998.
4. 1997 FutureScapes survey by ActivMedia.
5. The following discussion of Eli Lilly is based on the author's interview with Josh Plaskoff.
6. The following discussion of TRW's Space and Electronics Group is based on the author's interviews with Glenda Simpson and Bob Esposito.
7. The following discussion of IBM is based on the author's interview with Jonathan Judge.
8. The following discussion of Boeing is based on the author's interviews with Linda Fischer.
9. The following discussion of Re/Max is based on the author's interviews with Michael Stefonick.
10. The following discussion of KnowledgePoint is based on the author's interview with Michael George.
11. 1997 FutureScapes survey by Activmedia.
12. *Electronic Mail & Messaging Systems* newsletter.
13. Based on interviews by the author in Singapore.
14. 1997 Olsten Forum on Managing Workplace Technology.
15. The following discussion is based on the author's interview with Omar Leeman.
16. Internet Business Network, publishers of *Electronic Recruiting News*.
17. Forrester Research.
18. The following discussion is based on the author's interviews with Randy Madden.
19. The following discussion is based on the author's interviews with James Cullinan.
20. The following discussion is based on the author's interviews with Tim McEneny.
21. The following discussion of Advanced Micro Devices is based on the author's interview with Patrick Guerra.

22. Forrester Research.
23. First coined by the author in *The Digital Estate* (New York: McGraw-Hill, 1996).
24. The following discussion of Rowe.com is based on the author's interview with Richard Rowe.
25. The following is based on the author's interviews with Robert Yurkovic.

CHAPTER 4

1. The following discussion is based on the author's interviews with Donna Iucolano.
2. The following discussion is based on the author's interviews with Elizabeth VanStory.
3. The following discussion is based on a presentation at the 1998 Internet Commerce Expo by Jim Kessler.
4. The following discussion of SNS is based on the author's interviews with Fred Douglas.
5. The following discussion of American Skandia is based on the author's interview with Wade Dokken.
6. Study conducted by Truckers News.
7. The following discussion of Fidelity Institutional Retirement Services Company is based on the author's interview with Lisa Wesley.
8. The following discussion of government technology usage is based on the author's interviews with John Thomas Flynn.
9. The following discussion of Land O' Lakes is based on a presentation at the 1998 Internet Commerce Expo by Michael Shilling.
10. The following discussion of Dayton Hudson is based on a presentation at the 1998 Internet Commerce Expo by Michael Shilling.
11. The following discussion of ANX is based on the author's interview with Thomas Hoy.
12. A 1997 survey conducted by The Futures Group, Inc. showed that companies with revenue in excess of $10 billion place more importance than the norm on industry experts (33 percent) and the Internet (30 percent).

CHAPTER 5

1. The following is based on the author's interviews with John Nadeau, owner of the Old Acton (ME) Airfield and Gravel Company.
2. Based on information supplied by Mergers and Acquisitions Marketplace.

3. The following discussion of onsale.com is based on the author's interview with Jerry Kaplan.

4. The following discussion of MuniAuction is based on the author's interview with Myles Harrington.

5. The following discussion of Priceline.com is based on the author's interview with Jay Walker.

6. The following discussion of Trade Direct is based on the author's interview with Tony DiPollina.

7. The following discussion of Moai Technologies is based on the author's interviews with Anne Perlman.

8. The author served on the executive committee of the News in the Future program at the MIT Media Lab while at IBM.

Chapter 6

1. The following discussion of Thinking Media is based on the author's interview with Owen Davis.

2. The following discussion of Orange plc is based on the author's interview with Stephen Boulton-Wallace.

3. The following discussion of Aptex is based on the author's interview with Michael Thiemann.

4. The following discussion is based on the author's interview with Mary Kelly.

5. Based on a Forrester Research study of 41 companies that use E-mail and the Web for customer service.

6. Presentation at the May 1998 @d:tech Chicago conference.

7. The following discussion of WorldStreet is based on the author's interview with Alexis Kopikis.

8. The following discussion of Chrysler is based on the author's interview with Richard Everett.

Chapter 7

1. The following discussion of Symantec is based on the author's interview with Mike Gelardi.

2. The following discussion of Business Evolution is based on the author's interview with P.V. Kannan.

3. The following discussion of iVillage is based on the author's interviews with Candice Carpenter.

4. The following discussion of Talk City is based on the author's interview with Peter Friedman.

5. The following discussion of theglobe.com is based on the author's interview with Todd Krizelman and Stephan Paternot.

6. The following discussion of Gillette's research team is based on the author's interview with Bob Kleinrath.

7. The following discussion of Instinctive Technology is based on the author's interview with Jeffrey Beir.

8. The following discussion of online focus groups is based on the author's interview with Paul Allen.

9. Based on a discussion at the 1998 @d:tech Chicago conference, chaired by the author.

10. The following discussion of Buckman Laboratories is based on the author's interview with Robert Buckman.

11. Based on the author's interview with Cameron O'Reilly in Sydney.

CHAPTER 8

1. International Data Corporation.

2. U.S. Department of Labor statistics.

3. Survey conducted by CIO Magazine.

4. Fall 1996 study conducted by California State University at Northridge.

5. The following discussion of UOL Publishing is based on the author's interview with Scott Kline.

6. The following discussion of Real Education Inc. is based on a presentation by CEO Robert Helmick.

7. The following discussion of Chrysler Financial is based on the author's interview with Karen Cowan.

8. The following discussion of General Motors is based on the author's interview with Mark Hillman.

9. The following discussion of the University of Phoenix is based on the author's interview with Terri Hedegaard-Bishop.

10. Based on the author's interviews with the students and teacher.

NET FUTURE WEB ADDRESSES

1-800-Flowers   www.1800flowers

7-Eleven   www.7-eleven.com

A.M. Best   www.bestline.com

Nevada Telecommunity Project
   ctr.cstp.umkc.edu/NevadaTelecommunity

Acses   www.acses.com

ADP   www.adp.com

Advanced Micro Devices   www.amd.com

Allen & Gerritsen   www.a-g.com

Altos Education Network   www.altosnet.com

Amazon.com   www.amazon.com

Amdahl Corp.   www.amdahl.com

America Online   www.aol.com

America West   www.americawest.com

American Skandia   www.americanskandia.com

American Tech   www.powriter.com

Ameritrade   www.ameritrade.com

AMP   http://connect.amp.com

Antonelli's Meat Fish and Poultry Shop   www.antonellis-
   meat.com/antonellis-meat.web/antonellisgif.html

Applied Materials Inc.   www.appliedmaterials.com

Aptex   www.aptex.com

Artshots Graphic Studio   www.artshot.datastar.net

Atlanta Internet Bank   www.atlantabank.com

ATT   www.att.com

Auction Universe   www.auctionuniverse.com

Auto-By-Tel   www.autobytel.com

Automotive Industry Action Group   www.aiag.org

Avon   www.avon.com

Bank of America   www.bankamerica.com

Bank of Montreal   www.bmo.com

Bank Rate Monitor   www.bankrate.com

Bargain Book Warehouse   www.bargainbookwarehouse.com

BarnesandNoble.com   www.barnesandnoble.com

Bay Networks   www.baynetworks.com

BellSouth   www.bellsouthcorp.com

BidFind   www.vsn.net.af

Bionetwork   www.bionetwork.com

Bloomberg   www.bloomberg.com

BMG Music Service   www.bmgmusicservice.com

Boeing Co.   www.boeing.com

BonusMail   www.bonusmail.com

Books.com   www.books.com

Booz, Allen & Hamilton   www.bah.com

Boston Edison   www.bedison.com

Boston Globe   www.boston.com

Bottom Dollar   www.bottomdollar.com

Buckman Laboratories   www.buckman.com

Burlington Northern and Santa Fe Railway Co.
    www.bnsf.com

Business Evolution   www.businessevolution.com

Cadence Design Systems   www.cadence.com

California Virtual University   www.california.edu

Camelot Music   www.camelotmusic.com

Canada Trust   www.canadatrust.com

Canadian Imperial Bank of Commerce   www.cibc.com

Capitol Records   www.hollywood&vine.com

Career Mosaic   www.careermosaic.com

CareerPath   www.careerpath.com

CDNow   www.cdnow.com

Cendant   www.cendant.com

Charles Schwab   www.schwab.com

Chase Manhattan   www.chase.com

Chevron Corp.   www.chevron.com

Chrysler   www.chryslercorp.com

Chrysler Financial   www.chryslerfinancial.com

CIA for kids   www.odci.gov/cia/ciakids

Cisco Systems   www.cisco.com

Citibank   www.citibank.com

CityAuction   www.cityauction.com

Clarin   www.clarin.com

Clayton College and State University   www.csc.peachnet.edu

Coach University   www.coachu.com

Colletta di Castelbianco   www.colleta.it

CompareNet   www.compare.net

CompuBank   www.compubank.com

CompUSA   www.compusa.com

Counsel Connect   www.counsel.com

Countrywide Home Loans   www.countrywide.com

CSX Technology   www.csx.com

Cummins-Allison Corp.   www.cumminsallison.com

Cyberhomes.com   www.cyberhomes.com

Cybermeals   www.cybermeals.com

Dayton Hudson   www.dhc.com

DBC   www.dbc.com

Dealaday.com   www.dealaday.com

Dell   www.dell.com

Delta Airlines   www.delta-air.com

DigitalThink   www.digitalthink.com

Dow Chemical Co.   www.dow.com

Duke University   www.duke.edu

E Stamp   www.estamp.com

E*Trade   www.etrade.com

E.I. du Pont de Nemours   www.dupont.com

Eastman Software   www.eastmansoftware.com

EBay   www.ebay.com

Eddie Bauer   www.eddiebauer.com

Edmunds   www.edmunds.com

Educational Development Resource Centre
    hednet.polyu.edu.hk

Egghead   www.egghead.com

Eli Lilly   www.lilly.com

E-Loan   www.eloan.com

EMI Music Publishing   www.emimusicpub.com

Encyclopedia Britannica   www.ebig.com

ESPN   www.espn.sportszone.com

Excite   www.excite.com

FairMarket   www.fairmarket.com

Federal Express   www.fedex.com

Fidelity Investments   www.fid-inv.com

First Chicago NBD   www.fcnbd.com

Ford Motor Company   www.ford.com

Ford PreOwned Showroom   www.fordpreowned.com

Fore Systems   www.fore.com

Foundation Health Systems of California   www.hsintl.com

Fuld & Co.   www.fuld.com

Futures Group   www.tfg.com

Futurestep   www.futurestep.com

Garden Escape   www2.viaweb.com/gardeners/index.html

General Mills   www.genmills.com

General Motors   www.gm.com

GeoCities   www.geocities.com

Gibson Guitars   www.gibson.com

Gillette Co.   www.gillette.com

Gist Communications   www.gist.com

GoTo.com   www.goto.com

Graduate Center at Marlboro College
   www.gradcenter.marlboro.edu

Graduate School of America   www.tgsa.com

Haggle Online   www.haggle.com

Hard@Work   www.hardatwork.com

Hewlett Packard   www.hp.com

Hollywood Stock Exchange   www.hsx.com

Home Shopping Network   www.internet.net

Howard Press   www.howardpress.com

Huntington Bancshares   www.huntington.com

Hyatt   www.hyatt.com

IBM   www.ibm.com

ICat   www.icat.com

I-Escrow   www.iescrow.com

InfoSpace   www.infospace.com

InfoTest   www.infotest.com

Instinctive Technology   www.instinctive.com

Individual Investor   www.iionline.com

Intel Corp.   www.intel.com

Internet Mortgage   www.internetmortgage.com

Internet University   www.caso.com/luhome.html

Investorama   www.investorama.com

Iron Works   www.ironworks-gasgrills.com

iVillage   www.ivillage.com

J.C. Penney   www.jcpenney.com

Jennicam   www.jennicam.org

JobSmart   www.jobsmart.com

John Hancock   www.johnhancock.com

Journal of Commerce   www.joc.com

Kaiser Permanente   www.kaiperm.org

Kansas City Power and Light   www.kcpl.com

Kasbah   kasbah.media.mit.edu

Kelley Blue Book   www.kbb.com

KinderCare   www.kindercare.com

Knight Ridder   www.kri.com

Knowledge Ecology Fair   www.c-o-i-l.com/kefair

KnowledgePoint   www.knowledgepoint.com

Kosher Grocer   www.koshergrocer.com

Land O' Lakes   www.landolakes.com

Learning Junction
     www.teamscape.com/html/body_products.html

LearnItOnline   www.learnitonline.com

Lee   www.vfc.com

LendingTree Inc.   www.lendingtree.com

Liberty Mutual   www.libertymutual.com

LifeQuote   www.lifequote.com

Lucent   www.lucent.com

Lycos   www.lycos.com

McGraw-Hill   www.mcgraw-hill.com

Mail Boxes, Etc.   www.mbe.com

Manheim Online   www.manheim.com

MapsOnUs   www.mapsonus.com

MasterCard   www.mastercard.com

Matthew Bender   www.bender.com

Maytag Corp.   www.maytagcorp.com

MCI   www.mci.com

Mergers and Acquisitions Marketplace
  www.mergernetwork.com

Meta Network   www.tmn.com

Miami City Web   www.miamicity.com

Microsoft Expedia   expedia.msn.com

Microsoft Investor   investor.msn.com

Mining Company   www.miningco.com

Mirabilis   www.mirabilis.com

Moai Technologies   www.moai.com

Mobil   www.mobil.com

Monster Board   www.monsterboard.com

Montague Institute   www.montague.com

Motley Fool   www.fool.com

MuniAuction   www.muniauction.com

Music Boulevard   www.musicblvd.com

Narrative Communications   www.narrative.com

National Center for Supercomputing Applications
  www.ncsa.edu

NationsBank   www.nationsbank.com

NCR   www.ncr.com

NECX   www.necx.com

Net Perceptions   www.netperceptions.com

Netcentives   www.netcentives.com

NetGrocer   www.netgrocer.com

NetMarket   www.netmarket.com

Netscape   www.netscape.com

New York Stock Exchange   www.nyse.com

New York Times   www.nytimes.com

NewsLibrary   www.newslibrary.infi.net

North Hampton School
  www.sau21.k12.nh.us/nhes/camp/camp.html

Norwich University   www.norwich.edu

Office Depot   www.officedepot.com

Onsale   www.onsale.com

Open Sesame   www.egenie.opensesame.com

OptiMatch   www.neural.com/optimatch

Orange plc   www.orange.co.uk

Outsource Solutions   www.sallysilver.com

Owners.com   www.owners.com

Paine Webber   www.painewebber.com

Papa John's   www.papajohns.com

Party Creations of Georgia   www.party-creations.com

PatroNet   www.tr-i.com

Paul Bunyan Telephone Co.   www.paulbunyan.net

Personnel Decisions International   www.pdi-corp.com

Pie Gourmet   www.piegourmet.com

PlanetAll   www.planetall.com

Playboy   www.playboy.com

PriceDrop.com   www.pricedrop.com

Priceline.com   www.priceline.com

PriceScan   www.pricescan.com

Pristine Real Time Trading Room   www.pristine.com

Procter & Gamble   www.pg.com

Qualcomm   www.qualcomm.com

Quick & Reilly   www.quick-reilly.com

Quicken.com   www.quicken.com

Quote.com   www.quote.com

Re/Max   www.remax.com

Real Education   www.realeducation.com

Reuters   www.reuters.com

Rockwell   www.rockwell.com

Root   www.root.net

RoweCom Inc.   www.rowe.com

Sabre   www.travel.sabre.com

Sapient Health Network   www.shn.net

Scholars.com   www.scholars.com

Sega of America   www.sega.com

Shell Oil   www.shell.com

SHL Aspen Tree Software   www.aspentree.com

ShopFind   www.shopfind.com

Shopping.com   www.shopping.com

Sicherheit und Privat   www.offshore.com.ai

Silicon Graphics   www.sgi.com

SkillsSearch Corp.   www.skillsearch.com

Slate   www.slate.com

Smart Kids Toys   www.smartkidstoys.com

Smartcalc   www.smartcalc.com

SNS   www.sns.ca

Society of Competitive Intelligence Professionals
   www.scip.org

Software Training University   www.stlu.com

SonicNet   www.sonicnet.com

Sony   www.sony.com

Southern California Gas Company   www.socalgas.com

Southwest Airlines   www.southwest.com

Springhouse Corp.   www.springnet.com

Stockpoint   www.stockpoint.com

Store 24   www.store24.com

Strategic Resource Solutions   www.srs.net
Streamland   www.streamland.com
Streamline   www.streamline.com
SUNY   www.suny.edu
SyberWorks   www.syberworks.com
Symantec   www.symantec.com
TalkCity   www.talkcity.com
Telekurs PayServ Ltd.   www.tdf.ch
TheGlobe.com   www.theglobe.com
TheStreet.com   www.thestreet.com
Thinking Media   www.thethinkingmedia.com
Thomson Financial Publishing   www.interdata.com.au/
Thompson Publishing Group   www.thompson.com
Ticketmaster   www.ticketmaster.com
Time Warner   www.pathfinder.com/corp
Time.com   www.time.com
TotalE!   www.totale.com
Toyota   www.toyota.co.jp
Trade Direct   www.trade-direct.com
TransCanada Pipelines Ltd.   www.transcanada.com
Tribal Voice   www.tribalvoice.com
Tripod   www.tripod.com
TRW   www.trw.com
Ubarter.com   www.ubarter.com
U.S. Air   www.usair.com
U.S. Clearing   www.quick-reilly.com
U.S. Defense Department   www.defenselink.mil
U.S. West   www.uswest.com
Ultima Online Network   www.owo.com
Unisys   www.unisys.com
United Airlines   www.ual.com

United Parcel Service   www.ups.com

University of Colorado   www.cuonline.com

University of Maryland   www.umd.edu

University of Phoenix   www.uophx.edu

University of Tennessee   www.utk.edu

University of Texas at Austin   www.utexas.edu

UOL Publishing   www.uol.com

Vanderbilt University   www.vanderbilt.edu

Virtual Berkeley
   www-adtp.berkeley.edu/virtualberkeley/virtualberkeley.html

Virtual High School   www.vhs.concord.org

Virtual Source   www.vsource.net

Virtual-U   virtual-u.cs.sfu.ca/vuweb/page.html

Volvo   www.volvocars.com

Wall Street Journal Interactive Edition   www.wsj.com

WallStreetCity   www.wallstreetcity.com

WebPricer   www.trac.org./webpricer

Webstreet Securities   www.webstreetsecurities.com

Wedding Photographers Network
   www4.theknot.com/phnhome.html

Wells Fargo   www.wellsfargo.com

West Group   www.westgroup.com

West Publishing   www.westpub.com

Wharton Business School   www.wharton.upenn.edu

Wit Capital   www.witcapital.com

Word Of Net   www.wordofnet.com

WorldStreet   www.worldstreet.com

Wrangler   www.vfc.com

Yahoo!   www.yahoo.com

Ziff-Davis University   www.zdu.com

INDEX

ABOUT THE AUTHOR

Chuck Martin is the author of the New York Times Business Book Best Seller, *The Digital Estate: Strategies for Competing, Surviving, and Thriving in an Internetworked World*, a guide to the basic do's and don'ts of understanding and using the Internet in everyday business. He is a well-respected leader, speaker, and cyberexpert in the rapidly growing interactive marketplace. He is a former vice president of IBM and was founding publisher of *Interactive Age*. He is president of the Net Future Institute, which focuses on the future of E-business and the Internet.